FOUR SCREENPLAYS

Carl Theodor Dreyer, 1889-1968

FOUR SCREENPLAYS

791.43

Indiana University Press

BLOOMINGTON & LONDON

Fire Film *by Carl Theodor Dreyer*
first published by Gyldendal, Copenhagen, 1964
© *Gyldendalske Boghandel, Nordisk Forlag A.S. 1964*

This translation copyright © *Thames and Hudson Ltd 1970*

Published 1970 by Indiana University Press

Library of Congress catalog card number: 70–122543
ISBN: 253–12740–8

Printed in Great Britain

CONTENTS

FOREWORD

The editor of this volume has, to my delight, selected the scripts of precisely those four of my films which I myself like best and rate highest – partly because they were difficult to make, partly because they gave me unusual opportunities for stylistic experiment. Each of the four posed new and very different theoretical and practical problems, which I had first to investigate and then to surmount. Yet I enjoyed the difficulties, because they compelled me to explore fresh paths and provided me with experiences which later stood me in good stead. Although this was not my conscious aim, I ended up with a dramatic form which, I believe, has characteristics in common with that of tragedy.

This applies particularly to *La Passion de Jeanne d'Arc* and *Vredens Dag*. The former meets at least one of Aristotle's requirements, namely unity of time and place, while the latter fulfils another of his conditions: a great central scene, in which, as the result of some unexpected and shocking incident, one of the principal characters acquires a new insight into another such, and discovers qualities which he has not previously encountered in the person concerned. This startling revelation has a decisive influence on the further development of the action, and foreshadows the highly dramatic cathartic effect of the final act.

If I take this opportunity of drawing attention to these features, it is because I am convinced that presently a tragic poet of the cinema will appear, whose first problem will be to find, within the cinema's framework, the form and style appropriate to tragedy. Every experiment in that direction is therefore of value.

CARL TH. DREYER

INTRODUCTION

Even somebody totally unversed in the skills of film script writing can appreciate that a work of art in words must undergo many changes before it can become a work of art in moving pictures.

We have all seen films that kept to the plot of a novel or play with great fidelity. They were seldom good. The autonomous film artist does not set to work at one end of a novel, translating page by page into moving pictures; nor does he photograph a play scene by scene.

All Carl Dreyer's films have literary models; none of them, with the exception of *Ordet*, is particularly faithful to the original.

He alters as he sees fit; often with the paradoxical result that the spectator sees the film version of a favourite novel or play that he admires, and goes into raptures over what seems to him like a miracle. It was exactly as he remembered it!

Whereas the truth of the matter is that a good film seldom retains more of the original than its theme and spirit. If everything shown on the screen had been as the spectator thought he remembered it, the film version would undoubtedly have struck him as tedious and monotonous.

The film scripts published in this volume constitute an archive which sheds much light on the early stages of a film artist's work: his choice of a subject, his reshaping of the literary model, and above all the painstaking, almost novelistic elaboration of the manuscript prior to shooting, which was characteristic of Carl Dreyer. (It is worth recalling at this point that the world-famous director, who died in March 1968 in his eightieth year, was originally a writer.)

Though a verbal presentation was, for Dreyer, a necessary intermediate stage, he never attached any importance to achieving a style which would stand up to literary criticism in every particular. It is easy to demonstrate that his scripts contain clichés bordering on the banal; but they sufficed for his purposes – as notes helping him to fix his visions. At no point in the work of preparing the scripts for publication did he wish to make stylistic improvements, even though he constantly expressed his dissatisfaction with certain passages.

The four scripts are published as they came from his hand when the film was made; only a few obvious errors have been corrected.

Comprehensively, the scripts reflect the integral nature of Carl Dreyer's vision. He commits to paper not only pictorial effects, but even the most transient moods and impalpable atmospheres. All those elements which coalesce into an artistic whole only on the shooting-floor and in the cutting-room, he finds it natural to epitomize in the novelistic form that best enables him to abide by his primary intentions: the development of the plot, the atmosphere, and the feelings that each shot is intended to evoke in the spectator. Of the practical details of procedure the scripts say next to nothing.

The original scripts are annotated on the blank left-hand pages with manuscript jottings about properties, lighting, sound effects, panning shots, plot and similar practical matters.[1] Dreyer used to make these

---

[1] As an example of Dreyer's terse production notes here are two left-hand pages of the script of *Jeanne d'Arc*:

Jean Ayme (?), hard (snaps his fingers)
        jumps up
        with Marnay (?) who holds him back.
Simon sucks his teeth
    shouts, shrugs his shoulders.
Maillard 1. in profile against the floor, shouts at her.
      2. contemplating.
Pilotte, hair
Gitenet, beard
Nikitine, feet
Ridez laughs.
Jean Ayme shouts traitor at Houppeville
Ridez laughs so that his belly bounces.
Polonsky 1. soothes, 2. looks at her mildly.
Arrua protests with indignant look at Silvain
  (gets up, sees Joan kneeling)

notes on the eve of shooting, and add last-minute impromptus and inspirations – a method not normally permitted in rationally organized film companies.

The reader of fastidious literary taste will at once seize on a discrepancy between Carl Dreyer's exacting standards, where the art of the film is concerned, and his apparently uncritical approach to the selection of literary sources. The material for *Blade af Satans Bog* (*Pages from Satan's Book*, 1919) he owed to that utterly banal purveyor of edifying pot-boilers, Marie Corelli; while the famous film *Du Skal Ære Din Hustru* (*Master of the House*, 1925), which marked his breakthrough and gained him the entrée to French film studios, was the result of collaboration with Svend Rindom, who wrote comedies and, in the 1930s, the scripts for a series of films which contributed to a decline in the character of the Danish cinema.

Marnay: how did you greet . . .
cold silence: group stands up to see
                              Delauzac, large eyes
all prick up ears
Jean Ayme disc. w. Barnay if it is poss. (see 24)
              together (??) (sees Larive)
Simon shouts traitor at *Jean d'Est* (??)
Polonsky looks at her mildly
Maillard panorama (cold silence)
Ridez – –
Groups cold silence
A clenched fist
Two hands raised in the air
A quick movement of the hand.
Dacheux hand to forehead
Argentine profile
Bac hand under cheek
Persitz hand in ear, looks at fingers
Awl-marks on his fingers
One who hesitates and wants to ask
cleans his teeth with his tongue, sucks, smacks his lips
An impatient one snaps his fingers
One points to the inkstand, proud (Vielsa) (??)
A man clutches his head: is he mad?
The group on the left stands up to see Houppeville.
Martoff and Persitz (from below).

Whether, during the early years, Dreyer's scripts represented his own choice or that of a film company which then proceeded to commission his services, is not in every instance clear. Be that as it may, it tells us something about his artistic mastery that, instead of allowing himself to be frightened by prevailing standards of aesthetic judgement, he relied on his ability to make a good film even from mediocre material. He is one of those sovereign artists who are able to transmute the tinsel of triviality into the pure gold of art. Nor does the transformation always occur at the script stage. In his younger days he undertook to solve problems which at the outset must have seemed formidable. And solved them.

It is fair to say that he solved them ruthlessly. From every source he took only what he could use; and this he reshaped with a boldness and wilfulness which, to anyone who has never tried to put himself in the film-maker's position, may well appear as a violation of the original artist's rights. Dreyer was incapable of thinking along such lines, and never accepted conventional ideas about the sacrosanct nature of the source.

Had it not been for this ruthlessness *vis-à-vis* his originals, his pioneering works would have been no more than cinematized literature and theatre.

In an article written in 1939,[1] Dreyer emphasized the importance of the director preparing his own scenario in his own way:

It is he who by his selection and linking of motifs determines the film's rhythm. The preparation of the scenario is therefore in the strictest sense the director's legitimate business; and if he doesn't fight tooth and nail against any encroachment on it, it is because he has failed to understand the real nature of the director's function.

Allowing others to prepare a scenario for a director is like giving a finished drawing to a painter and asking him to put in the colours.

This uncompromising independence is characteristic of Dreyer. A

[1] 'Filmsteknik og drejebøger', *Berlingske Tidende*, 26 January 1939. Reprinted in Carl Dreyer, *Om Filmen*, 2nd edition (Copenhagen, Gyldendal, 1964).

comparison between his original sources and his carefully elaborated scripts reveals his method of going to work. The *theme* of the original work he treats with due reverence; but in the pursuit of his own purpose, which is to restate the theme in moving pictures, he is without scruples. He simplifies and stylizes, shuffles the narrative elements around and introduces new ones as required. The dialogue is reduced to an absolute minimum and made subordinate to – in many instances replaced by – visual images.

Whereas the dramatist must resort to the artificial device of soliloquy in order to reveal his characters' feelings, Dreyer achieves a richer and much more expressive effect by presenting dialogue in visual terms. He dramatizes introspection and creates not only a palpable atmosphere but a distinctive and complementary intellectual suspense.

So paramount is the part played by psychology in Dreyer's films that first and foremost his scripts emphasize the shifts of mood which condition his characteristic camera rhythms.

Carl Dreyer seldom theorized about his work and never felt the urge to offer a comprehensive statement of his views on the cinema, though from time to time he produced aphorisms which were very much to the point. In 1933, for example, he wrote:[1]

All good films are characterized by a certain rhythmic tension, which is induced partly by the characters' movements as revealed in images, and partly by the tempo, rapid or less rapid, at which these images succeed one another. For the first kind of tension, much importance is attached to the lively use of a moving camera, which even in close shots adroitly follows the characters; so that the background constantly shifts as it does when we follow somebody with our eyes. As for the succession of images, it is of some significance for the adaptation of stage plays that in each act of most plays there is as much action off stage as on, which can yield material for new elements and consequently for new rhythms.[2]

[1] 'Den virkelige talefilm', *Politikens Magasinet*, 19 November 1933. Reprinted in Carl Dreyer, *Om Filmen*, already cited.

[2] Dreyer instances here the third act of Kaj Munk's *Ordet* – the first indication that he was contemplating a film version. 'If *Ordet* was filmed, all the scenes in the sick-room, of which theatre audiences learn only by report, would be appropriated for the film. The

This thesis is equally valid for the stylized early Renaissance of *Jeanne d'Arc* and the heavy rural realism of *Ordet*. In range and scope Dreyer recalls the greatest of the French naturalists, and his theory of rhythmic tension is not so far removed from the sentence in Ronsard's *Abrégé de l'Art Poétique* which inspired Flaubert so much: 'The sentences in a book should move like the leaves in a forest, all unlike each other in their likeness.'

The point of departure for each of the scripts included in this volume is a pre-existing literary work, which Carl Dreyer has rewritten for filming. By referring to the original works it is possible to follow the director's working methods and to see how, even at the script stage, he carries into effect his thesis on rhythmic tension.

These texts are the director's secret recipes. Until their publication in Danish in 1964 they were known only by a few historians of the film, most notably Ebbe Neergaard, whose book on Dreyer's art[1] is of fundamental importance; and after him the Frenchman Jean Sémolué, whose book on Dreyer,[2] basing its premises on Neergaard's detailed studies, is the first in a major language. Between these two works came one Polish and one Italian monograph on Dreyer as an artist of the cinema, and another Italian book which deals with Chaplin and René Clair as well as with Dreyer. It is in fact noteworthy that most of the major works so far on Dreyer and on his individual films have appeared in Italy, among them illustrated books on *Jeanne d'Arc* (1945), *Vampyr* (1947) and *Ordet* (1956).

This publication of the literary bases of Dreyer's most famous films likewise owes its origin to Italian initiative, in that the Milan firm of Rizzoli approached the director about the possibility of publishing them in Italian translation. Any such documentary publication had been far from Dreyer's mind: he took the view that the only significance his

---

actors' comings and goings to and from the sick-bed would help to create the two kinds of tension which to a very large extent determine a film's rhythm.' The programme outlined here was realized when Dreyer made *Ordet* twenty years later.

[1] Ebbe Neergaard, *En Filminstruktørs Arbejde* (Copenhagen, Athenaeum, 1940).

[2] Jean Sémolué, *Dreyer* (Classiques du Cinéma; Paris, Editions Universitaires, 1962).

scripts could have, irrespective of any intrinsic literary value with which others might endow them, was as supplementary notes to his work in his primary artistic medium, the film. 'I would ask you to remember', he wrote to the editor, 'that my film scripts were never written with publication in mind, but purely and simply for internal use, within the four walls of the studio.' But, while he did not hesitate to keep a sharp eye on what was going on, he readily gave his consent to the project.

It is not easy to attach a comprehensive label to Carl Dreyer's art. One can call it realistic, but such a designation will apply primarily to his camera work, which is the subject of this introduction only in so far as it concerns the visual rendering of the dialogue.

A study of Dreyer's art at the script stage will reveal a relationship with literary expressionism, whence it is only a short step to surrealism. Once this connection has been observed, it becomes possible to discern also a close kinship with that brand of romanticism which is inspired by dreams and strongly tinged with neuroticism. Like Hoffmann, Poe and Sheridan Le Fanu, Dreyer is fascinated by the workings of the human imagination at the level which borders on the obsessional, exemplified particularly in those collective mental aberrations that find their expression in fear, hatred and persecution.

All four films are played out at two levels. The outer world rests, to all appearances, in harmony: everything in the actual picture has the dense, existential texture, the intimate, familiar quality, of a domestic scene by Chardin. What takes place, however, within the domestic setting is fantastic, and, as the action develops, gradually becomes unaccountable to reason, absurd and evil.

It is an over-simplification to say that Dreyer's primary source of inspiration is romantic terror literature; nevertheless, it is the truth, in so far as his dominant motif is fear, its origins and consequences, and above all the sufferings inflicted on the individual by a spiritually conformist society, driven by a fear for the salvation of the soul, and a terror of condemnation by the neighbours, which camouflage themselves as rectitude, civic virtue and devotion to duty.

The question which preoccupies Carl Dreyer more than any other is the relationship between the individual and the group. What, in our culture, is the position of those who differ markedly from the majority: the passionate lover, the madman, the genius or the man of intense faith, when faced with the lukewarm and the normal, the average and the hypocritical? And what about their righteous judges, who do not hesitate to cast the first stone?

The film of Carl Dreyer's which answers these questions most exhaustively and explores to greatest effect the artist's imaginary world is *Vredens Dag*, which to my mind contains elements of each of the others: the supernatural and the fantastic, which dominate *Vampyr* and *Ordet*; the powerful faith which forms the *leitmotif* both of *Jeanne d'Arc* and of *Ordet*; the question of justice, and the passing of judgement, found in *Jeanne d'Arc* in conjunction with the assertion of power, and the intolerance, which also preponderates in parts of *Ordet*; and finally fear, which is the underlying theme in all of them. This complex of overlapping motifs coalesces in Dreyer's strongest artistic impulse: the hope of freeing humanity from its bondage.

As the reason for this feeling of bondage, Dreyer's French biographer Jean Sémolué has postulated a deep-seated intolerance, which has its roots in the austere, earnest Scandinavian brand of Protestantism. This is, of course, a generalization, and necessarily imprecise, but not without truth. Sémolué's impression of the singular propensity of Scandinavians to point out with loving solicitude every mote in their brother's eye derives, beyond question, from his impressions of Dreyer's film, and especially of *Vredens Dag*. But since this particular film is based on well-documented historical facts and gives convincing artistic expression to an oppressive sense of sin that dominated the first centuries after the Lutheran Reformation, and since, moreover, moral and religious formalism have clung so tenaciously to life that they were still a very real issue in 1954, when Dreyer made *Ordet*, one cannot dismiss out of hand the outside oberver's impression of a peculiarly uncompromising, censorious attitude, especially to sexual relations.

Vredens Dag is an attempt to explain in psychological terms how intolerance and scandal are exploited by the spiritual authorities in order to strengthen their hold on the ignorant and easily-influenced inhabitants of a Danish town in the sixteenth century. The Lutheran Reformation, with its strict moral outlook, is, in Dreyer's view, an authoritarian ideology. Its religious formalism breeds carping criticism, fear, hatred and persecution, which in this film culminate in a human sacrifice.

The source of the film was the Norwegian playwright Hans Wiers-Jenssen's historical drama of the age of witchcraft trials, *Anne Peders-dotter*.[1] The play is about an elderly priest's youthful wife and her illicit love for the priest's son by his first marriage – a relationship countered by the ecclesiastical authorities with a witchcraft trial, in the course of which Anne Pedersdotter is induced by superior spiritual force into admitting that she has procured her old husband's death by witchcraft.

The historical element is emphasized in Wiers-Jenssen's play, which is concerned with the delusions, superstitions and ignorance that existed in the past. For Dreyer such delusions were by no means a thing of the past. It was his experience that in our more enlightened age they repeat themselves in other forms, and that they occur with a frequency directly proportional to the closeness of the conventional and ideological strait-jacket in which social life is confined.

In the film, therefore, the emphasis is shifted from the historical to the universal; and the centrepiece, despite the telling presentation of the witchcraft trial, is the delineation of an erotic relationship, which is punished with inhuman severity, because the young lovers disregard all fear of conventional morality's latent sexual hatred. Since the Lutheran Reformation every erotic relationship outside marriage had

[1] Following its Kristiania première in 1906 *Anne Pedersdotter* had won widespread acclaim abroad. It had been in the repertoire of a succession of English theatre companies from 1911 onwards, and a translation by John Masefield was published in Boston, Mass., in 1917. In Italy the Ibsen actress Emma Grammatica had taken the initiative in a production of the play at the Teatro Nazionale in 1918, and in 1921 an Italian translation was published by a Milan firm. The play was also well known in France and America in the early 1920s. It was thus internationally famous when Carl Dreyer saw it in a Copenhagen production in 1925.

In Norway the first printed edition of the play appeared in 1962.

The film script is by Carl Dreyer in collaboration with Poul Knudsen and M. Skot-Hansen.

become a sin; a liaison between two young people, one of whom was married, could only be expiated by death, irrespective of whether the young wife married to the old man had had her thwarted natural sexuality to contend with.

A comparison between Wiers-Jenssen's and Dreyer's versions of the central scene in which the two young people meet for the first time will at once suggest that Dreyer has taken large, almost improper, liberties with the play. Whereas Wiers-Jenssen's dialogue is hesitant and shy, Dreyer goes straight to the point and underlines the spontaneous erotic outlet represented by an exchange of words that may well seem as frivolous as anything in a woman's magazine. He announces the coming conflict quite unmistakably by letting the old dean order his young son to give his new 'mother', who is the same age as himself, a kiss. The triteness of the words, however, or what may seem like it, has no bearing on the artistic effect. Dreyer is aware that the greatest banalities often have the greatest air of authenticity; that everything depends on the intensity of feeling.

The dialogue, therefore, is deliberately restricted. Only the barest minimum is spoken. Everything essential is left to the camera.

A good example of this extremely thorough translation of dialogue into visual terms is provided by scenes 278–93. They demonstrate Dreyer's complete autonomy. What Wiers-Jenssen expresses in verbal exchanges, Dreyer's picture-poetry renders far more intense through a sequence in which the dialogue is cut away till only the bones remain: Anne's passion and her craving for sexual satisfaction. She is pure pleasure and desire, a personification of sexual appetite on the borderline of desperation and violence, as contrasted with Absalon, the disciple of Luther, at once infatuated and terrified, who does not dare to satisfy the appetite which, after all, his master has more or less legitimized. He feels love as a sin; for Anne it is a right.

In the film religious anxiety and hatred of sex are whipped up into a mass hysteria resembling a collective mental disorder, with strong elements of religious mania, insanity and repressed sexuality. The over-agitated minds can be assuaged only by a human sacrifice, and the *leitmotif* then becomes a macabre kind of black mass, celebrated by cool reason in the shape of priests, learned men who understand the human mind, and in a spirit of cold rationalism release the blind forces of evil against the two women: first the petrified, simple old crone, whose denunciation as a witch opens the action and whose death by burning is shown with powerful realism; then the young lover Anne, for whom an identical fate is assured.

But stronger than the superstitious citizens' terror of witchcraft is the old women's hatred of sex, and strongest of all is the priests' fear of seeing their power slip from between their fingers. And so Anne, young and hungry for love, becomes the next victim of the righteous.

Carl Dreyer made this film in 1943 during the German occupation of Denmark. Immediately after the première he left the country, and until the end of the war worked for Swedish film companies: his work had become a potential source of danger to him. *Vredens Dag* can hardly be regarded as a Resistance film, but it contained unmistakable elements of the irrationality that was characteristic of Nazism: witch-hunting, mass hypnosis, assertion of power, and the primitive, always latent forces which, in certain conditions, can be exploited by any authority that knows how to license the gratification of blood-lust as an act of justice; whereby a judicial process conducted without witnesses or counsel for the defence culminates in a death sentence passed on the sole basis of a forced confession. Nobody with eyes in his head could fail to see how dangerous this great artistic achievement might be for the artist.

Ordet, like *Vredens Dag*, is a play that has overflowed from its circumscribed stage setting into Dreyer's preferred *mise en scène*, a Danish landscape, which plays an active part in the story and releases feelings and perceptions beyond what can be expressed on the stage.

The basic theme is the same: life-denying, censorious, fanatical religiosity. The action is played out by characters for whom life is real, life is earnest, and who find few moments of relief from their oppressive Lutheran ideology, let alone of playfulness or frivolity.

Of all Dreyer's films *Ordet* is the truest to its original: Kaj Munk's play of 1932, whose première Dreyer attended. As early as 1933 he recorded his first ideas on the cinematic possibilities of this play; and for the next twenty years he was at work on a project for a film version which matured only in 1954.[1] Like *Vredens Dag* the film opens with a scene which at the same time familiarizes the spectator with the milieu and prepares the ground for a plot that is to diverge increasingly from everyday reality, and culminate in a veritable miracle.[2] In order to attune the spectator to the mental pressure under which the family at Borgensgård is living, and to reveal the attitude of each of its members to the central problem of conventional Christianity versus real faith, Dreyer himself added the opening scenes, which are not to be found in the play. Broadly speaking, they are his own work, inspired by a passage in Kaj Munk's memoirs, but they blend harmoniously with the spirit and tone of the play. His range in this film is wider than in the others: the delineation of the characters is not restricted to a few dominant traits such as faith, fear, arrogance and disapprobation. The range is wider, but Dreyer has, while cautiously changing the order of events in the play with a view to cinematic effect, disciplined himself so strictly that digressions detrimental to its unity are nowhere allowed. His style is rich and loaded with pertinent detail, but he never diverges by a single step from the highroad of the play. His mastery here lies precisely in this limitation.

He could, for example, have exploited the very tempting possibilities for making fun of the intolerant mission people. He could have cari-

---

[1] The Danish première of *Ordet* took place on 10 January 1955.

[2] 'The aim of the film must be to induce in the audience a tacit acceptance of the author's idea, as expressed in the closing stages of the film, namely that a sufficiently strong faith confers on its possessor the power of performing miracles.

'With this aim in mind the audience must be gradually prepared, beguiled, inveigled into a mood of religious mysticism. To make them receptive to the miracle they must be led to that special sense of grief and melancholy which people experience at a funeral.

'Once they have been brought to this state of solemnity and introspection, they can more easily allow themselves by degrees to be persuaded to believe in the miracle – simply because in being made to think about death they are led on to think about their own death – and so, unconsciously, they hope for the miracle and therefore jettison their normal attitude of scepticism.

'The audience must be made to forget that they are seeing a film, and must be persuaded (or, if you prefer, hypnotized) into thinking that they are witnessing a divine intervention, so that they go away gripped and silent.'

Previously unpublished manuscript in the Carl Dreyer archive.

catured them ever so slightly in order to raise a laugh; but he grasps fully the seriousness underlying their stubborn formalism and gives it the degree of respect desiderated by Kaj Munk, in order to make plausible the reconciliation between the two warring religious sects. His moderation in the use of effects, however, does not mean that he has become meek and mild or relinquished the pungent, uncompromising criticism of religious self-righteousness found in *Jeanne d'Arc* and *Vredens Dag*, where the portrayal of the priesthood has a satirical edge worthy almost of Daumier. The later Dreyer has not become milder; he has merely learned more about the tools of his art. When he makes such sparing use of satire, it is precisely because of his awareness that hypocrisy is exposed far more effectively by a serious presentation than by ridicule. He is the same severe, uncompromising critic of organized religiosity as he was in 1928, when making *Jeanne d'Arc*.

Dreyer's position as an artist remained basically unchanged during the quarter-century that separates these two films. Their theme is essentially the same: the contrast between the agonies of the tormented, defenceless human body and soul, and the monumental composure and insensibility of the powers that be. *Jeanne d'Arc*, unlike *Vredens Dag* and *Ordet*, is completely stylized in its décor and in the minutest disposition of the action – testimony of how early Dreyer mastered the application of Aristotle's rules for the classical drama: unity of action, time and place. The film's time-span is less than twenty-four hours, the place is the fortress at Rouen, and the action centres round the final phase of Joan's trial, her conviction and death at the stake. Since in point of fact the trial lasted for eighteen months, Dreyer's first task was to produce a script which would incorporate its most dramatic moments. The raw material for the script was in all essentials Pierre Champion's edition, published in 1921, of the official record of the trial. A book on Joan of Arc by Joseph Delteil was bought as an intended basis for the script, but not utilized. The script is thus Dreyer's unaided work, even if at the film's première Delteil figured as joint-author.

The action proceeds with clockwork precision, not one foot of film seems superfluous, and despite the abridgement and concentration of the trial's historic course nothing seems to be missing. The trial has been transformed into art, yet with fidelity to history, by a selection of episodes which serve the artist's purpose: the confrontation between Joan and her judges, and the decisive central scene in which she is confronted with herself, when it dawns on her that she has betrayed her faith and her king. To save herself from the stake she has endorsed her guilt as a heretic; but as she sits alone in her cell she realizes the truth and remorsefully withdraws her confession. This is the real climax of the tragedy. Confronted with herself, she sees through her motive – fear of death – and is filled with a self-contempt that she can dissipate only by withdrawing her confession.

For all the physical and mental suffering which Falconetti's soulful performance conveys to the spectator, *Jeanne d'Arc* is not predominantly realistic: it has the quality of a legend rather than of real life. As regards the style, many of those features which in real-life tragedies always obtrude, and which serve to confuse the feelings, have been omitted. On this subject Dreyer himself has made the apt observation that 'it is remarkable what a commonplace, undramatic course the greatest tragedies pursue. This is perhaps the most tragic thing about tragedies.'[1]

Still on the question of style, there is no trace of humour, unless we interpret the grotesque effect produced by the clerical examining judges as a stylized comic element – but these prelates, fat and thin, with their self-indulgent sophistries, exist in the film solely as a foil to Joan's sufferings. The sequence with the jugglers and tightrope-walker, likewise, has as its only object to enhance the sense of Joan's complete isolation from the crowd, and of human justice as something utterly absurd.

Vampyr, first shown in Berlin in 1932, takes place, like *Jeanne d'Arc*, in a closed world, a nightmarish prison of the spirit, as is made clear by the actual pictorial style: in *Jeanne d'Arc* by the stiff, Byzantine-style décor, which reinforces the formalism of the judicial process, and in *Vampyr* by the misty photographic effects, which convey direct to the spectator the feeling of nameless dread.

---

[1] 'Lidt om Filmstil', *Politiken*, 2 December 1943. Part of a speech made at the Students' Union, 1 December 1943.

The original inspiration for *Vampyr* was Sheridan Le Fanu's ghost story 'Carmilla', which has a certain kinship with Edgar Allan Poe's tales of parapsychology. Its subject is psychic abnormality. The vampire of Le Fanu's story is not one of those relatively harmless family ghosts from the period of the terror novel; it is a young and beautiful woman of excellent family, apparently normal, but afflicted with the urge to seek death and 'a sinful and unnatural love'. She is the incarnation of human wickedness and perversion, seductively beautiful, and disfigured only by two needle-sharp canine teeth, which she sinks in the throats of her fair sisters; a very daring story for its time, in its exposure of facts which were strictly taboo.

This monster of a beauty – who in her unnatural ways is related to other female figures of romantic literature (such as the sorcerer Coppelius's preternaturally beautiful daughter Olympia in Hoffmann's story 'The Sandman', and Hawthorne's 'Rappaccini's Daughter') – is on a journey, accompanied by an older woman who pretends to be her mother. On the way they meet with a driving accident, in which Carmilla is injured. She is unable to continue the journey, and the 'mother', who has urgent business, therefore leaves her at a neighbouring castle, the owner of which has a beautiful young daughter. Carmilla, having recovered from the effects of her accident, strikes up a very intimate friendship with the daugher – intending, as we shall see, to suck blood from her throat.

Of Le Fanu's story Dreyer has preserved only the vampire motif and the atmospheric suggestion of some lines about a landscape shrouded in mist, which may have influenced the camera work: 'Over the sward and low grounds, a thin film of mist was stealing, like smoke, marking the distances with a transparent veil; and here and there we could see the river faintly flashing in the moonlight.'

A couple of lines about 'when the door creaks suddenly, or the flicker of an expiring candle makes the shadow of a bedpost dance upon the wall' recur as the inspiration for a shot in the scene where Nikolas (Allan Gray)[1] visits Léone's sick-room: 'The light is whirling

---

[1] The character in question, who features in the credit titles as Allan Gray, is consistently called Nikolas in the script, because the part was played by Baron Nicolas de Gunzburg, who financed the making of *Vampyr*.

round. The shadow of the handrail flickers nervously on the wall.' The description, in the story, of the man in black who accompanies a masterful old woman in a highly servile manner recalls the scene in the film where the doctor, Marc, 'with great servility . . . greets the blind woman [the vampire] as she comes up the stairs' and 'follows her with exaggerated and ill-placed attentiveness'.

From Le Fanu's story Dreyer has also borrowed the castle as an appropriate *mise en scène* for part of the action; the gothic churchyard, on the other hand, with all its horrors, has not taken his fancy as a place of residence for the vampire, who in the film is metamorphosed from the beautiful young woman of the story into a hideous old witch, and who must therefore have her own dramatic setting, the hideous, desolate house.

A more detailed comparison of the individual films and their motifs reveals their interconnection. Dreyer has his favourite themes, to which he returns and on which he composes new variations. The examination scene in *Jeanne d'Arc* (1928) corresponds with a similar scene in *Vredens Dag* (1943); Joan's death at the stake is paralleled by Herlof's Marte's. The supernatural element in *Vampyr* recurs in *Vredens Dag*, in Anne's ability to 'call' the living and the dead, and in *Ordet*, where John recalls the dead Inger to life.

OLE STORM

LA PASSION DE JEANNE D'ARC

The Passion of Joan of Arc

At the Bibliothèque Nationale in Paris it is possible to see one of the most famous documents in the history of the world – the official record of the trial of Joan of Arc.

The Bibliothèque Nationale's original record of the trial of Joan of Arc is shown on the screen. An invisible hand turns over the manuscript pages.

. . . If you turn over the pages, yellow with age, which contain the account of her martyrdom . . .

Page after page is shown of this unique document with its lines as straight as arrows, its marginal annotations, and the naïve miniature drawings for which the notaries have found time and space.

. . . you will find Joan herself . . . not the military genius who inflicted on the enemy defeat after defeat, but a simple and natural young girl . . . who died for her country.

The last pages are turned. Then the picture disappears and gives way to the first scene of the film, which shows

1 The prison, where Joan is sitting, praying. The flagstones, the floor in Joan's cell. We see two straws and a hand, Joan's hand, which lays the straws on the floor in the form of a cross.

2 Scenes from the church are shown: the chalice is brought out.

3 In the prison we see Joan kneeling before her straw cross – this most

fragile and exalted of crosses. She prays in ecstatic joy, at one moment bending right forward so that her forehead touches the flagstones, the next moment kneeling with her hands folded and her eyes raised to heaven as if she saw beings visible only to her. From time to time she mutters a short prayer.

4 THE CHURCH

A young monk makes his way through rows of kneeling priests. He is the Usher Massieu, who is on his way to summon Joan and conduct her to her first examination.

5 THE PRISON

Joan in front of her little cross. Suddenly the two straws spin round in a mysterious gust of wind. What is it? Joan sits for a moment, overcome with astonishment, then puts the straws back in the form of a cross. Again a hostile power attacks this cross and scatters it over the flagstones. Joan doesn't know what to believe. Can it be one of her voices? A divine intervention? Once again she replaces the cross. Then there is a roar of laughter from the door behind her. Joan turns and sees three soldiers, who have been standing in the half-open door, blowing at her straw cross through a long tube.

 Enter the soldiers. They are tormentors and bullies of the worst kind. They continue to jeer at her.

6 Now the jailer appears, an elderly man, followed by a blacksmith. Joan turns in terror and looks up at them. When she sees the chains in the blacksmith's hands, her eyes fill with tears, and she shrinks back a step. The jailer seizes her by the foot, and the blacksmith puts the ankle-chains on her.

7 While he is thus occupied, Massieu enters. He is an engaging young man of twenty-five, healthy, vivacious and open; he radiates youth, health and life. He remains standing by the door until the others have left the cell. The jailer, who goes out last, certifies that the prisoner is the Maid. The door closes behind the jailer. And now that Massieu is alone with this woman, whom he has heard described as a dangerous

witch and an object of fear – he is afraid. He prays inaudibly and crosses himself. He has brought with him a small stoup and aspergillum, and as he stands by the door he sprinkles Joan eagerly with holy water. Joan, who has dragged herself over to the boards which serve as her bed, looks at him in gay surprise, and with a slight smile says:
Come a little nearer, I shan't fly away!
Massieu, astonished, approaches her, asks if she is Joan, the Maid, and when she confirms this begins to read the summons:
. . . that you summon the aforesaid Joan, commonly called the Maid, to appear before us . . .
Joan declares herself ready to follow him. Massieu calls for the jailer. They lead Joan out.[1]

8 THE CHAPEL
Bishop Cauchon takes the chair for the trial. To either side of him sit the Inquisitor, Lemaître, and Jean d'Estivet, who is to present the case against Joan. These three men are surrounded by the other forty-one clerics, all men of learning, thoroughly versed in the art of dragging confessions out of accused persons.

A special table is reserved for the notaries.

Cauchon gives orders for the accused to be brought in.

9 Every face turns towards the entrance. They all see Joan for the first time. It is so quiet in the chapel that you can hear the grating noise of the chains round Joan's ankles.

10 Joan comes forward. Through the pointed, coloured windows the sunlight falls obliquely into the room in long shafts. Suddenly Joan finds herself in the middle of one of these shafts and stops for a moment. She becomes aware that every eye is turned towards her; she sees that they are hard, cold and uncomprehending. For a few seconds it seems as if she is going to collapse, overcome by the cold, remorseless atmosphere. On one side a completely human, simple, young country girl; on the other the flower of this century's talents, learned doctors, the

---

[1] The entire introduction, i.e. 1–7 inclusive, was cut immediately before shooting began.

fine fruits of the university, every prodigy in Christendom . . . the instruments of reason – and of death. The personification on one side of innocence, on the other of magnificence. The terrible, relentless way in which they look at this girl in man's clothes, all these bishops, all these ascetics and members of orders with their newly cropped tonsures! These learned gentlemen regard her man's shoes and short hair as something loathsome and indecent. They believe as one man that it will be an easy matter to get the upper hand over this child.

11 With a harsh movement Cauchon orders Joan over to the seat for the accused.

12 She remains standing for a moment, drooping under the heavy burden of her chains. Then she sits down. Her face is pale and marked with grief and suffering. She lets her eyes wander over these rows of men in clerical garb – alone and unaided she must battle with them to save her name and her life. She leans towards Massieu and says a few quiet words to him as if to remind him of some promise. Massieu says to Cauchon:
The accused begs humbly for leave to go to confession . . .
The bishop, who is engaged in thumbing through some documents which one of the prelates, Loiseleur, has just brought him, discusses the request briefly with the Inquisitor, and replies that he is obliged to deny her this favour because of her indecent dress.

13 Then he opens the session and orders Joan to take the oath. With a gesture he indicates that the Bible is to be fetched and placed in front of Joan. She kneels, folds her hands over the book and recites the oath:
I swear by the Holy Gospels to speak the truth, the whole truth and nothing but the truth, concerning the mission which has been entrusted to me by the King of Heaven.

14 There is a hush in the room. At this moment, when everything is quiet, a small door opens, giving direct access to the castle from the chapel. It is Warwick, the English governor and general, who enters. The respect shown to the new arrival by some of the soldiers in his vicinity suggests

that he is a person of some importance. As the Commander-in-Chief of the English army of occupation he is the real, though unrecognized, driving force behind the trial. He has come for the purpose of speeding things up, but he keeps in the background – like an accomplished butler who supervises from a distance and sees that everything is proceeding smoothly. For the moment he remains standing just inside the door; presently he comes further forward and is hidden by columns. At one point we see him in conversation with Loiseleur.

15 Joan has sat down again, and the hearing begins. Cauchon asks Joan her name. She answers:
At home I am called Jeannette . . . Here they call me Joan!

16 Cauchon asks her age. Joan thinks and counts on her fingers:
Nineteen . . . I think.

17 Cauchon, after smiling to his neighbour, asks:
Can you say Our Father?
Joan nods. Scenes from her childhood come rushing into her memory. Her eyes are moist with tears, and when Cauchon asks:
Who taught it to you?
Joan can hardly produce a word, for her sobs are lying like a knot in her throat. She answers so softly that hardly anybody can hear:
My mother . . .

18 The Promoter, Jean d'Estivet, whispers to Cauchon:
Tell her to say the Our Father! If she refuses, it will be evidence of her being possessed by the Devil.
Cauchon nods and tells Joan to say the Our Father. She refuses. Jean d'Estivet and Cauchon exchange glances. Cauchon tells her urgently to do his bidding, but Joan refuses again, for she is afraid that memories of her mother and her home in Domrémy are going to overwhelm her.

Cauchon puts further pressure on her: she is to repeat the Our Father immediately and unconditionally. She declines to do so.

19 Cauchon rebukes her for this stubbornness and lets the examining judge take over the interrogation. The latter makes an inclination of the head and asks:

You say that you are sent by God?

Joan confirms this with a nod and adds:

To save France!

The judges burst out laughing. Joan's eyes are raised to heaven, as if it was heaven that gave her courage and found the right words for her. Her expression, which is filled with the glory of a heavenly vision, is almost unearthly as she answers:

That is why I was born!

More contemptuous laughter from the judges. The examining judge confers with the other judges. Their expressions show that they are setting a new trap for Joan.

20 Finally he says:

So you believe that God hates the English?

Joan does not immediately understand the question, and the examining judge has to repeat it. Then Joan gives one of her brilliant, inspired answers:

I know not whether God loves or hates the English . . .

21 Disappointment on the judges' faces. Joan continues, with a strength which suddenly reveals a new side of her character, and turning towards the English soldiers:

But I know for certain that the English will all be driven out of France . . .

Commotion and protests among the soldiers: why should Joan be allowed to insult England? But Joan continues inflexibly:

. . . except for those who are going to die here!

The soldiers are furious. They can no longer contain themselves. One of them makes a movement towards the accused. Massieu leaps to her defence. But Cauchon intervenes and orders silence; he has to use all his authority to restore order among the judges. The hearing continues.

22 Cauchon asks:

You have told how Saint Michael appeared to you . . . how did you greet him?

Joan explains that she has always greeted Saint Michael in the way one should greet a saint. One of the judges tells her to show how she greeted Saint Michael.

23 With touching simplicity Joan kneels, goes through the motion of taking off her cap, and bows reverently before the imagined saint. She gets up again, while the judges talk together.

24 Cauchon continues:
In what form did he reveal himself?
Joan does not immediately grasp the question. Half the judges shout to one another.
   Hundreds of questions fly across the room: Did he have wings? Was his head like an ordinary man's? Was he wearing a crown? Under this deluge of questions Joan makes a movement as if to say that she cannot answer them all at once.

25 Finally, when quiet is more or less restored, Cauchon formulates his question more carefully:
What was Saint Michael wearing?
But Joan does not answer.

26 An elderly canon is seen to rise, go over to the bishop and whisper something in his ear. There is a suggestion of pruriency about this man. The bishop nods and turns to Joan:
How can you know whether the person you saw was a man or a woman?
Joan is silent. She realizes that another trap is being laid for her.

27 Cauchon is reluctant to give up the ground he has won. He asks a new question:
Was he naked?
Every ear strains to hear the reply, for now Joan has to answer. And again she produces one of her brilliant, careful answers:
Do you not believe that God would have clothes for him?

28 Cauchon realizes that his stratagem has failed, but nevertheless he pursues the matter further:
Did he have any hair on his head?
But Joan, who now feels that she is on firm ground, smiles and answers with artless inspiration:
Why should he have had it cut off?

29 Cauchon sees that he will get nowhere with Joan by this method. He confers with those sitting nearest him and then gives way to the examining judge, who begins to question Joan about her dress:
Why are you wearing men's clothes?
Joan refuses several times to answer and remains sitting motionless, stiff as a ramrod. The judge says:
Are you willing to wear a woman's dress?

30 Massieu leans towards her and advises her to accept this suggestion, which he thinks must be very easy for her to do. But Joan looks at him with the air of one treasuring a great secret, and says no to the judge. When the judge presses her to tell him why she refuses, she answers:
When I have completed the task which God has entrusted to me, then I will wear women's clothes again.
Whispering among the judges –

31 An indication that another trap is being prepared. Then one of the judges says:
So it is God who has commanded you to go about in men's clothes?
Joan answers unhesitatingly:
Yes!
A smile of triumph spreads from face to face among Joan's judges.

32 The Promoter, Jean d'Estivet, complacently makes some notes. Then he leans forward over his desk, smiles and asks in an insincere tone of voice:
And what reward do you hope to obtain from the Lord?

33 Joan, whose expression is that of a saint, folds her hands on her breast and raises her eyes to heaven:
The salvation of my soul!
She remains sitting in the same position; her look conveys the impression that she can see into the furthest corner of heaven.

34 But Jean d'Estivet is incapable of controlling himself. He gets up, goes right up to her, spits in her face and hisses:
Do you not understand that what you are saying is blasphemy?
Then he goes back to his place. But on Joan's face there lingers the expression of one who is far removed from this world. From time to time throughout this episode two of the judges, Nicolas de Houppeville and Martin Ladvenu, have been seen to show signs of sympathy for the accused.

35 After this last outrage on the part of the Promoter, de Houppeville can control himself no longer. Provoked to the limit, he rises and shouts:
This is unworthy . . .
The whole room turns to him in amazement. He continues fearlessly:
. . . it is persecution!

36 He leaves his place; Ladvenu tries to restrain him, but he approaches the bishop and says to him:
We are treating this woman like an enemy – not like a human being on trial!

37 Then he casts a look full of tenderness at Joan, who at this moment is drying her cheeks, still wet from Jean d'Estivet's spittle. Houppeville continues:
For me she is a saint!
He goes over to her, genuflects before her, and turns to go out through the door.

38 Warwick has followed these proceedings with an attentive eye. He whispers a few words to an officer, who follows Houppeville the length of the chapel.

39 When he reaches the porch the officer takes two soldiers with him and follows on Houppeville's heels.

Each of the judges in the room understands the fate in store for Houppeville, and is seized with fear. An icy, unquiet silence prevails.

40 Paul Jorge [the name of one of the actors] prepares to rise and ask the meaning of this incident.

41 Cauchon stops him with a movement, and gives the order for the session to continue. He asks Joan:
Has God promised you anything?
Joan gives an absent-minded nod. Cauchon presses her to tell him what it is that God has promised.
Can you not tell us what it is that God has promised you?
Cauchon asks with his most ingratiating smile, but Joan shakes her head. Cauchon tries to persuade her:
You must tell us.
But Joan declines to answer:
That has nothing to do with your trial![1]

42 Cauchon maintains the contrary, and Joan tells him to ask the assembly. Cauchon turns to the judges and asks:
Has this question any bearing on the trial?
He orders those who consider that it has to raise their hands. Nearly every hand goes up. Then it is the turn of those who take the opposite view. Ladvenu is the only one to raise his hand, but when he sees that he is entirely alone he takes it down again.

43 And Cauchon is able to say to Joan that, since the relevance of the question to the trial has been unanimously agreed, she is obliged to answer. He repeats his question:
What has God promised you?
Joan does not answer.

[1] Translator's note: a correct translation of Dreyer, and historically accurate.

44 Cauchon continues:
Has God promised you that you will be released from your prison?
Joan confirms this with a nod. Dalleu speaks in a low voice to Cauchon, who asks:
When?
After sitting for a while, lost in thought, Joan answers:
I do not know the day or the hour!
A further exchange of words between Cauchon and d'Estivet; then Cauchon makes a sign for Massieu to take the accused back to prison. Joan rises to go.

45 She takes a few steps, turns and asks:
May I not be relieved from carrying these chains?
Cauchon can see no reason for complying with her request. But he sees the opportunity of imposing a condition which he knows will be unacceptable to Joan:
Will you take an oath never to bear arms against England again?

46 Joan answers unhesitatingly:
No!
Then she is led away. Her chains clank as they drag over the flagstones. The judges leave their places.

47 They break up into groups, according to their friendships or the order to which they belong. We see one group consisting of Dominicans, another of canons, a third of mendicant friars. The entire assembly talks and whispers. Monks' cloaks, homespun tunics and cowls, caps and hats. Here a fat old abbot, here a short, slim monk. Respectful inclinations of the head, sanctimonious smiles, violent outbursts of laughter. The witty ones recognizable by their thin lips and legs. In the background beardless students, solemn as popes, in earnest discussion.

But round the judges' table a discussion is going on between Cauchon, Lemaître, Jean d'Estivet, the learned Thomas de Courcelles, Loiseleur, Beaupère, Pierre Maurice and Warwick. Warwick stays in the background, as if wishing to underline that he has no part in the conspiracy against Joan; but it is clearly understood that he has the last word in the matter. They are considering what procedure to adopt. The point is to lose as little time as possible in getting Joan to compromise herself. Loiseleur propounds a scheme which receives general approval. Warwick is asked a question, which he answers in the affirmative. An order is given to a secretary, who at once leaves the chapel.

48 THE PRISON

Massieu has brought Joan back. The door closes behind her. Overcome by fatigue, she sits on her bed. In front of the judges she has restrained her weeping. Now that she is alone, the pent-up tears pour from her eyes.

49 THE CHAPEL

The conference is still going on. Loiseleur is dictating to the notaries. At intervals one of the other judges interposes a word or a suggestion.

50 THE PRISON

Joan is still shaking with sobs. Suddenly she sees a cross slowly forming on the floor close to her feet. It is the shadow of the window grating. She knows this cross and loves it. It always comes when she is feeling lonely and unhappy. She has no doubt that it is God who sends her solace and encouragement in this way. She dries her eyes and produces from a hiding-place a piece of handiwork, with which she occupies her hands and her thoughts when she is not before the judges. It is a crown of plaited straw – very simple, pretty and childlike. Soon she is completely absorbed in this work, to which she devotes all her love. We see the Joan from Domrémy who 'is second to no woman in Rouen, when it comes to spinning or sewing'. From time to time she looks at the cross on the ground.

51 The conference in the chapel. Loiseleur finishes his dictating. The notary reads back to him.

52 THE PRISON

We see only Joan's hands which are occupied in plaiting her crown. The shot is taken in such a way that the crown and the cross on the ground can be seen together.

53 The conference in the chapel. The notary finishes his reading aloud and what he has read is approved. Meanwhile the secretary has returned. He hands a document to Warwick, who passes it round. It goes from hand to hand, and finally to the notary.

54 In the little ante-room leading to Joan's prison. The soldiers are playing with a small English dog. An old serving woman comes with food for Joan in an earthenware bowl. One of the soldiers seizes the bowl; he selects the best piece of meat and gives it to the dog. The latter swallows the meat and licks the soldier's fingers. With the same fingers he picks out another piece of meat and gives this also to the dog.

55 A short scene from the conference, featuring two documents. A hand – that of the notary – is engaged in copying the signature from one document to the other.

56 THE PRISON
The soldier comes in with Joan's food, followed by the dog. Two other soldiers appear in the door, for these rascals never lose an opportunity of tormenting their victim. As the soldier hands Joan the food, his eye falls on her ring. He demands it from her, but she implores him to let her keep it: it is her mother's ring. But the soldier is determined to have it, even if he has to use force. He calls to the other two soldiers to come and help him, and puts the bowl of food on the ground in such a position that the dog naturally takes advantage of it.

57 Just as the first soldier has finally succeeded in forcing the ring from Joan's finger Loiseleur appears in the open door. He appears to be filled with genuine indignation at the sight of the ill treatment to which the three rascals are subjecting Joan. The soldiers have turned round. They are afraid. Loiseleur threatens them and quickly goes up to the soldier who has wrested Joan's ring from her. The soldier is compelled to hand over the ring to Loiseleur, who thereupon orders the three ruffians out of the cell.

58 Loiseleur shuts the door. He is alone with Joan. He looks all round

him and goes over to Joan, who regards him with deep amazement, an amazement which embraces gratitude as well; for after all it is he who has just saved her from the soldiers' cruelties. He remains standing a few paces from her, looks at her in a serious and friendly way and says:
I have great sympathy for you!
A feeble smile appears at the corners of Joan's mouth, but her expression of astonishment remains.

59 Loiseleur has stopped by the cross; when he takes a pace forward the cross disappears; but Joan fails to notice this, absorbed as she is in wondering why this prelate has come to visit her. Loiseleur, who has now come right up to Joan, hands her the ring, which she receives gratefully. Then she again fixes her look of enquiry on the prelate, whom she has previously seen among her judges.

60 Finally he says to her in a low whisper:
Would you recognize your King's signature?
Joan nods, though without understanding the purpose of his visit. From his cowl he produces a letter which he hands to Joan. She takes it. She shows with a smile that she recognizes Charles VII's signature. Then she returns the letter and says:
I can't read!

61 Loiseleur reads the letter aloud for her, as follows:
To our dearly beloved Joan. Charles, the King, hereby informs you that he is preparing to advance on Rouen with a mighty army. He is sending you a faithful priest, who will stand by you. Have confidence in him.
The reflection of an inner joy shines in her eyes. Her face lights up during the reading and she smiles. Loiseleur does not move from the spot. He stands watching her, motionless and pale. He gazes at her with the eyes of a snake, while Joan sits with an absent smile, completely absorbed in her own joyful thoughts.

62 Loiseleur suddenly raises his head and pricks up his ears. Immediately behind the cell wall there is a secret room, where a man can remain

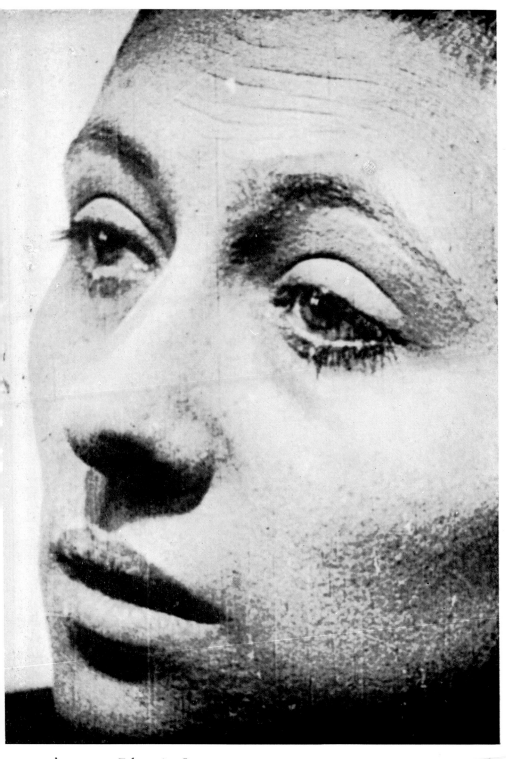

JEANNE D'ARC 1927. *Falconetti as Joan.*

JEANNE D'ARC Scene 10: *Joan before the judges.*

JEANNE D'ARC *Two priests.*

Scene 79: *Loiseleur (Maurice Schutz) and the supreme judge Cauchon (Eugène Silvain).*

hidden, spying on the prisoner through a judas, or chink in the wall. Alternating with the scenes between Joan and Loiseleur are close-ups of Cauchon spying and eavesdropping behind the chink.

63 Loiseleur moves away from Joan and goes towards the hiding-place; he is perfectly aware of its existence. When he reaches the chink, he and Cauchon look at each other. First Cauchon's serious eye is shown through the chink, then – likewise through the chink – Loiseleur's small, cunning, contracted eye. Loiseleur catches sight of the crown and says:
Your martyr's crown.
Then he turns to Joan, who is still sitting with the King's letter in her hands. He offers to hear her confession.

64 She turns to him with a look of joy, hardly daring to believe in this happiness. She drops a pretty curtsy, then kneels with folded hands in a charming attitude suggestive of a penitent child. He advises her strongly to speak to him with an open heart. Here she is not before her judge, but before her king. God can hear her!

65 Joan confesses her sins like a schoolchild reciting a lesson. Cauchon and his attendants follow the scene attentively from the secret room. With a ledger on his lap the notary takes down everything that Joan says, but it is clear that she is saying nothing of any significance, for all the skill with which Loiseleur presents his questions. So it is not long before Loiseleur gives her a sugary smile and rattles off the absolution. He makes the sign of the cross over her and stands up.

66 Cauchon and his confidants have left their hiding-place and now come into the cell. The soldiers bring in chairs and a table for the scribe. The judges group themselves in a circle round Joan, some sitting, others standing. Loiseleur places himself behind Cauchon. In addition to the judges, Massieu also is present.

67 Cauchon gestures to Lemaître who says to Joan:
You profess to be a daughter of God? . . .

Joan agrees with a nod, and Lemaître continues:
Then why will you not say Our Father?
Joan sits motionless for a moment. The judges look at her with watchful eyes. A perceptible change comes over Joan. Her expression is transfigured. A heavenly light spreads over her face, she folds her hands and begins to pray. The sight of this small and helpless woman, turning to God in captivating innocence, makes an involuntary impression on some of the judges. The gentle Massieu in particular can hardly restrain his tears.

Joan has said the Our Father. Jean d'Estivet is thus obliged to eliminate this important point from his charge-sheet.

68 Lemaître continues with the hearing:
Has God told you that you will be released from your prison?
Joan smiles and gives Loiseleur a secret, confidential glance. His eyes gleam back at her in complicity. She answers:
Yes . . . and by means of a great victory!

69 The judges are astonished and cross-examine her. They ask her to explain precisely what she knows, and how she has come to know it. But Joan answers:
I know that God will soon come to my help in a miraculous way!

70 Jean d'Estivet hastens to write down this important answer. With great secrecy he grips Loiseleur's hand in gratitude. Cauchon, Lemaître and some of the other judges plot together.

71 Lemaître leans forward and begins to question her:
Has God promised you that you will go to Paradise?
Joan knows instinctively that they have laid a trap for her. In her uncertainty she looks for help from Loiseleur, who indicates to her with a slight smile that she is to say yes. Lemaître is satisfied with her answer but takes good care to conceal his satisfaction. In a tone almost of boredom he says:
So you are certain of being saved?

2 Again Joan resorts to Loiseleur. He gives the same sign as before, and Joan says yes.

Massieu's eyes are as if riveted to Joan's lips, and now when she answers yes he forgets where he is, forgets that Cauchon is just beside him, and almost without thinking says to Joan:
Do you realize that this is an extremely important answer?
Cauchon pounces on Massieu and bursts out:
You had better hold your tongue!
Massieu wants to explain, but Cauchon cuts him short and orders the hearing to continue.

3 Lemaître presents his next question, which is only one link in a chain of questions carefully prepared and ingeniously related:
Since you are so certain of your salvation . . . why do you need to go to confession?
Joan is already floundering in the net. She has the feeling that her answer may decide her destiny. She is like a hunted animal that looks for the smallest gap in the chain of beaters in the hope of escaping its pursuers. The judges never take their eyes from her. Ladvenu and Massieu are the only ones whose faces show signs of sympathy and compassion. Loiseleur, seeing that his plan is working out to perfection, gives Cauchon a slight nudge with his knee. There is a pause.

4 Lemaître realizes that the moment is ripe for presenting the final question which will settle the issue:
Are you in a state of grace?
For a few seconds it is so still that you could hear a pin drop. Joan tries to catch Loiseleur's eye, but he adroitly avoids meeting her look of entreaty. Joan is obviously at a loss how to answer.

5 But then the honest and fair-minded Massieu moves convulsively forward and shouts:
Don't answer, Joan – this question is too dangerous . . .
Cauchon, enraged, rises in all his majesty and bellows with the full power of his lungs:
Be quiet, will you, in the Devil's name!

Massieu defends himself. He explains that nobody has the right to ask such a question of an accused person, least of all when the accused is a young girl standing on her own with nobody to advise her. But Cauchon will tolerate no insubordination. Massieu is forced to kneel there and then and ask for pardon, and must consider himself fortunate not to share de Houppeville's fate.

76 When peace is restored Cauchon gives orders for the hearing to continue. Lemaître, still seething, asks:
Answer now! Are you in a state of grace?
Joan opens her mouth to answer, but appears to have second thoughts – and remains silent. She looks in the direction of Loiseleur, who is apparently absorbed in his own reflections. He is abandoning her to her fate. In his view she is a certain prey; whether she answers yes or no, she is doomed to perdition. But now that Joan has collected her thoughts again, she gives this admirable answer:
If I am not, may God put me there! And if I am, may God so keep me!

77 Joan has broken the chain of beaters. She realizes this and smiles. But her judges, who have sat there greedily waiting for the prey to fall into the net so that they can hurl themselves on it – these judges now sit not knowing what to say or where to look. They gaze at each other in speechless amazement. Some of them unconsciously make the sign of the cross. Loiseleur is beyond doubt the most disconcerted. All of them feel that they have suffered a defeat. This battle is lost; now they must try to win the next one. A short conference takes place. The judges rise to go.

78 Joan throws herself at Cauchon's feet, embraces his knees and begs him:
I implore you to let me come to Mass!
Cauchon thrusts her away so brutally that she hits the bed. She remains lying on the floor.

79 Loiseleur has hastily stolen over to Cauchon and is whispering something in his ear. Cauchon's face lights up. He whispers to the others,

letting them in on Loiseleur's plan. Then he approaches Joan and says to her in his mildest voice:

Joan, if you were allowed to go to Mass now . . .

Joan looks up at Cauchon. Her eyes are already gleaming with hope and expectation. Cauchon continues:

. . . would you consent to give up your men's clothes?

When Joan hears this condition, her hope is extinguished as rapidly as it was kindled. Her expression reflects the deepest disappointment. Her judges repeat Cauchon's question, but she declines their offer. One of them helps her up. She sits on the bed, and all those taking part in the session crowd round her, saying that she must adopt the dress which is appropriate to her sex, if she wants to obtain so great a blessing, and if she wants to live up to her pious feelings.

80 Finally Cauchon says:

Then you would rather keep your men's clothes than come to Mass?

Joan explains through her tears that she is not allowed to do otherwise:

I cannot do anything else . . . it is not in my power!

But Cauchon, unable to control his anger, persists:

. . . this shameless costume . . .

Joan tries in vain to make them understand that this form of dress does not pollute her soul with sin, and that wearing it is not in conflict with the Church's laws. Ignoring Joan's remarks, Cauchon rages:

. . . abominable in the eyes of God . . .

Joan writhes under these denunciations, she implores him to show mercy, but he scourges her pitilessly:

. . . You are no daughter of God . . .

Joan weeps and sobs.

81 Cauchon shows no sympathy. He lowers his voice, bends right over her and hisses:

. . . but a child of the Devil!

Joan cries out and collapses.

The judges watch her for a moment. Ladvenu full of sympathy. Then Cauchon turns to Massieu and says:

Go and prepare the instruments of torture!

Massieu can hardly believe his ears. Are they really going to torture Joan? But a look from Cauchon prevents him from saying anything. He goes out through the door, giving Joan a look of compassion as he does so.

82 The soldiers, who have witnessed the examination, escort him out, and in the ante-room they reproach and abuse him:
Why did you make signs to her and give her good advice?
They threaten to throw him into the Seine if this happens again.

83 THE PRISON
The judges leave Joan, Loiseleur being the last to go. Before he leaves the cell he approaches Joan and pats her hair sympathetically:
Do not grieve . . . place your trust in God, he will not forget you!
Joan turns her tear-stained face to him; full of gratitude for his kind words, she kisses his hand. Then Loiseleur goes out.

Joan is left in solitude for a mere moment, before the soldiers enter in order to bait her in their usual manner. Joan takes no notice of them. One of them tickles her in the ear with a straw. Joan gets up laboriously and sits down on the bed. One of the soldiers suddenly catches sight of the straw crown. He laughs, picks it up, turns it round in his hands, and finally places it on Joan's head. Outraged by this form of sacrilege, she removes it and puts it on the bed; but the soldier replaces the crown on her head, at the same time giving her several slaps in the face. He steps back and peeps through the hollow of his hand, as if to see her better.

84 The other soldiers roar with laughter and say in mocking tones:
She looks just like a daughter of God, eh?
He takes an arrow from his quiver, and places it in Joan's hands.

She lets him do this without resistance. Another soldier takes a pitcher of water, and sprinkles Joan with his fingers. All three bow low before her as if she was a saint, and finally kneel and say:
Saint Joan, pray for us!
Then, still bowing, they step back and go out.

Joan sits for a moment by herself. Without changing her position she prays silently to God. She is praying to the Almighty for strength and courage to endure her trial by torture.

35 Enter Massieu. He is to fetch Joan and bring her to the torture-chamber. He is amazed at finding her decked out in this way, but he gives her such comfort as he can, and leads her out.

36 THE TORTURE-CHAMBER
The judges have already arrived and are taking their places. They consist of Pierre Cauchon, Lemaître, and nine doctors and prelates. The two executioners, Maugier Leparmentier and his assistant, are putting the instruments in order and making other necessary preparations.

37 Enter Massieu with Joan. She is told to come nearer. Cauchon tells one of the younger judges to bring a stool for Joan.

38 The judge who helps Joan to her seat says:
Look at all these kind, sympathetic men . . .
He points at Cauchon, who sits surrounded by his collaborators. Not one face expresses any feeling of friendliness towards the accused. The judge continues:
Do you not consider that these learned doctors are likely to be endowed with more wisdom than you . . .

39 Joan nods half absent-mindedly. The judge is pleased with his happy idea and is about to continue his course of instruction when Joan interrupts him:
. . . but the wisdom of God is even greater!
The judge, who has spoken to Joan as one speaks to a child which stubbornly refuses to listen to reason, shrugs his shoulders and gives up. There is nothing to be done about this woman's arrogance.

90 Cauchon has raised his hands to his face, outraged by such obstinacy. Now he leans forward in his chair and says with great emphasis:
Suppose we were to tell you now that your visions did not – as you believe – come from God . . .

Joan looks up quickly, as if unable to believe her ears. She searches the faces of her judges, one after the other. Cauchon continues:

. . . but are sent to you by the Devil, who wants to bring your soul to perdition?
Joan sits for a moment, deep in thought. Then a smile spreads across her face. Almost unconsciously she shakes her head – and smiles again. Assuredly the Devil has no power over her and is not going to obtain it either.

91 One of the judges asks:
If the Devil appeared in the form of an angel, how could you be certain whether it was a good or a bad angel?
For a moment the smile fades from Joan's lips. She does not answer. Cauchon looks at her for a long time and then says:
It is Satan to whom you have knelt, not Saint Michael!
Joan finds this idea so comical that she has to laugh. She cannot help herself; it is not a provocative laugh, only the spontaneous laughter of a healthy person. But Cauchon strikes the table in anger. Joan stops laughing. Cauchon gazes fixedly at her for some time without saying a word. There is complete silence in the room.

92 Cauchon gets up, approaches Joan in a dignified manner, leans towards her and says:
How can you believe that it is God who guides your steps when you see the abyss opening before your feet?
Joan is serious again. Cauchon continues, pronouncing the words with steadily increasing emphasis:
Do you not understand that it is the Devil who has turned your head . . .
He pauses briefly, then continues:
. . . who has deceived you . . .
Then after another short pause:
. . . and betrayed you?
While Cauchon has been speaking a change has come over Joan. It is clear that she is tormented by doubts. God has promised her that she will be set free. Why has God not kept his promise to her? Why does he let her stand alone against all these churchmen, these learned doctors? She even asks herself whether she has the right to talk as she

does in front of all these gifted and erudite men. Is it true that she is full of pride? Is it the Devil who has possessed her and insinuated in her mind everything that she believed to have come from God?

3 Cauchon, judge of character that he is, has no difficulty in seeing what is going on in this young woman's heart. While Joan is wrestling with her doubts he orders a small table to be set in front of her. He puts a document on the table and then places a pen in her hand. Half absent-mindedly she lets him do all this, but when Cauchon tries to persuade her to sign she tells him that she is unable to read. Cauchon tells the notary to read the declaration aloud:

. . . I declare that I am guilty of the crimes with which I am charged, and which the Devil has misled me into committing. I confess that my visions are the work of the Devil, and I am ready to return to the path of truth and, before all the world, to recant . . .

4 When the notary has finished reading aloud, Cauchon tells Joan warningly that she must sign the declaration, and adds:

The Church is opening her arms to you . . .

Joan's expression makes it clear that she has almost overcome her doubts. Her faith in God and belief in her mission are on the point of gaining the upper hand.

Cauchon threatens her:

. . . but if you do not sign, the Church will turn her back on you and you will stand alone . . .

Joan's crisis is over. Once again she sees clearly the path she must follow. Quietly she puts away the pen. Cauchon sees this and thunders:

. . . alone . . .

But a heavenly light shines from Joan's face. She smiles. With her eyes raised to heaven she says:

. . . alone – with God!

5 Cauchon, realizing that his prey is about to escape him, increases his exertions and displays all his powers of persuasion. Does she know that the Church has the means to compel her? Is she familiar with the secrets of the torture? Cauchon's threats make no impression on Joan.

She feels safe with her God. Her face is transfigured by a beautiful light as she says:

I would rather die than deny God's acts.

Enraged by Joan's pig-headedness, Cauchon loses patience. He orders Joan to be put to torture. While the executioners are taking care of her the judges gather together in a group.

One instrument of torture after another is displayed for Joan's benefit. With an executioner at her side she is conducted past the various appliances. She looks at each one for a long time, trembling with fear. Occasionally the executioner demonstrates with a gesture how one of the instruments is operated. They are trying to frighten Joan out of her senses.

When the executioners have completed their preparations and the torture can begin, Cauchon goes up to Joan and invites her once again to sign the declaration. She refuses and says:

Even though you torture my soul out of my body I shall confess nothing . . .

Cauchon gives orders for the torture to begin. Joan lets out a scream of pain. She is seen to raise one hand. They all think she is indicating her readiness to sign. A judge holds the document out to her, but Joan thrusts it away so violently that it falls on the ground. Somebody picks it up. And Joan says vehemently:

And if I should confess anything, I will afterwards declare that it was only by using force that you made me confess.

96 Joan collapses. The executioner bends over her. She has fainted.

97 The executioner and Massieu carry her out while the judges confer on what procedure to adopt next.

98 THE PRISON

Massieu has gone on ahead to notify Joan's keeper, who sends a man out with a message for Warwick. Massieu prepares Joan's bed and takes the little crown in his hands; he looks at it for a moment, then flings it into a corner. Enter the executioner and his assistant, carrying Joan between them. They lay her on the bed and go out. Before

Massieu leaves the cell, he gives one of the soldiers instructions to keep an eye on Joan.

99 THE TORTURE-CHAMBER

The judges confer. Cauchon thinks the torture should continue, and asks the judges to vote on this proposal, but only one of them is in favour of continuing. This is Loiseleur, who says:

It is medicine for her soul!

Ladvenu gives Loiseleur a look of hostility.

00 THE PRISON

Joan is lying on her wretched bed. The chains, the brutal soldiers, terror, fatigue, and finally the torture have exhausted her strength. She is unrecognizable. Her face is as white as a sheet. Deep shadows under her eyes. When the scene opens, she is lying in a feverish doze. She breathes rapidly and with difficulty.

A soldier with a hard, repellent face is watching at her side. Joan opens her eyes and says:

I am thirsty!

The soldier looks at her with an unfeeling, hostile expression. Then he takes the bowl of water and pours the water over the floor.

01 THE TORTURE-CHAMBER

The judges have not yet concluded their conference. They still seem unable to agree on whether the torture shall continue or not. However, Master Erard wins a majority of the votes when he declares:

This heart is much too hardened . . . there is no hope of our getting a re-cantation this time – we will have to wait!

Cauchon disagrees. A confession would be valuable, even if it was subsequently withdrawn. But Erard continues:

. . . and she might die at our hands!

Cauchon yields to this argument. Even Loiseleur defers to Erard and admits that it would be very damaging to all their interests if Joan died at the hands of the executioner. She would then be certain to enjoy a martyr's glory. Having decided to give up the torture they leave the torture-chamber.

102 THE PRISON

Enter Warwick. He goes over to the bed and bends over Joan – not with any feeling of sympathy. Joan opens her eyes for a moment and meets his cold, hostile gaze. Then she relapses into her state of lethargy.

Warwick goes from the bed towards the door, which he has left standing open behind him. Two doctors whom he has sent for come into the cell. He follows them over to the bed, where he speaks the famous words which for sheer brutality are without parallel in history:
I would not have her die a natural death on any account . . . she has cost me too much for that . . .
The doctors begin to examine Joan. They feel her thighs and right side.

Meanwhile Warwick has gone from the sick-bed over to the door.

103 Enter Loiseleur with the news that Cauchon is waiting in the adjoining room. Warwick is about to go when one of the doctors approaches him and says:
She has a fever, we shall have to bleed her . . .
Warwick shows signs of unease, and asks whether this is really necessary.
The doctor insists that it is. Warwick consents, adding:
But take good care that she does not do away with herself . . . she is very crafty.

104 The doctor turns back to the bed to prepare for the blood-letting. Warwick accompanies Loiseleur into the adjoining room, where Cauchon and some of the other judges are waiting. Cauchon enquires after Joan. Warwick answers in a manner which cannot be misunderstood:
She is very weak. . .
The two men exchange glances. Cauchon and the judges have come to extort a confession from Joan. 'whether because they were afraid of her escaping in this way and dying without having made a recantation, or because her weakened physical condition raised hopes of her soul being easier to purchase'.

Cauchon explains to Warwick how he wants to proceed. Loiseleur joins in the discussion and proposes a drastic remedy. Cauchon approves

Loiseleur's idea and tells Massieu and another young monk to fetch the holy vessel.

05 While this is going on, scenes are shown from the sick-bed and Joan's blood-letting. One of the doctors goes out in order to report that the blood-letting is finished. The patient is better and can undergo examination without danger.

Cauchon, Loiseleur and some of the other clerics come into the cell. Warwick remains with the doctors in the adjoining room.

06 Joan is lying with closed eyes. Cauchon goes over to the bed and bends over Joan with a benevolent, paternal expression. He touches her on the temples. Joan opens her feverish eyes. He asks her in a friendly manner how she is. She makes a movement with her head and at the same time gives a feeble smile. Her eyes shift from Cauchon to the others; what is going to happen now? She is evidently taken by surprise.

07 Cauchon guesses her thoughts, calms her and says:
We have come to give you comfort and strength . . .
A tiny glimmer of gratitude passes over Joan's face. Cauchon and the others install themselves, sitting and standing round her bed.

Cauchon, with the same benevolent air and kindly smile, asks whether Joan has anything to say to him, whether perhaps she has any wishes. Joan holds him for a long time in her gaze, which the fever has made still more penetrating. Then she makes a feeble movement with her head. Cauchon arranges the pillow under her and comes close to her in order to hear better. Joan, whose laboured breathing makes it difficult for her to speak, says in a weak voice:
I am afraid that I am going to die . . .

08 Cauchon speaks some words of consolation to her in his capacity of priest. Joan continues:
. . . If I should die, I implore you to have me buried in consecrated ground!
Joan tries to read the answer from Cauchon's face; she sees only utter benevolence and charitableness. In addition, all the judges now seem

full of affection and sympathy. They tiptoe round her bed, first one and then another coming close up to her. They tuck the blanket round her and touch the place where she has been bled. Some of them kneel and pray for Joan. She regrets not having been more amiable towards these men who are revealing their true feelings, now that they see her in such misery. She feels every confidence in them and in Cauchon. He has caused her great suffering; now, however, he appears no longer as a judge, but as one who has come to show her goodness and compassion. And when Cauchon strokes her hair and says:
The Church is merciful . . .
Joan smiles trustfully.

109 Cauchon continues:
She does not close her heart against those who return to her . . .
Joan, in her weakened state, does not know how to express her gratitude. She squeezes Cauchon's large hand in her tiny one, which is absolutely white. But Cauchon says in a gentle voice:
What would you say if we gave you the Sacrament?
Joan cannot believe her ears. She asks one question after another, which Cauchon answers only with nods and his paternal, benevolent smile. Joan has to find an outlet for her joy, and with her two small hands she takes Cauchon's great fist and places it against her cheek.

110 Cauchon signals to Loiseleur, who opens the door. Enter Massieu with the Eucharist. Cauchon helps Joan sit up in bed. Beside herself with joy and anticipation, she follows the preparations and keeps looking at Cauchon with gratitude. Then she says joyfully:
I am a good Christian . . .

111 The judges in the cell send up a prayer of thanks to God for restoring this lost sheep to the fold. Joan smiles happily.
    Then the notary places a document in front of Joan and offers her a pen. Joan looks in amazement at the document, which she recognizes: it is the same declaration which was placed in front of her for her to sign during the torture scene. Her look of astonishment shifts from the notary to the document and from the latter to Cauchon.

112 She explains once more that all the accusations in the document are what God has commanded her to do. She cannot recant like this without denying her God. Cauchon bends over her and says:
The Sacrament . . . is it not a great blessing?
Joan nods, and her expression seems to want to say: of course, everybody knows that the Church has no greater treasure.
   Cauchon continues:
. . . But you will never share in the Church's blessings, if you do not expiate your sins.

113 He indicates to Joan that she must sign. One of the judges approaches with a wafer. An expression of misery and pain lies on Joan's face as she sits there, sick, feverish and racked with doubts. On one side she sees the wafer, which is more precious to her than life itself, on the other side the document, which will make her confess that she is an agent of the Devil.

114 As if talking to herself and her conscience, she says:
I am a good Christian . . .
As she sits there, alone with all these men, she is the picture of utter despair and loneliness. They all gaze at her with fixed stares. Nobody speaks to her. Finally Cauchon breaks the silence. In a quiet voice he advises Joan to sign and save her soul; but Joan has now mastered her temptation. She hands back the paper. Her body is broken. But the strength of her spirit is unaltered.
   For a moment they are all struck dumb.

15 Cauchon gestures, ordering the Sacrament to be carried out. The tears run down Joan's cheeks, when she sees the priests going out with the sacred vessel.
I love God . . . I love Him with all my heart!
she says.

16 Loiseleur, who has accompanied the procession into the adjoining room, tells Warwick the outcome.

117 In the cell the atmosphere has changed abruptly. Cordiality is replaced by coldness, gentleness by severity. The judges are overcome by a feeling which can almost be called irritation – irritation with Joan and what they call her pig-headedness.

118 Jean d'Estivet reproaches her harshly for allowing her vanity to take precedence over the salvation of her soul. He concludes with these words:
If you die in this hour, you die as an infidel . . .
Joan, goaded by the mental torture to which she has been subjected, answers in words conjured up by her *sancta simplicitas*; but Jean d'Estivet, revelling in the pain his speech has given Joan, obliterates her with the wounding words, which sting like the lash of a whip:
Your soul is doomed to perdition . . .
To which one of the others adds:
. . . to everlasting torture in the flames of Hell!

119 Groaning under the burden of the injustice and malice they are heaping on her, Joan turns for comfort to Cauchon, whose hand she has just pressed to her cheek; but Cauchon has no comfort to give. He draws back and says coldly:
Joan, you are a child of the Devil!

120 She looks at him in unaffected terror. Then it is as if a veil gradually falls from her eyes; as if the whole truth is revealed to her in a flash of lightning. They have lied to her in order to trap her. In her overwrought and exhausted condition she loses all self-control. Fever and ecstasy take charge of her features. As a stream of reproaches pours from her lips they all gaze at her in terror: is this the last flare-up before death, is it madness? All of them feel themselves face to face with something unfamiliar and extraordinary. Slowly they draw away. Cauchon rises and backs round his chair.

121 Foaming at the mouth, Joan continues to pour out a torrent of words:
You say that I am a child of the Devil . . .
and she continues:

JEANNE D'ARC *The English governor Warwick, played by an anonymous café-proprietor.*

Scene 62: *Cauchon listens to Loiseleur's conversation with Joan in the prison cell.*

JEANNE D'ARC *Close-up of two judges.*

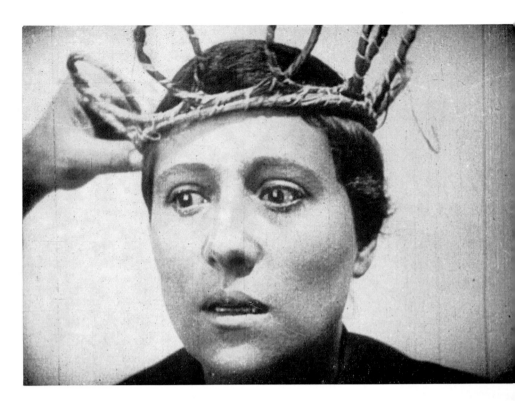

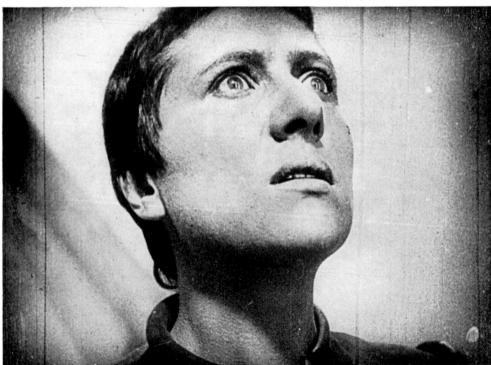

JEANNE D'ARC Scene 83: *Joan with the crown of straw.*

. . . but I say it is you who have been sent by the Devil to torment me!
She stands up in bed, pointing at each judge in turn.
  A violent storm of anger breaks out:
Blasphemy! She is possessed! This is monstrous!
The judges huddle together in their agitation and terror, and gradually
withdraw.

122 And now Joan falls back on her bed, exhausted. She groans and gasps
for breath. She wipes the sweat from her forehead with her sleeve.
For a moment there is silence. Only her groans can be heard. The judges
look at each other, not knowing what to do. Then they turn to Cauchon
who is pondering. It is he who breaks the silence with the following
words addressed to Massieu:
There is nothing for it . . . give the executioner his orders!
While the doctors who have entered during the preceding scene are
attending to Joan, the judges leave the room.

123 By the time the judges come out into the castle yard, there are already
rumours of what has happened in the cell. The inhabitants of the castle
crowd round to hear the news and learn of the preparations now in
hand for the penultimate act of the drama. From the castle yard a small
door leads out to the churchyard, which lies outside the castle walls.
The judges make for the churchyard.

124 THE PRISON
Some soldiers have come with a stretcher. They lift Joan onto it and
carry her out.

125 THE CHURCHYARD
One group of judges after another is seen moving forward to the spot
from which they are to witness the impending ceremony.

126 Joan, lying on the stretcher, is carried into the churchyard.

127 The churchyard, which is surrounded by walls, is very big, but only a
few graves can be seen in it. They are all covered with flat stones after

the custom of the Middle Ages. In those days churchyards served as a meeting-place at certain festivals, and the judicial authorities of the Church often used them as a stage for important announcements and abjurations, which they wanted known to as many people as possible; they formed a theatrical setting, with graves and gravestones as sets. A stench of putrefaction arose from this earth filled with dead bodies. The poisonous smell of nothingness. The smell of stones, corpses and worms.

Against the buttress of the church two platforms have been erected and covered with red velvet. On one of them the entire assembly of judges is sitting in state: Pierre Cauchon, the Inquisitor, and a host of jurists in scarlet caps and purple skull-caps. The other platform is for Joan.

128 Escorted by English soldiers, Joan's little procession comes slowly to this place.

129 Everywhere in the churchyard, and even on the walls, there are thousands of people, heads jostling. The great majority of them are favourably disposed towards Joan. When she is carried in, every neck is craned to catch a glimpse of her. For her part Joan tries to read her destiny in their faces. From the way they look at her she gets the impression that their feelings towards her are friendly. Joan, who for months has lived remote from this earth, is visibly moved. She smiles at the tiny flowers which greet her from the grass. She almost touches them with her hand and imagines that she is caressing them. But when she looks in the other direction, her eye falls on two gravediggers who are engaged in opening up an old grave. She sees the worms swarming in the skulls which are thrown up, and she is filled with the fear of death. Once more she ponders over the words which the members of the judicial body have addressed to her, and she thinks sadly of her fellow-countrymen, who seem to have forsaken her completely.

130 The tiny procession approaches the platform reserved for Joan. Loiseleur comes forward to meet the procession and assist her. She smiles happily at this man, whom she believes to be on her side. She is helped to a seat on a little stool.

31 Her face is as white as a sheet. She closes her eyes, which have been hurting intensely, bows her head and places her hands on her breast – to all appearances indifferent to everything happening around her. Erard, Massieu and two notaries take their places at Joan's side.

32 Loiseleur goes back to the larger platform where he takes his place near Cauchon, who now gets up and declares the session opened.
Joan, for the last time I order you to abjure. Are you willing to sign?
Joan sits motionless and expressionless. She hears nothing, and smiles distantly.

33 One of the prelates takes his place at Joan's side. He begins an admonitory sermon, taking as text the words from Saint John's Gospel: 'The branch cannot bear fruit of itself except it abide in the vine.' Inspiring terror at one moment, speaking sanctimoniously the next, he warns, he threatens, he implores, he mocks, he calls her a cunning traitor, cruel, greedy, a liar, a heretic, a witch. His anger rises in measure with his words and finally reaches a point where it overflows in a torrent. He is unquestionably a powerful speaker.

34 But the stream of words appears to flow over Joan's head without touching her. The past and the present mingle in her thoughts; yet nothing of what goes on around her escapes her notice. She looks towards the open grave. She cannot see the actual gravedigger, only the earth which he is shovelling up from deep down. Then she hears a shout of command.

35 In the densest part of the crowd the soldiers are clearing a passage to allow a carriage into the churchyard. The new arrivals are the executioner and his two assistants.

36 Erard is enraged at Joan's apparent lack of interest in what he is saying. He raises his voice and shouts furiously:
. . . This woman's arrogance fills one with disgust . . .
Joan's attitude remains unchanged. She does not move. Erard's voice trembles as he continues:

There has never been a monster in France like the one which has appeared in the form of Joan.
He pauses, leans towards her, and with a threatening gesture shouts at Joan:
It is to you, Joan, I am talking . . . it is to you I say that your king is a heretic!

137 Now Joan turns towards him. She can withstand all his invective, when it is her own person and her own honour that are at stake; but this accusation directed at her king deeply outrages Joan's love of France and of Charles, the king. Her expression is one of anger and indignation as she says:
Indeed, my lord, I am ready to maintain, even at the risk of my life, that my king is the noblest man in all Christendom . . .

138 A ripple of applause can be heard among the spectators. The soldiers, who are standing side by side in closed ranks, turn threateningly.

139 Thrown out of his stride by Joan's answer, the preacher embarks on a tirade, which Joan answers confidently; finally, not knowing how to respond, he shouts to Massieu:
Make her be quiet!
The spectators derive much derisive enjoyment from this little scene.
   Order has been restored on the platform. Massieu has persuaded Joan to keep quiet. The preacher is approaching his peroration. He points to the judges and declares they have proved incontestably that Joan has violated the Church's doctrines in deed as well as in word; and asks her if she has anything to say in answer to this. She reflects for a moment and, while the spectators stand on tiptoe to see what is happening, she rises to her feet and says:
I alone am responsible for everything that I have said and done . . .
Joan draws a deep breath before continuing. All those standing round her gaze at her expectantly. Then she says:
. . . If I have done any wrong, I am to blame, and nobody else!

140 She sits down calmly. Erard, however, is almost inclined to interpret her words as a declaration that she is now ready to recognize the error

of her ways. He leans forward towards the notary, who hands her a paper. Several of the judges have come forward, also one of Warwick's secretaries. There is so much tumult and confusion round Joan that she has difficulty hearing. Sommaire explains:

It is the abjuration . . .

Joan does not understand what this means. What is the meaning of 'abjure'? She turns to Erard to ask his advice.

Explain it to her!

Erard orders Massieu. The latter asks to be excused, but after glancing at Erard he does not dare to insist, and is obliged to advise Joan of the danger she will incur by refusing. He says to her:

If you do not sign you will be burnt!

41 Among the crowd thronging the place the word 'burnt' can be heard flying from mouth to mouth. Around Joan on the platform the air is filled with shouted words. Joan asks Massieu for advice; he tells her that when the Church advises her to sign she must do so. Once again she turns to Erard and asks him to tell her whether she must abjure. He answers:

Either you sign – or you will go to the stake!

and he points at the executioner, who at this moment approaches at a sign from Warwick. Now Joan understands the cruel death in store for her, and she is afraid. Jesus Christ also was afraid when He learned that His hour was come. Fear has overcome her spirit and is affecting her feelings as well as her judgement; with the threat of the stake hanging over her she now begins to consider the proposition which has been put to her. Almost unconsciously she turns her face towards the grave. She sees shovelful after shovelful of earth piling up . . . a human skull appears among the lumps of soil. Worms are writhing in the eye-sockets. The spectators shout:

Sign, Joan, sign!

42 But she does not hear them. She is breathing heavily and feeling giddy. She looks vacantly at her surroundings like somebody coming out of a faint, not knowing where he is. In a whisper which is barely audible to anybody but herself she says:

I have done no wrong . . . I believe in the twelve articles of the Creed and in God's Ten Commandments!

143 Even Erard's heart bleeds at the sight of such deep unhappiness. His tone changes, and his voice becomes almost syrupy as he says:
Joan, we have great sympathy for you!
Warwick gives a sign to the executioner, who is approaching with a rope.

144 Now Loiseleur mounts the platform and takes up a position on the other side of Joan. He says to her in a low voice:
You have no right to die . . . you must continue to fight for France . . . for the King of France.
Joan feels a pang in the pit of her stomach when he pronounces the name of her country and her king, which mean everything to her and are never out of her thoughts.

145 The spectators follow with anxiety and deep involvement everything taking place on the platform. Those standing round her, who have witnessed her fear, make all kinds of golden promises if only she will consent to sign. Cries of 'Sign, sign!' resound from mouth to mouth, and Loiseleur urges her earnestly to follow this advice.

Joan is dazed, and no longer understands a thing. Anxiously she explores the eyes of those standing round her. Her terrible uncertainty is reflected in her expression. The moment has arrived when she begins to yield to the unremitting pressure. And when, at this very moment, the executioner rises up before her, she surrenders.

146 She casts a frightened glance at her surroundings; then she slowly kneels and bows her head. Sommaire seizes the document which has been placed in front of Joan for her signature and reads it aloud, sentence by sentence. Sentence by sentence Joan repeats his words, smiling feebly and speaking in a peculiar mechanical way which betrays the fact that she is far away, absorbed in her own thoughts. During the reading Erard gestures with the pen to the larger platform to inform the judges that Joan is going to sign. The tension among the spectators is at breaking point.

The reading is concluded. Joan gets to her feet. Erard puts a pen in her hand; round Joan the excitement is palpable. People seem to be afraid of her dying.

47 But Joan is like somebody who has escaped from a great danger, whose relief now finds expression in a tremendous joy, almost resembling gaiety.

48 She draws a circle, explaining as she does so that she is unable to write. But this is not good enough for Erard. So Loiseleur steps forward and guides Joan's hand, enabling her to write the word JEHANNE, followed by a cross. When Joan has signed, Erard, with the document raised over his head, gives a wink of triumph to let the judges know that he has succeeded in his task. The document passes from hand to hand until it reaches Loiseleur, who says cheerfully to Joan:
You have done a good day's work today . . . you have saved your soul!

49 And he hurries away to give Cauchon the document.
Among the spectators the tension is released in shouts of joy. But one or two English soldiers, who have seen Joan's smile, go up to her and shout at the priests around her:
She has only made fools of you!
The priests push them away. Cauchon, who has received the document, now gives a signal for Joan to come forward and hear her sentence of judgement.

50 Joan descends from the platform, leaning on Massieu. In his enthusiasm one of the spectators forgets himself and bursts out:
Long live the Maid! . . . Long live France!
Two soldiers turn abruptly, force their way through the crowd, seize the unfortunate man who has given vent to his patriotic feelings, and lead him away.

51 Joan has come before her judges' great platform. Cauchon takes the document from his secretary and begins to read it aloud:
In as much as you have at last renounced the error of your ways, we release you from excommunication from the Church . . .

Cauchon pauses for a moment. Joan stands before her judges with folded hands. A smile of gratitude is sketched on her face. She lowers her head to conceal her joy.

Then Cauchon continues:

But in as much as you have rashly sinned we condemn you . . .

Joan looks up with an expression of fear and surprise. Cauchon continues his reading:

. . . to perpetual imprisonment, there to eat the bread of sorrow and drink the water of affliction . . .

Joan stands for a moment, dumbfounded. It is as if she cannot grasp the meaning of what she has just heard. She feels as if her heart is in her mouth. Her eyes have the expression of a hunted animal. Then she hides her face in her hands and weeps. Cauchon gives a sign for Joan to be led out. She staggers away, leaning on Massieu's arm.

152–3 THE GATEWAY LEADING INTO THE CASTE YARD

Joan meets the two soldiers who earlier maintained that she had made fools of her judges. They heap abuse upon her, and Massieu has to protect her.

154 THE PRISON

Joan is escorted in by the jailer. He makes her sit down on a stool and starts cutting off her hair. Joan is seized by a new and dispiriting fear. Although she is in pain, she manages to weep inaudibly, sobbing without a sound. When her weeping eases off for a moment she whispers:

Oh, I am so tired, so tired . . .

But the jailer is concentrating entirely on his work. The locks of hair fall on the ground. Joan weeps ceaselessly. The events in the churchyard pass in succession before her eyes, but now she sees them in relation to one another, from a new angle and with a sharper perception. She realizes that it is the fear of death which has caused her to panic. She regards what she has done as the greatest sin she has ever committed. She is unable to forgive herself for having told lies through fear of death. Bitter are the tears which well from her eyes, from sources almost dried up, as Joan asks herself how she may still atone for her sin and repair the damage she has done. She turns to the jailer and says with an air of entreaty:

Oh, I am so tired . . .

The jailer mumbles something incomprehensible. Sympathy is not to be expected from this quarter. Joan feels like an outcast; it is hard to imagine a greater humiliation for a woman than to be shorn of her hair. And Joan is a woman.

At last the cutting operation is concluded.

55 Joan gets up and sits on her bed. She is like somebody who is on the verge of collapse from lack of sleep, and who does mechanically whatever he is told. Unconsciously she raises her hands to her face, shudders and looks at her hands with dread, as if they were unclean. She feels ashamed. What has she done? She has denied her God. She thinks of Peter's denial, of his threefold denial before cock-crow.

56 The jailer, who has left Joan by herself for a moment, now returns with a broom. Almost without thinking, and with a melancholy smile, Joan follows the broom as it sweeps up her hair – hair from Orléans and from Rheims. The jailer sweeps it up onto a shovel. He glances round the cell to see if there is anything else he can sweep up while he is about it. His eye falls on the plaited straw crown, the martyr's crown, which has landed in a corner. Joan sees the broom gathering in the crown. That too! It is as if in this little incident Joan sees a sign from God. She bitterly laments the glory she has lost by her abjuration.

The jailer leaves the cell. Joan sits by herself. She thinks of what she has done. This document signed by her hand is a denial, a denial of God. How she wishes she could tear it to shreds! She is in consternation over the enormity of her sin. Her soul is drowning in remorse. She flushes, she shakes her head violently: No! No! No!

She strikes her breast. She feels that she is damned eternally, eternally abandoned by God. She raises her head in bewilderment. She thinks of Hell. She stands up as if to cry out in remorse. Then suddenly she recalls the executioner and the stake at which her flesh will burn. She collapses again on her bed. She sits there in agony, her head hidden in her hands. The door opens. The jailer comes in. Now Joan

rises, having made her decision. She hurries over to the jailer and
shouts:

Go and fetch the judges . . . I take back . . . I regret . . . I have lied . . .

She looks at him with tear-stained eyes and gives him a push to make
him go and tell the prelates. She is seized by a deadly fear, she is
terrified that a new fit of weakness will master her before she can put
into effect the decision she has just made. She knows that this decision
will probably lead to her death, but this she feels strong enough to meet.
And now that the first step has been taken she trembles with impatience.
She is weary of the struggle and longs to be free.

157 The spectators of the scene in the churchyard have still not returned
to the town, but have encamped in a large open space where booths
selling cider and other drinks have been set up. They are grouped in
families on the grass, some of them are crowding round the booths,
and the younger ones are dancing and singing to the sound of music.

The preceding prison scenes alternate with short shots of this folk-
life: dancing bears – acrobats – jugglers – a musician – a hobby-horse –
a dance-leader – a man with a stick over his shoulder and a cask hanging from the stick – penny in the bucket – another musician who has
fastened together a drum and a flute, which he holds in the left hand,
with the drum-stick in his right. A wild dance – a man selling birds –
dwarfs – contortionists.

The following prison scene is interrupted by glimpses of the preparations round the bonfire which is to be lit in the castle yard: a man
carrying firewood to the stake, a broken carriage-wheel in the fuel, etc.

158 The jailer now finds Cauchon in conversation with Warwick at the
entrance to the chapel. The jailer explains briefly what has happened
in the prison. Warwick and Cauchon exchange eloquent glances. At
the same moment Loiseleur comes out from the chapel. In a few words
Cauchon puts him in the picture and tells him to assemble some of the
judges and notaries.

159 Meanwhile Joan sits waiting impatiently in her prison. It is evident
that she does not make a sacrifice such as hers without doing her nature

an injury. She is racked by deep despair and her nerves show it. She shivers; her teeth chatter. She wrings her hands so that her knuckles are completely white.

60 Finally Cauchon enters, followed by various judges and notaries. They find the young girl dissolved in tears, her face contorted. It is a poor, helpless girl of twenty whom they have defeated.

During the following scene Cauchon exudes an air of benevolence and satisfaction. In contrast with his earlier demeanour he is now calm and equable. His feelings are pleasurable, but it is not a malicious pleasure; he is sure of his prey!

They sit down, and Cauchon asks Joan why she has sent for them. With a sob, but also with an expression of determination, she answers: *I have committed a great sin . . .*
She has to break off, choked by tears.

61 The judges comfort her and try to alleviate her grief, so that she can continue:
. . . I have denied God in order to save my life.
The judges look at one another. Not one of them is so hard-hearted as to be untouched by the young woman's genuine distress.

62 Even Cauchon is moved. It is a moment before he speaks. Then he says:
So you still believe that you are sent by God?
Joan nods in confirmation.

63 Again the judges exchange looks. The notary raises his head from his book. He examines the judges' faces searchingly, looks at Joan and writes in his notes: 'Fatal answer.' Cauchon has stood up. However dulled his human feelings may be, it still goes against the grain with him to send Joan to the stake, even though she herself is asking to die. He says in a friendly tone:
But, Joan, you have admitted in front of everybody that you were misled by the Devil.

Joan, who has gradually regained her self-control, does not answer immediately. It is only when the judges press her that she replies:
Everything I said was for fear of the stake!
Cauchon holds a whispered consultation with the others, but it is clear that they all regard it as wasted effort to continue. Cauchon says:
Have you anything else to tell us?
Joan shakes her head. The judges rise to go. When Cauchon goes into the adjoining room his eye falls on Warwick, who has just come up the stairs and now gives Cauchon a look of enquiry. Cauchon merely says:
It is all over!
Warwick receives the news with no indication of surprise.

Meanwhile the judges have started to go down the stairs, when Cauchon holds the last two back. They are Ladvenu and Massieu. Cauchon drops his voice and gives them an order.

164 The two monks go into the cell, where they find Joan sitting with her hands in her lap. She is now calm and decided. What is she thinking about? About her home in Domrémy – or about death? Massieu and Ladvenu remain standing by the door. Joan does not see them, so preoccupied is she with her own thoughts. They approach with cautious steps, as people do involuntarily in the house of death. Ladvenu calls to her. She looks up, surprised to see him.

Then Ladvenu says:
Joan, I have come to prepare you for death!
For a moment silence reigns, so deep that Joan's breathing can be heard. Then she says in a barely audible voice:
Now . . . already?
Ladvenu, struggling with the tears which are muffling his voice, answers yes. Another long, long silence. Then Joan asks, almost as if fearing the answer:
What kind of death?
Ladvenu, choked by his feelings, is unable to speak. He makes a sign for Massieu to answer on his behalf. Massieu says:
At the stake!
A slight shudder passes over Joan's face, but in her soul there is no longer any struggle or doubt.

65 Ladvenu, who has now regained his self-control, gives Massieu a quiet
order. Massieu goes out hurriedly. When he has gone Ladvenu says:
How can you still believe that you are sent by God?
Joan smiles, as if she knows more than other men, and answers:
His ways are not our ways!
After a pause she adds:
Yes, I am His child!
Ladvenu, moved by this persistent faith, says presently:
And the great victory?
Joan looks at him as if amazed at his asking such a stupid question.
She answers:
My martyrdom . . .
Ladvenu nods. He looks at her as at a saint descended from heaven. Yet
he cannot refrain from asking one more question:
And your release?
Joan answers with a look of ecstasy in her eyes:
. . . Death . . . !
Her purity and the sincerity of her faith in God are almost dazzling to
Ladvenu. He gets up. He pities the unhappy Joan, and is troubled over
this soul which is endangered beyond hope of salvation. He turns to
Joan and asks her if she wants to confess. She accepts his offer gratefully
and kneels.

66 Massieu has gone to fetch the Eucharist. A procession of priests, wearing
surplices and stoles, and carrying lights in their hands, comes out of the
chapel and goes in the direction of the castle yard, singing litanies.

67 Everyone in the castle yard kneels; the women are in tears. To every
entreaty the priests answer:
Pray for her!

68 Presently the procession arrives at Joan's cell, and she prepares to receive
the Eucharist. Ladvenu takes the consecrated Host in his hands, shows
it to Joan and says:
Do you believe that this is the Body of Christ?
Joan receives the Body of Christ with touching meekness. She weeps

copiously as once again she finds Him from whom she has so long been kept apart. In the fullness of her heart she raises her voice and offers to Jesus prayers of a childlike gentleness and moving quality.

The cell door stands open.

169 In the ante-room Loiseleur has come into view. He hears Joan talking with her Saviour and is deeply moved. Even this man's eyes well over with tears. He is afraid he will be unable to stifle his emotion and withdraws.

170 The solemn ceremony is over. The monks leave.

171 The jailer comes in with a coat which Joan is to wear.

172 Meanwhile rumours are circulating among the crowd in the area behind the churchyard that Joan has withdrawn her abjuration. Now they set out in swarms for the castle, pressing over the lowered draw-bridge leading into the castle yard, where the English soldiers control the flow in such a way that they keep the invaders concentrated in one corner of the yard. Through the gate hundreds of curious sightseers can be seen climbing up into trees and standing on the parapets of the bridge in the hope of seeing a tiny fragment of the unaccustomed spectacle.

173 In between, scenes from the prison are shown. Joan is wearing a coat that comes down to her feet, which are bare. Her earlier calm seems to have disappeared. She prays and weeps incessantly. Ladvenu and Massieu, who have returned to fetch her, lead her away.

174 Joan has arrived at the castle yard. In her coat she appears to many of those present as a vision from God. An old woman approaches, hands Joan a cup of milk, weeps and kneels. The poor child, who is herself in need of comfort, offers the woman such comfort as she can, but the English soldiers put an end to this scene.

75 The stake is erected in the middle of the castle yard.[1] The fuel is piled up on a foundation of stone. The post to which the victim is to be tied projects over the fuel. The intention is for thousands of people to witness with their own eyes that the Maid has really been burnt. A notice-board is fastened to the stake, with the following inscription: 'Heretic, Relapsed, Apostate, Idolatress.'

Further away there is a platform for the judges and the English nobility; another is reserved for the preacher and for spectators.

76 When Joan has taken her place at the stake one of the judges, Nicolas Midi, stands and begins his sermon:
In the name of the Lord, amen!

77 For Joan it is as if his voice has reached her from far away. She weeps incessantly, as she watches the executioner's final preparations; she sees him bending over

78 His coal-bucket; later she sees him, with a knife in his mouth, uncoiling the rope which is to fasten her to the stake.

79 Nicolas Midi continues his sermon:
. . . Like a rotten member we cut you off from the body of the Church.
The preacher turns to face Joan directly; she listens attentively and gives an unconscious nod. At the same moment she sees a flock of doves taking off and flying into the heavens. Then Nicolas Midi ends his short address:
Joan, go forth in peace . . . the Church is unable to protect you!
Joan, who retains to the end her respect for the Church's servants, inclines politely and gratefully in his direction.

80 In a loud voice she prays:
Dear God, I accept my death willingly and gladly . . .
Her face becomes more serious and more anguished; she continues:
. . . but I entreat Thee, if Thou lovest me, that my suffering may be short . . .

---

[1] The burning actually took place not in the castle yard but in the market-square of Rouen.

181 Her lament, mild but strongly spoken, rings through the hushed square. Everyone holds his breath to hear the condemned Joan's last words; every eye turns towards her and watches for her smallest movement. They are deeply affected by the simplicity she shows, face to face with death. Many are in tears, even some of the English soldiers.

182 At the end of her prayer she says to Ladvenu, with tears in her eyes: *Where will I be tonight?*
Ladvenu exhorts her to have faith in God: with the help of the Almighty she will attain her place in Paradise. The English soldiers grow impatient, and one of their officers approaches the platform and says: *Look here, priest, are you going to be all day?*

183 Ladvenu insists on his right to prepare the young woman for death. And he says to Massieu, who is bringing him a small missal: *Joan wishes to have a cross with her when she dies!*

184 Ladvenu instructs Massieu to fetch one from the chapel, and with the little missal in his hand he reads the prayers for those under sentence of death.
  One of the English soldiers has heard Ladvenu's words to Massieu. He extracts two bits of wood from a faggot lying ready for the bonfire, and joins them so that they form a modest little cross.

185 Joan, who has followed his movements, is touched. She takes the cross lovingly and reverently, and covers it with kisses.

186 The English captain is now losing patience, and orders the executioner to do his duty.

187 Massieu returns with the processional cross. He shows it to Joan; she is inexpressibly happy as she takes it with both hands, kisses it with tears in her eyes, and addresses ardent prayers to it.

188 Now her eye falls on the executioner, who has climbed up on the other side of her in order to tie her to the stake. He drops the rope; she picks it up. She is bound brutally to the stake.

Ladvenu remains standing. During Joan's prayer he remains holding the crucifix in front of her, so that throughout she can see her Saviour. When the executioner has secured Joan he descends. Ladvenu continues to speak words of comfort to Joan.

All around her are now in tears. Loiseleur weeps. Even Cauchon weeps. The executioner has made his final preparations.

189 In his hand he holds the flaming torch which is to set the bonfire alight.

190 Joan suddenly catches sight of the fire, but her first thought is not for herself: she thinks only of Ladvenu, who seems to have forgotten the danger he is exposed to. She shouts to him:
The fire! Get down!

191 But she implores him urgently to continue right up to the end holding the cross raised before her eyes.

192 The flames crackle and climb higher.

193 Suddenly a deathly hush descends on the square. A dull silence. Only the crackle of the flames and the mumbled prayers of the priests can be heard. Oppressed by this stillness, some of the spectators fall on their knees, and others follow their example. Many of them light wax candles.

194 The flames leap from one faggot to another . . . they advance in little jumps over cavities and gaps in the fuel. Sparks fly, smoke whirls up; through the smoke, which occasionally conceals Joan, can be seen part of her

195 Face, which is raised to heaven, and her mouth, which is whispering prayers. Then her eyes seek Christ, whom Ladvenu continues to hold up towards her; Christ who, like herself, is enveloped in smoke.

196 Through the smoke she sees the executioner stirring the fire,

197 And a soldier on his knees trying to get near enough to the bonfire to throw the martyr's crown on it.

198 She also sees Massieu, who is sprinkling holy water on the bonfire from his stoup.

199 Meanwhile the judges have risen. The clerics are not allowed to witness the actual execution, but their departure is in the nature of a flight. The eyes of most of them are filled with tears. They all cross themselves as they withdraw.

200 The English soldiers force a way for them through the crowd, but as the priests approach the spectators the latter draw back of their own accord to avoid contact with them. On every face you can read contempt, in every quarter you can hear the traitors being taunted as such.

201 Suddenly the first tongues of flame lick round Joan's feet. She squirms. The things of this earth are vanishing, and Joan's thoughts are now only of the King of Heaven. In spite of the pain and terror she does not forget her Christ – indeed it is as if, with every second that passes, she is coming steadily closer to Him.
Jesus!
she begins to scream in her long death-struggle.

202 The weeping crowds repeat the name of Jesus.

203 Innumerable tongues of flame, growing constantly in size, number and fierceness, are now fanning round her.

204 The rope binding her to the stake begins to burn.

205 Joan is frantic with terror:
Jesus!
she screams in her agony.

06 The echo repeats her cry in the sad and silent square. The bystanders pray in chorus, while the women weep and wail:
Intercede for us . . .
Others continue:
. . . now and in our last hour.

07 Joan's coat is already in flames, consumed by the fire as far as the knees. Her feet are burning.

08 But the executioner continues piling fuel on the bonfire. An ominous, infernal silence prevails.

09 Joan screams:
Jesus! Jesus!

10 But the bystanders, who during these final scenes stand as if paralysed by the fire and by Joan's cries, are seized by a mood compounded of fear and ecstasy. Outbursts of anger and indignation against the oppressors can already be heard. The English soldiers take up a threatening posture.

11 The flames climb steadily higher.

12 The notice-board fastened over Joan's head goes up in flames and falls into the bonfire.

13 A last vision is caught of Joan's face, contorted in terror. She pronounces once more the name of Jesus, lets her head slump and gives up the ghost. The tumult grows among the bystanders, clenched fists are raised in the air.

14 Threatening words can be heard. Then somebody in the crowd gives free expression to what everybody is thinking and shouts:
You have burnt a saint!
The cry is taken up, until it is heard from every throat.

215 The rope fastening Joan to the stake has burnt through and falls in
ashes. Joan's body totters and sinks into the bonfire.

216 At a sign from Warwick the soldiers pursue the mob out of the castle
yard with thrusts of their lances, through the gate and over the draw-
bridge, which is then raised. Many fall victim to the soldiers' brutality
or are trampled to death.

217 The smoke rises in a column, concealing Joan.

218 On Warwick's orders the executioner rakes through the fire. Normally
no trace of Joan should remain – but what is this? Joan's heart is un-
damaged. He shows it to Warwick and pours oil on the flames, but
still the heart will not catch fire. He tries in vain, with the help of sul-
phur and coal, to make it burn: the flame leaps up, guided by his
expert hand, but when the fire subsides again the executioner finds the
heart still intact. Convinced that he is witnessing a manifest miracle, he
looks questioningly at Warwick, who answers curtly:
Throw this lot in the Seine!

219 In his anguish the executioner falls on his knees before Ladvenu,
terrified that he will be condemned for having burnt a saint.

*As the sun went down Joan's heart was sunk in the river, the heart which
from that time became the heart of France, just as she herself was the
incarnation of the eternal France.*

VAMPYR

Vampire

A man is walking down the narrow riverside path that winds its way towards the spot where a ferry crosses to the other bank. It is a summer evening, after sunset. The traveller, Nikolas, is carrying a rucksack, and in his hand a pair of fishing rods. He wants to spend his holiday in solitude, which is why he has come to this remote region in search of peace.

He arrives at the old inn and finds the door closed. The inn is lying in profound silence, as if all its occupants have gone to bed. Nikolas rattles at the door, but it is well and truly locked. At this moment he sees a reaper walking along with his scythe over his shoulder. He looks at the man curiously as he walks down towards the ferry. He shouts after him:

Hullo, you there!

But the reaper, not hearing his cry, continues on his way. The landscape is bathed in a grey, dim twilight; every object has a tinge of unreality. Nikolas goes round to the back of the house. There he discovers a window in which a light can be seen. He comes nearer, knocks on the window pane and listens; but not a sound reaches him. Simultaneously the light goes out. Nikolas knocks again. Silence still. But now a window is opened quietly on the floor above, and a timid child's voice asks:

Who's there?

Nikolas runs his eye up the façade of the house and discovers a little girl of thirteen with a gentle, frightened face. She says to him:

I'll come down and open the door.

She gestures, indicating that he is to go to the front door. Then she carefully closes the window.

As Nikolas stands waiting he glances down in the direction of the ferry. The ferryman – who has a white beard – boards the ferry-boat which begins crossing the river. He goes backwards and forwards, pulling laboriously at the iron chains which run rattling and squealing round the ungreased wheels.

Meanwhile the little girl has opened the door of the inn. She is a strange child. She looks rather small for her age and wears spectacles. Her eyes are moist, as if she has just been crying. When she talks to somebody she tilts her head backwards.

Nikolas enters, and the girl shuts the door behind him. He slips his rucksack from off his shoulders. As he is doing so a door opens a few inches and a face appears, staring inquisitively. The little girl gives a sign to Nikolas to follow her up the stair leading to the guest rooms. She lights a candle in a little enamel candlestick of the kind found in country districts, and hands him the candlestick.

On the floor above, the doors out onto the passage are standing open. The rooms are poorly furnished, the beds without bedclothes, the windows dirty, as if they have not been cleaned for a long time. The little girl conducts Nikolas to a spartanly furnished room. On a table he finds a candlestick with a half-used candle, beside which are lying another candle and a box of matches. He lights the candle. The girl, who has remained standing in the doorway, says with an inclination of the head:

Good night, sir!

Nikolas: *Good night!*

The girl disappears and shuts the door behind her. He glances round the room. Over the bed hangs one of those copperplate engravings, framed in glass, that are so common in the country. Nikolas looks at the engraving for a moment. It represents something like 'Death pays a call'. Then from a neighbouring room he hears a woman sobbing.

Close-up: Nikolas turning and listening. He opens the door a few inches. A man's voice is heard trying to calm the woman, but she is incapable of mastering her despair. She breaks out, in a voice choked with tears:

Oh, why did he have to die – why should I have to lose him . . . why, why?

Man's voice (consolingly): *Don't cry!*

Woman's voice (in despair): *My little boy, my little boy!*

The weeping eases off.

Woman's voice: *Oh God, oh God!*

We hear a door opening, followed by footsteps; then everything is quiet again. Nikolas, who had lifted the light to look at the engraving, puts it down, and after locking the door crosses to the window to pull down the blind. First, however, he looks out across the river, where he sees the reaper with the scythe sitting on the railing of the ferry-boat, while the ferryman continues his monotonous progress up and down – like the ferryman on the river separating life and death. Then Nikolas draws down the blind. It is one of those blinds, often seen in the country, that have some painted motif: a temple, a forest or the like. He takes out his watch. The sound of the watch continues during the following shot, which shows the shadow of the house creeping slowly over the ground – a symbol of time passing.

A moment later we return to the room. Nikolas has been asleep for some time. Somewhere in the house a clock strikes eleven; then we hear the footsteps of somebody approaching and knocking on the door: two knocks – and again two knocks. In his deep sleep Nikolas seems to hear the knocking without taking it in fully. He reacts while still half asleep, turns his head towards the door and sees the handle slowly turning. Then the door is opened, inch by inch, as if by an invisible hand. A man enters the room, wearing a full-length dressing-gown. Without a sound he approaches the bed and leans over Nikolas.

Are you asleep?

Almost unconsciously Nikolas opens his eyes and meets the stranger's enquiring gaze.

Wake up!

Nikolas looks at him in astonishment and asks, almost in a whisper:

Who are you?

The stranger, whose whole bearing and behaviour indicate unease and nervousness, straightens up, crosses the room, pulls up the blind, and stands so that the moonlight falls on his face, which shows traces of recent suffering. He takes out a handkerchief and mops his brow with a nervous movement . . . like a man dreading a catastrophe. Then he says:

Sh!

Nikolas looks at him in growing amazement. The stranger continues to stand there, as if his thoughts are somewhere quite apart. Then he seems to remember where he is and why he has come. He again goes right up to the bed and leans over Nikolas. In broken syllables he stammers out the words:

She mustn't die . . . do you hear? . . . She's dying, she's dying!

The stranger speaks like a man in dire need, one who in his agony doesn't know where to turn for help. Suddenly – without transition – he turns away and crosses to the door. There he stops, apparently absorbed in his own thoughts. Absently he raises a thumb to his lips, looks at it and licks it. Then he puts a hand in his dressing-gown pocket and takes out a parcel the size of a book. He puts the parcel down, takes his leave with a polite inclination of the head, and goes out.

Nikolas sits half up in bed, tormented by doubt. Has he been dreaming? Has there really been anybody in his room? He lights a match and looks at his watch. It is five past eleven. Then he gets up, goes to the door and tries it; it is firmly locked. He looks at the blind; the blind is up. And on the table lies the parcel. Some words are written on it:

To be opened after my death!

Nikolas is unable to go back to sleep. A dying man has called on him. He cannot ignore this call! He must go and look for the man who has asked for help. He starts putting his clothes on.

Outside, the shadow of the inn creeps further and further over the ground – time is passing.

Nikolas has crept stealthily down the stairs and stolen out of the door without waking the people in the inn. The moon is shining, so that everything is clearly visible. He takes a few steps, then stops irresolutely. Which way shall he go? It is, in truth, a hopeless task that he has undertaken, since this stranger has given him no information whatsoever. As he stands like this, he suddenly catches sight of a shadow gliding down the white road. It is the shadow of a man – a man with a wooden leg – followed by the shadow of a dog. Nikolas stands stock-still for a moment, utterly bewildered. Yes, it quite definitely *is* a shadow – and *only* a shadow. There is no man or dog to be seen. The man's shadow stops, turns slowly and looks all round. With mounting astonishment Nikolas watches to see what will happen next.

The man's shadow walks on and joins a group of other shadows engaged in digging a grave in the shadow of a tree. We see these shadows of gravediggers as they dig their shovels deep in the earth and throw up shadows of shovelfuls onto a heap of earth which likewise is a shadow. One of the shadows in the grave stops when the shadow of the man with the dog comes up to him. After a short conversation between the two men, the shadow of the man with the dog turns, takes a few paces in the direction whence he came, and beckons to somebody.

Nikolas looks in the same direction and sees a weird procession: two men's shadows, sharply outlined against the light road, walking slowly along, carrying a dead body. The limply hanging arms and dangling legs show clearly that it is a human body. The whole procession of shadows is utterly fantastic. Nikolas follows the happenings with the keenest attention; the shadow of the man with the dog gives an order; they start laying the body in the grave; then the shadow of the man with the dog moves away.

Nikolas has an impulse to follow this shadow. A voice inside him tells him that there must be some connection between the apparition in the room of the inn and this phenomenon of the shadows. He follows the shadow, which suddenly leaves the road and disappears through a door or opening in the wall of a factory. This factory is, strictly speaking, only the ruins of a factory which has been derelict for many years. Half of the window panes are broken, and those remaining are covered in dirt and cobwebs. The tumble-down factory looks dismal and fantastic in the moonlight and makes one think of a gigantic churchyard.

Nikolas enters the factory by the same opening through which the shadow disappeared. The room Nikolas enters is a small, bare, square room, full of rubble and stones, through which Nikolas carefully threads his way. There are two doors. Nikolas tries one, which leads into a room with no other exit; then he opens the other and comes into a room with another door. When Nikolas opens this latter door, he finds a steep staircase behind it. Nikolas treads gingerly on the stairs to see if they creak; then he goes up the stairs. When he reaches the top, he finds himself facing another door. Just as he is about to open this, he hears through the door footsteps echoing over the tiled floor. Nikolas stands rooted to the spot. The steps come nearer, and as they do so we see under the door a steadily increasing shaft of light. He can hear that they are the footsteps of a man. He watches the door as if hypnotized. The man on the other side has stopped; now the door handle moves, and a key is turned. Then the footsteps die away.

Nikolas, who has hardly dared to draw breath for fear of giving himself away, tries the door handle. To his surprise the door opens. The man, whose steps can no longer be heard, has evidently unlocked the door for an expected visit. Nikolas opens the door wide and goes in. He finds himself in a room resembling a corridor. A little way along there is a door. Nikolas tiptoes up to it and opens it. The room into which it leads is empty. Nikolas is about to turn back into the corridor when he hears a door slam. He peeps out through the partly open door. There now enters, by the door through which he himself has passed a moment ago, an old woman of erect bearing, who holds her head high and proudly. She must be very old. Her skin is pale as wax, yellowish and drawn tight over her cheek-bones. Her movements are stiff and resolute; she supports herself on a stick, which strikes the tiles with sharp, regular clicks. The old woman is blind. Her eyes are covered with a film and have a dead look. Her lips are thin. Her whole face bears the stamp of cruelty.

The moonlight shines through the window, outlining its cruciform frame sharply on the floor or the wall. When the blind woman reaches the window, she opens it with her stick before continuing on her way, and the shadow of the cross disappears. She goes through the door behind which Nikolas has hidden, and he decides to follow her. Suddenly she stops, throws her head back and sniffs the air like a dog. Nikolas stops too. She turns abruptly and says:

Who's there?

Nikolas waits as quiet as a mouse. The blind woman is reassured and walks on. Nikolas follows. But at the first turn of the corridor she vanishes.

Nikolas stands speechless for a moment. Then another remarkable thing happens: a sound which has no connection with the preceding scene reaches his ear. It is the sound of music, and the tune being played has a dancing rhythm, faintly reminiscent of a slow mazurka. Nikolas listens for a second, then takes a few steps in the direction of the sound and turns into a corridor, at the end of which there is a door. When he opens this, it is as if the music, cooped up behind the closed door, now rushes at him like a wave falling back to its original level. The music seems to come from some apertures in the wall. They are like organ pipes; at all events the music swells from them as from an enormous organ. The same blind woman now appears in a corner of the room. She stops. She makes a sign with her stick, and the music stops.

From the opposite corner of the room a curious figure now comes towards her: a lame man as thin as a beanstalk. But in spite of his lameness he moves with great agility; he looks remarkably like a great wading bird. Involuntarily he uncovers his head and holds his hat in his hand while talking to the blind woman. She gives him a curt order and walks on, finally disappearing in the factory's labyrinth of passages and corridors.

The shadow of the man with the wooden leg sits down on a bench on which his real 'ego' is also sitting . . . A man comes up to him. They whisper together. The new arrival is an unpleasant character with pig's eyes, a flat nose, a low forehead and sparse, stiff bristles, He has an underhung jaw and a powerful chin. There is something bestial about his appearance. The two men walk over to a window niche, where a man is lying asleep on the floor, huddled up like a dog. As the one-legged man wakes the sleeper with a kick from his wooden leg, the man with the pig's eyes pulls out his knife and tests the cutting edge with his thumb. The sleeper has sharp features and a hardened expression, as if his face has been carved in wood. As he gets up he scratches his un-shaven cheek with a bent forefinger. Then all three disappear.

[. . .]

Nikolas catches sight of a little house, an old, deserted dwelling with windows which have been painted over white, and which in the moon-light resemble glass eyes.

He goes into the house and enters a corridor. There is a smell of mould. Everything is old, dirty and dilapidated. Dust and cobwebs in every corner. Perhaps inhabited, perhaps not, very little furniture. An old cupboard, a chair, an umbrella lacking its cover, a greasy hat on a hat rack. In the corridor there is a door with reinforced panes of glass; the corridor leads to a staircase descending to the gloomy depths of a cellar. There is a death-like hush in the house.

Is there anybody here?

asks Nikolas in a loud voice.

No answer. The silence seems even deeper after the sound of his own voice. Opposite the staircase a door is standing ajar. Nikolas opens it cautiously. The room he looks into is peculiar in the extreme. It is depressingly untidy and dirty. Collections of eggs, birds and mussel shells, distilling-flasks and glasses of all sizes, dusty and filthy, some spiders under glass cases, a doctor's scales with weights the colour of verdigris, books, apothecary's glasses containing leeches and other crawling things. The skeleton of a child. A parrot on its perch. But not a single living human being.

Nikolas goes through a door into another room. As he does so he gets the feeling that there must have been people here quite recently. In the middle of the floor stands a black wooden coffin on two wooden trestles. On the floor wood shavings and bricks; on the window ledge a bowl of dirty water, soap, a brush and a comb; and standing against the wall a saw and other carpenter's tools. Nikolas goes through this room in turn. The house's inhospitable atmosphere is beginning to oppress him; he has the feeling that he is not alone, even if the room is empty. He walks on tiptoe, looks all round, and opens and closes the doors cautiously.

The third room is completely empty. Dust is lying so thick that it muffles the sound of his footsteps. Flakes of plaster are lying on the floor; they have peeled off from the wall and ceiling, on which there are rusty stains made by the rain dripping from the leaky roof. In the window there is a potted plant hanging, withered, from its stake.

Facing him a door. This leads into a room with a tiled floor which makes the echo sound harsh and cold. Some large boxes bar his way. Then he suddenly thinks he sees, directly opposite, a long corridor opening out of a wall with no door in it.

When he reaches it, there is no entrance after all, but an uninterrupted wall, into which he has bumped; he lights a cigarette, by the light of which he sees that he is standing close up against a whitewashed wall which is split, cracked and full of mould. He turns round and discovers that he is now in an old laundry room. It has not been used since time immemorial. Everything is covered in dust. On the copper are standing some rusty bird-cages and mousetraps. Old paraffin lamps are lying in a heap on the floor; but what astonishes Nikolas most is a collection of children's clogs standing neatly in rows. They are not quite as dusty as the other things in the old laundry room.

For this reason he goes through the empty room and back to the spot where a door leads out to the staircase. There he stops, and now he hears – in the quivering stillness of the old house – hounds baying and a child weeping. Then a scream, a half-suppressed child's scream, as if a hand had closed over the mouth of the screamer.

It comes from the cellar, but just as Nikolas is about to descend he hears steps on the staircase above. Somebody is coming down. He sees only this person's hand, as it fumbles its way slowly down the handrail. He can only guess at the owner of the hand. The hand continues to glide down, and Nikolas, summoning all his courage, says:

Good evening!

But the hand only rises and gestures to him to be quiet. The person stops on the staircase. Not a sound. Then the hand resumes its downward gliding movement. Nikolas realizes that it is the hand of an old man. The figure continues down to the staircase landing, and Nikolas takes a few steps towards him. He sees that it is a slender, elderly man. His hair hangs in tangled wisps. He pokes his head forward in an attentive attitude. He is wearing spectacles, and his face is marked by unctuous servility, coupled with relentless malignity. He looks like a usurer. This man is Marc. At this moment everything about him indicates that he is listening.

Nikolas: *I . . .*

But Marc interrupts him with a violent movement and bids him be quiet.

Marc: *Sh!!!*

VAMPYR 1932. *The vampire (Henriette Gérard) looking down into the coffin of the apparently dead Nikolas (p. 119).*

VAMPYR *The reaper at the ferry (p. 79).*

VAMPYR *Nikolas (Baron Nicolas de Gunzburg under the pseudonym of Julian West) in the derelict factory (p. 84).*

The old manservant Joseph (Albert Bras) (p. 93).

He continues to the staircase leading down to the cellar, descends two steps and leans over the handrail – we see his neck – and stands there for a long time listening, as he leans towards the depths. Then he comes back up to Nikolas, and his gaze is fixed and tense.

Marc: *Did you hear?* . . .

Nikolas: *Yes, the child* . . .

But now Marc's bearing changes. He looks as if he has woken from the hypnotic state which his intense interest in the cellar has induced. He suddenly becomes aware that he is facing a stranger. His face clouds over with suspicion.

Marc (sharply): *The child?*

Nikolas: *Yes.*

Marc: *There's no child here.*

Nikolas: *But . . . the dogs . . .*

During this exchange he has more or less pushed Nikolas before him to the front door, without ever actually touching him. But his intention is clear enough.

Marc: *There's no child here, and no dogs either.*

Nikolas: *No?*

Marc: *No!*

(Opening the front door)

Good night!

Marc has succeeded in getting rid of Nikolas, and without further comment he shuts the door.

Nikolas stands irresolutely for a moment outside the door, while he reflects on his visit to this extraordinary house. Then he sets off slowly down the road, until at a turn of the road he catches sight of the three disembodied shadows that took their orders in the factory from the blind woman. The group is recognizable by the man with the wooden leg. Nikolas follows the three shadows, feeling instinctively that they will lead him to the man who has asked him for help.

In the house, meanwhile, Marc has turned back to the stairs. From the depths of the cellar he hears steps approaching and the sound of a stick striking the ground; with great servility he greets the blind woman as she comes up the stairs.

Marc follows her with exaggerated and ill-placed attentiveness. He opens for her the door into the consulting-room, and closes it behind her. The blind woman continues on her way without taking any notice of him. Her head is tilted back slightly, as is often done by blind people. She moves forward, cold and unbending. As she crosses the consulting-room, she is on the point of stumbling over a large box lying open on the floor. Marc kicks it hurriedly aside and draws up a chair for her at the table. She ignores him completely. When she sits down, he takes her stick and puts it carefully on the table. Marc stands motionless and expectant. Then she slowly takes a medicine bottle from her pocket. With her bony hand she holds it out to Marc. When he takes it she raises her face towards him for the first time. He looks at her; they appear to exchange a conspiratorial glance: an order is given and received.

At this moment an explosion of laughter is heard from the parrot. Marc tears off his spectacles – which rest a little way down his nose – polishes them and gives the parrot a near-sighted, malicious and knowing look. Then he goes to a shelf on which he places the medicine bottle with the poison label.

We go from the sinister house to a neighbouring castle. A shot of the road, where we see Nikolas on his way to the castle.

The camera moves to a certain window on the ground floor of the castle, behind which we see a man getting up and taking a lamp. This is the man who, at the inn, visited Nikolas in a dream. We can call him Bernard. He leaves the room.

THE INTERIOR OF THE CASTLE

Bernard enters a room arranged as a sick-room. A woman is lying there in bed; it is his daughter, whose name is Léone. A nurse is looking after her. Léone is a woman of twenty-six. She is very pale, as if suffering from anaemia. Bernard goes up to the bed. The nurse stands beside him and says:

The wounds are nearly healed!

Bernard holds the lamp so that the light falls on Léone's throat. In the middle of her throat, where the jugular vein shows blue under the white skin, we see two small marks, reminiscent of those that appear after a cat- or rat-bite. There have been two wounds, but they are now closing and healing. Bernard prepares to go. He turns in the door, because Léone has stirred. She moves her lips as if in a horrible dream, and her face takes on an expression of terror. She stammers out:

The blood! . . . The blood! . . .

Then she seems to calm down. Bernard goes back to the bed. Léone opens her eyes, recognizes her father, gives him a feeble smile and takes his hand. Bernard looks at her with intensely serious eyes. It is evident that even if he does not *know* the cause of her condition, he has his suspicions about it. He takes a last look at his daughter and goes. In the door he turns to the nurse.

Bernard: *You mustn't lie down and go to sleep until the doctor has been here!*

The nurse promises not to do so. As he closes the door, Léone moves again. The nurse watches her closely.

THE CASTLE

Léone's sick-room. The nurse puts a chair by the bed.

THE PARK OF THE CASTLE

Nikolas jumps up on the wall ringing the castle. When he appears on the wall, his body forms a ghostly silhouette against the night sky (to suggest the shadows he is pursuing).

THE COURTYARD

The three shadows emerge from the shadow of the trees, steal across the moonlit courtyard and disappear into the deep shadows of the castle.

THE CASTLE

Bernard in the corridor, outside the door of his room. He still has the lamp in his hand. He goes into his room.

THE COURTYARD

Enter Nikolas (from another direction than the three shadows we saw in an earlier shot). He finds himself under the room that Bernard has just entered. Through the lighted window he sees Bernard putting down his lamp and recognizes him as the man who visited him in his dreams. At the same moment he sees the three shadows going diagonally across the ceiling of the room; at that moment Bernard leaves the window and goes across to a bookshelf. Nikolas rushes to the main door of the castle. He rings vigorously at the door. The bell gives a feeble ring. The echo dies away, and everything is quiet again. Nikolas rings again. Now he hears behind the door an old person's shuffling steps. He tugs at the door and shouts:

Open up . . . open up quickly . . . hurry!

The door remains closed, but inside he hears

A voice: *Who is it?*

Nikolas: *For God's sake . . . hurry . . . they're killing him! . . .*

Then the door opens, but only a few inches. Through the chink we see old Joseph, a faithful manservant. He is wearing only trousers and a shirt, which is open at the neck. His braces are hanging down his back. He is carrying a lamp in his hand. The manservant wants to know more, but at this very moment a long-drawn-out scream is heard, hideous and horrifying. For a moment this scream seems to paralyse the two men. The manservant puts his hand to his mouth in order not to scream himself. Mechanically he opens the door wide. The two men rush into the house.

THE STAIRCASE LANDING OUTSIDE
LÉONE'S ROOM
The nurse opens the door in terror. Her facial contortions show that the invalid has heard nothing, but that on the other hand she dare not leave her either.

THE DRAWING-ROOM
This adjoins Bernard's room. The manservant and Nikolas try to open the door into Bernard's room, but the body of the dying man is lying just behind the door, preventing them from opening it more than a few inches. The dying man's screams fill them with horror.

Joseph: *The other door!*

He gives Nikolas the lamp and hurries out to the other entrance to the room containing the dying man. When the manservant goes into the room, he finds his master slumped up against the door, with one hand still clutching the door handle convulsively, as if trying to escape the lethal weapon which has struck him just as he reached the door. His screams give way to gasps, and he has difficulty in breathing. Nikolas has put the lamp on the piece of furniture nearest the door. Now he comes up, and at a sign from the manservant makes the murdered man release his grip on the door handle. The dying man tries desperately to open his eyes and speak. Then it grows quiet, and in the silence only his laboured breathing can be heard. Suddenly he gives a deep sigh, at the same time opening his eyes and looking frantically around.

He looks up at Nikolas. An expression of surprise lights up his face for a moment. The manservant has intercepted this look and glances curiously at Nikolas. But the dying man's stare again becomes fixed and glassy. He stammers:

Water!

Nikolas gets up; on a table he finds a tray with cups and a jug of linden-tea. He pours out a little tea in a cup, which he lowers to the dying man. With a teaspoon he moistens the dying man's lips.

While Nikolas has been occupied with the tray, an old serving woman has arrived at the door connecting the death-room with the drawing-room. It is the housekeeper of the castle, the wife of the old manservant; they tell her to come in by the other door. She enters with the chamber-maid. The old housekeeper moves her hands incessantly under her motley apron.

On the staircase landing the nurse is still standing, terror-stricken, outside the open door of léone's room, listening and staring out into the darkness. Then Gisèle appears, wearing an apron-like dress, the sleeves of which are gathered in a tight band round her wrists. A very simple and slightly old-fashioned dress, which can easily be turned into a kimono. She thinks the scream has come from the sick-room, and is surprised to find the nurse on the stairs.

Gisèle: *Wasn't it her?*

The nurse: *No, it's down there.*

The nurse listens for sounds in Léone's room, while Gisèle runs down the stairs.

BERNARD'S ROOM

Enter Gisèle. She stops dead by the door, paralysed by the sight of her father lying on the point of death. She looks at the chamber-maid and the old housekeeper, who are clinging to each other, while the tears run down their cheeks. Beside herself, and with eyes dilated with terror, she goes to her father and kneels by his side. He understands that she is there. His face lights up for a moment, after which he closes his eyes again for a while, as if trying to draw breath for the few words he wants to say; but he has not sufficient strength left. He uses his last ounce of strength to draw a ring from his finger. He hands the ring to Gisèle, who recognizes it. It is a signet ring, the signet of which is formed like a tiny gold cross. She holds it in the hollow of her hand, while her eyes fill with tears. The dying man catches Gisèle's eye and, as it were, guides it over to Nikolas as if to say: 'This man will protect you.' His gaze becomes vacant, without consciousness, fixed and glassy. His breathing comes in jerks. Nikolas tries to moisten his lips but the liquid runs down his chin and thence onto his breast. His teeth are firmly clenched, and the corners of his mouth are sagging. The brief death-struggle has begun. While we see the little group by the door, which has been joined by the old coachman, we hear the dying man's death-rattle. Tears run down the coachman's furrowed cheeks.

ON THE LANDING
The nurse is still standing there. The death-rattle reaches her ears. She goes into Léone's room and shuts the door behind her.

BERNARD'S ROOM
Here the silence of death prevails. The group by the door follows with bated breath the last spasms of the death-struggle. Now the murdered lord of the castle is drawing his last gasp. The old housekeeper goes up to Gisèle, who is no longer weeping but merely stares uncomprehendingly at her father's lifeless body. The old housekeeper calls to her gently. Gisèle looks at her in surprise.

Gisèle: *Is he dead?*

The old woman nods. Gisèle looks once more at her father's face, then bursts into tears and without offering any resistance lets herself be led across to the wall, where she collapses into a chair, throwing her arms round the old woman and clinging to her hand. She says nothing. She only weeps and weeps. The coachman goes out.

Nikolas and the manservant carry the dead man across to a sofa. While the manservant is still in the room, Nikolas goes up to Gisèle. He helps the maid to lead Gisèle away. The latter is led out unresisting. He takes her by the arm. She hides her face in her hands and weeps heart-rendingly. The manservant remains in the room. He walks round in a curiously restless way; he makes a number of unconscious movements with his hands, as if wanting to make somebody or other keep quiet.

THE COURTYARD
The coachman crosses the courtyard, opens the door of the carriage entrance, and draws out a hunting carriage. He pulls it slowly and carefully, as if wanting to muffle the sound.

THE DRAWING-ROOM
The old housekeeper has gone on ahead in order to light a lamp. Nikolas gets Gisèle to sit down. Her gaze is vacant, and the only sound that comes from her is a suppressed sobbing.

Nikolas walks to and fro in this ante-chamber of death, deeply disturbed by the scene he has just witnessed. As he reaches the door, the old housekeeper is standing in front of him.

The housekeeper (in a low voice): *Couldn't you stay here . . . until . . .*

Nikolas replies with a movement of his head, then continues to pace the floor.

THE COURTYARD
The coachman leads a horse from the stable.

THE DRAWING-ROOM
Nikolas stops in front of Gisèle's chair and looks compassionately at her. She is sitting as motionless as a statue. Only her lips are trembling, as if she is praying quietly. Suddenly she senses his presence. She looks up at him imploringly and says in a voice choked with tears:

It's so dark here!

He takes out some matches and lights the lamps on an old piano, which is covered with a faded green silk cloth. The only sound is the monotonous tick-tock of an old clock, which suggests the dull beating of an almost exhausted heart.

THE COURTYARD
The coachman is hitching the horses.

THE DRAWING-ROOM
Nikolas lights another lamp, and as he puts out the match he looks at Gisèle. She is sitting with her hands in her lap, rocking her head backwards and forwards. Her eyes are glazed. She is doing all she can to prevent herself from breaking down completely, but when the first tears trickle down her cheeks she breaks into sobs. She lifts her clenched hands to her eyes and weeps. Nikolas goes over to her. He knows that he can do absolutely nothing, however much he wants to quench her sorrow. He bends over her, as if wanting to speak the words of consolation that she needs, but before he can say anything she bursts out:

How can anyone endure to live here?

Nikolas strokes her hair and goes to the window, from which he sees

THE COURTYARD
The coachman is putting on his cloak; he sits up and drives the carriage out.

THE DRAWING-ROOM
Gisèle jumps up at the sound of the carriage. In her anxious and over-wrought condition she endows every sound with meaning. She goes to the window, looks out and asks:

Where is he going?

To fetch the police! answers Nikolas.

The sound of the carriage dies away, but Gisèle remains standing with her face pressed against the window pane. Nikolas goes to a lamp, by the light of which he takes out the sealed parcel that the stranger gave him in the inn, breaks the seal and finds a book.

Nikolas tiptoes over to a chair, lifts it carefully, turns it towards the lamplight, and sits down without a sound. Sitting there, he begins to read the book from the beginning.

LÉONE'S ROOM

Léone is lying in bed. The nurse is sitting in the room with her sewing things. Suddenly she raises her eyes. A number of little furrows have appeared on Léone's forehead. Her breathing becomes irregular and laboured. Her face is twisted, as if she is tormented by fear and uncertainty. She opens her eyes, and her gaze is fixed and distant, as if held by someone a long way away. She looks like a medium under hypnosis. She is visibly no longer master of her own will, or she is under the influence of a power stronger than her own. In spite of her weakened condition she raises herself on her elbow and shouts very loudly:

Yes . . . yes!

as if someone has called to her. The nurse has put aside her sewing things and is throwing off the blanket in which she has wrapped herself for the night. Outside the dog howls – penetrating, long-drawn-out howls. Léone raises herself still further until she is sitting on the edge of the bed.

Léone: *Yes . . . I'm coming!*

The nurse hurries over to her, but Léone, who moves just like somebody hypnotized, is on her way to the door. The nurse blocks her path by pushing a chair in front of her. The nurse stands before her and stares hard at her to catch her eye. The chair prevents Léone from advancing. The nurse tries gently to wake her, as one talks to a child crying in its sleep.

Nurse: *You're dreaming . . . you're dreaming!*

Now a remarkable change comes over Léone; her tense expression relaxes. The hypnotic suggestion gradually seems to lose its hold on her, as if the other party has suddenly reconsidered and decided to wait for a better opportunity. She returns to her normal state of mind. She looks in surprise at the nurse, who leads her gently back to bed. Léone offers no resistance and even co-operates actively in getting into bed. The nurse sits down beside her.

Nurse: *What were you dreaming about?*

Léone: *A voice . . .*

Nurse: *That spoke to you?*

Léone: *That called . . . commanded . . .*

Nurse: *What did it say?*

Léone makes no reply.

Her eyelids close again. To all appearances she is sleeping the deep, sound sleep of an over-tired child. The nurse watches her anxiously. This peaceful and apparently quite normal sleep inspires her with fear rather than confidence. She goes into the adjoining room to rinse some medicine bottles and the like. At almost the same moment Léone wakes up with a start. She listens intently for the previous distant call; without a word she hurriedly throws off the blanket and steals out – so quietly that the nurse suspects nothing.

THE DRAWING-ROOM
Gisèle at the window with her forehead pressed against the cold pane. Nikolas is sitting reading the book.

Gisèle suddenly raises her head and looks out in the park.

Gisèle: *Léone! . . .*

Nikolas looks up.

Gisèle: *Look! . . . Look! . . . There, in the park!*

Nikolas hurries over to the window. The next moment they rush out into the hall; here they are joined by the manservant and the nurse, who come down the stairs in great agitation.

Nikolas: *Take the lantern!*

He points to the lantern which the coachman has left at the foot of the stairs. The manservant's wife, the old housekeeper, comes in with her husband's jacket. He hastily puts it on. Then they all hurry out to

THE PARK

By the time they are out there, Lèone is nowhere to be seen. They begin a thorough search of the park, which looks ghostly with its moonlit sandstone statues. Some of the tree trunks are painted white. They look like skeletons, swaying backwards and forwards. Spiders' webs shine like silver. From time to time a bird flies off in alarm.

We begin by following the manservant, as he makes his way through bushes and undergrowth with the lantern held high over his head like a luminous hour-glass. With his free hand he holds his jacket tightly round his neck. In the distance we hear Gisèle shouting anxiously:

Léone! . . . Léone!

We see the old housekeeper standing on the stairs and looking out into the park. Gisèle's cries can still be heard. Now we follow Nikolas and Gisèle, who are together. Suddenly Nikolas stops and calls to Gisèle. He points out a group at some distance from them. On a stone table covered with ivy a white figure is lying prostrate. Bending over her a dark shape can be dimly discerned – as far as can be judged, that of an old woman. The white figure is lying in such a way that its head hangs over the edge of the table, and the attitude of the dark figure suggests that its lips must be in contact with the prostrate woman's throat.

Nikolas and Gisèle, terror-stricken, make for the spot. Now the dark figure appears to notice them. Like a dog when it is disturbed, the figure turns its head irritably and stares at the newcomers with the dead eyes of a blind person. With a grimace resembling nothing so much as a snarl, it bends down again over Léone, but straightens up once more as if abandoning its plan, and just as it looks as if it will turn away and go it dissolves into thin air. Nikolas and Gisèle have reached the stone table. It is indeed Léone. Gisèle is already at her side. She looks in perplexity at Léone's thrown-back head. There is a gentle expression on Léone's lips, which are parted in a peaceful smile. Her hands are hanging down, white and limp. She looks in every respect as if she is dead. Nikolas puts his ear to her mouth to listen to her breathing . . . which is very weak . . . Gisèle cups Léone's face carefully in her hands and turns it towards her.

Gisèle: *Léone! Léone!*

Léone slowly opens her eyes and looks for a long time in astonishment at Gisèle, who says in a disappointed, imploring voice:

But it's me . . . Gisèle!

Léone's eyelids close again. Only a narrow strip of white can be seen between the closed eyelids. Gisèle shows signs of wanting to call Léone back to consciousness.

Nikolas: *Don't wake her!*

At the same moment the manservant comes up, and Nikolas takes the lantern from his hand, letting the light fall on Léone's face.

Gisèle: *Look . . . blood! . . .*

And she points at Léone's throat. The manservant opens his eyes wide and leans forward to look. Then he takes Léone in his arms, as if she was a child, and carries her to the castle. At the entrance the housekeeper is waiting. The nurse brings her a shawl or blanket; the housekeeper runs to meet the group and wraps Léone in the blanket. The little procession is now approaching the house. Nikolas runs on ahead to open the double door. The nurse goes up to the sick-room, shuts the windows and arranges the bed. Meanwhile the manservant carries Léone up the stairs. Gisèle follows behind. Nikolas shuts the double door, goes into the drawing-room and continues his reading of the diary. His jaw is set in determination. A page of the book is shown.

LÉONE'S ROOM

The manservant has laid Léone on the bed and now goes out. The nurse settles Léone and discovers the wound in her throat; she takes a wad of cotton-wool, moistens it with a disinfectant rinse from a bottle, and dabs the liquid on the wound. Léone shudders convulsively, puts her hand on the wound and groans. The nurse goes out.

Gisèle (calling softly): *Léone! . . . Léone! . . .*

Léone wakes up, but seems not to recognize Gisèle. She looks at her sister as if she has just woken from an evil and hideous dream. Then suddenly she seems to realize where she is. She shivers, puts her transparent hands to her face and weeps silently.

Gisèle (bending over her): *Why are you crying?*

Léone continues weeping for a little; then she says:

I wish I was dead!

Gisèle: *No, no . . . Léone!*

Léone (still weeping behind her white hands): *Yes, yes, yes . . . I am lost . . . I am sinking deeper and deeper into the darkness . . . I am afraid . . . I am afraid! . . .*

Gisèle gives her a comforting pat on the arm. Léone takes her hands from her face. The nurse returns. Léone glances round the room, as if looking for somebody.

Léone: *Where is . . . ?*

Gisèle hardly knows how to answer; she looks enquiringly at

The nurse, who asks: *Your father?*

Léone: *Yes!*

Nurse: *The master . . . is asleep!*

Léone smiles, gives a sigh of contentment and closes her eyes. She sighs again with relief and lies peacefully for a moment with closed eyes. Then a remarkable transformation occurs. A deathly pallor spreads across her face. Her breathing becomes more rapid. Her mouth opens. Her lips tighten. Then she opens her eyes. They are now hard, almost malevolent. Her face takes on an expression of lust when she sees Gisèle. The latter shrinks away uncomprehendingly, seized with fear and pain. The nurse gives her to understand that she had better go.

THE DRAWING-ROOM

Nikolas is there with the old housekeeper, who with old-world courtesy brings him a cup of strong coffee. Just as she is handing Nikolas the cup, Gisèle comes in. With a distracted expression she shuts the door mechanically and goes and sits down. The old housekeeper puts the other cup down beside Gisèle, who is completely absorbed by her recent strange experience. The other two look at her enquiringly.

Gisèle (back in the present): *I think Léone is dying!*

The old housekeeper goes. Gisèle shakes her head like somebody trying to get to the bottom of an insoluble mystery. Nikolas takes the cup and puts it in her hand. Mechanically she takes a gulp and puts the cup down; then she gives a sudden start, as if she has heard a piercing death-scream. She sits for a moment with her mouth agape and her eyes wide open. Then she stands up, rushes to the window and looks out. She seems surprised at not seeing anything and turns towards Nikolas.

Gisèle: *Didn't you hear something?*

Nikolas shakes his head, goes up to her and forces her to sit down on a chair; but she cannot refrain from turning towards the window.

Nikolas: *You're tired!*

He glances at her and turns back to his cup of coffee, which he put down a moment ago. Now he puts it very carefully on the table. An oppressive silence has settled over the house.

Gisèle: *Oh, this silence!*

She presses her extended fingers against her breast, as if trying to free it from the pressure of the silence. Nikolas watches her for a little. Then he goes to the piano and begins to play. At the first touch she rises, goes slowly across the room and stands behind him. She stands there with her hands behind her back, until the music finishes. Then she says very quietly:

Thank you!

A moment later she adds:

I'll try to get a little sleep!

She takes a few steps, turns and says:

You're not leaving us, I hope?

Nikolas rises and goes close up to her. She looks into his eyes like a trusting child. He gazes at her with infinite tenderness. Then he bends down and kisses her impulsively on the forehead. She gives him a smile of gratitude and goes into the adjoining room, where she lies down on the sofa and draws up a blanket over her. Nikolas stands gazing after her. A tear trickles from the corner of his eye down his cheek. From the other room he hears her voice:

Play something more!

He turns back to the piano and plays the same tune again. Gisèle's eyelids close. She sleeps.

As the last notes die away, the old manservant enters the drawing-room. Nikolas hastily turns towards him and puts his finger to his lips as a warning not to make any noise. The manservant says quietly:

The police are here.

Outside can be heard faintly the noise of a carriage rumbling over the cobbles in the courtyard. Nikolas leaves the room, together with the manservant.

THE COURTYARD
The two men emerge from the house and stand at the head of the steps. The carriage drives up the last few yards. The horse walks as if sunk in its own thoughts; then it stops abruptly. Joseph takes the lantern, which has been left on the steps, and slowly approaches the carriage. After a few paces he stops. Now he can see the whole carriage clearly – and the coachman is alone.

Joseph: *Are you alone?*

No answer! He takes a few more steps and repeats his question:

Are you alone?

Still no answer. Joseph turns to Nikolas, who in the meantime has come nearer. They look more closely at the coachman, who is sitting in a curious position with his legs stretched out stiffly against the dashboard of the carriage. He has the reins in his hand, but they are hanging loose.

Joseph goes still nearer to the carriage and lifts the lantern. The coach-man is sitting as if asleep. Nikolas clambers up behind the coachman's seat. Joseph hands him the lantern, which he holds in front of the coach-man's face. He sees two staring, glassy eyes. Half paralysed with terror, Nikolas hands the lantern back to Joseph. In the hope that the coachman is merely asleep, Nikolas puts his hand on his shoulder to waken him. But at the first touch the coachman's head sinks on his breast, and his whole body slumps forward.

Meanwhile the manservant has placed the lantern on the ground, and as soon as Nikolas has got down from the carriage the manservant draws his attention to blood dripping from the floor of the carriage – drip! drip!

Both men stand for a moment as if hypnotized by this fearful new discovery. Then Nikolas hurries into the house. During all this the other servants have gathered round the carriage. They shudder at the sight of the dead coachman and stare at the horse, which – with a corpse at the reins – has found its way home unaided. Joseph gets up onto the carriage . . .

THE DRAWING-ROOM

Enter Nikolas. He shuts the door very quietly behind him as if afraid that by making the slightest noise he will bring about still worse misfortunes. He tiptoes to the piano and extinguishes the two lights on it. As he is doing this, he cocks an ear to listen for Gisèle's breathing; then he resumes his reading of the diary, a page of which is shown.

As he reads we hear in the distance the sound of horses' hooves on the paving stones . . . also the sound of the carriage being put away. Then silence reigns again around the old house. Nikolas listens out into the silence. Is he awake, or are all these fearful happenings merely a long, horrible nightmare? The heart of the old clock is still beating. After a moment a deep sigh is heard from a corner of the room. Nikolas looks in that direction. A cello is standing there. One of the strings has slipped, and as he looks at it another string breaks. Then silence again wraps its mantle round the room.

Nikolas begins reading again, but now the hideous, piercing screech of the doorbell is heard throughout the house. Nikolas puts down his book, goes to the window and looks out. There he sees a man, who turns his back on him. Joseph comes running from the stable buildings. Nikolas gathers that the stranger must be the doctor, for he and Joseph start discussing Léone's condition.

Doctor: *How is she?*

Joseph explains to him that things are going rather badly. The young lady has been found in the park. In answer to the doctor's exclamation of surprise Joseph explains that she has climbed out of a window.

Doctor: *Was she alone, then?*

Joseph: *Yes, just for a moment.*

Meanwhile the doctor has come in, followed by the manservant, who is carrying his bag for him. When the doctor enters the ante-room, Nikolas opens the door. The stranger, who has hung up his hat, turns round. It is Marc, whom Nikolas met in the little house behind the factory. They look hard at each other for a moment.

Nikolas: *Good evening!*

Good evening!

answers the doctor, and it is he who eases the tension of the situation by saying to the manservant:

Let's go up . . . it's high time . . .

The doctor hurries to get in front of the manservant. As soon as his back is turned, Nikolas goes up to the manservant and makes him understand that he is to go in to Gisèle. The manservant goes into the drawing-room. Nikolas runs up the stairs behind the doctor.

THE SICK-ROOM

The doctor hurries in and goes straight to the bed. The nurse's face takes on an expression of fear. She is giving the patient camphor. Léone is paler than before. Her features are hard and sharp, her lips blue. It is painful to see her and hear her breathing. Beside herself, the nurse turns to the doctor and says:

It's going very badly!

Doctor (curtly): *Her pulse?*

Nurse: *Very weak!*

The doctor lifts the patient's eyelids, then examines her lips and gums. Next he takes Léone's wrist to feel her pulse. As he does so, he glances towards the door, where Nikolas is standing. An expression of surprise passes across the doctor's face; then he smiles the most fleeting of smiles. He lets go of Léone's hand and looks closely at her face. The nurse, who has been following his slightest movement, asks anxiously:

Is she dying?

Doctor (seriously): *Yes.*

He takes a few steps away from the bed and seems to fall into deep thought; then he says, as if talking to himself:

Perhaps we could save her . . .

Nikolas and the nurse follow him with their eyes. He speaks as if adding a link to the chain of thought he is forging for himself.

Doctor: *Will you give her blood?*

The question is addressed to Nikolas. He looks across at Léone. He feels certain the doctor is right, and if he does not immediately declare himself willing, it is because his feelings are divided between the obvious need to save Léone and his fear and uncertainty about this man. He looks at the nurse. Her anxiety has disappeared, and a gleam of confidence and hope shines in her eyes.

The doctor comes a step nearer and says, emphasizing each word:

Immediately . . . this very moment!

Nikolas makes no reply. He almost fails to notice the nurse, whose face reflects disappointment and sorrow. The doctor looks at him for a moment, then turns away and shrugs his shoulders.

Nikolas straightens up, takes off his coat, and rolls up one of his shirt sleeves. The nurse gets up with a happy smile and crosses to the table on which are bottles and instruments. The doctor, however, closes the door behind Nikolas, who has the feeling that he has let himself be caught in a trap.

THE DRAWING-ROOM
Joseph goes to the door of the room where Gisèle is. His face shows surprise when he discovers Gisèle on the sofa; she is sitting motionless, with her legs drawn up under her and her head leaning back against the wall, staring fixedly at him with wide-open, startled eyes. As if talking to herself, she says:

Why does the doctor always come at night?

The manservant goes up to her in order to calm her.

THE SICK-ROOM
By the time we return there, all the preparations for the blood transfusion are completed.

THE DRAWING-ROOM
Joseph returns from the room where Gisèle is. He has evidently succeeded in calming her. He goes and sits in the chair where Nikolas sat. He rests his head in his hand. He sees the open diary and begins reading it.

THE SICK-ROOM

The blood transfusion is now in progress. The only words are curt orders like: 'Now! – Quickly! – That's enough! – Give it to me! – Sit still!' etc.

THE DRAWING-ROOM

Joseph is reading the diary, which arouses his interest more and more. It is as if he finds a connection between what he reads and the fearful events that have taken place around him. An extract from the diary is shown.

THE SICK-ROOM

The blood transfusion continues. Marc has positioned himself outside the circle of light from the lamp, so that he can see Nikolas in bright light, while he himself sits in the dark. Nikolas watches Léone's face anxiously and closely during her struggle with death. Life slowly seems to return to her, and her breathing becomes more peaceful. She opens her eyes and looks at the people round her, but she is much too enfeebled to speak, and closes her eyes again. Marc keeps a close watch on Nikolas, who grows paler and paler. His eyes swivel slowly from Nikolas to the patient and back to Nikolas again.

THE DRAWING-ROOM

Another fragment of the diary is shown.

THE SICK-ROOM

The blood transfusion is completed. While Marc himself is looking after the patient, the nurse leads Nikolas into an adjoining room, where she makes him sit down and prepares his bandage. The doctor stands bending over Léone.

Doctor: *Is he in a bad way?*

Nurse (as she bandages Nikolas): *Yes, rather.*

Doctor: *Give him a tablet!*

The nurse brings a tablet which she gives to Nikolas with a glass of water. He puts the glass down on a table near him. Then she covers him up, puts out the lamp and goes into the sick-room, the door of which is ajar, leaving a strip of light visible. Meanwhile the nurse has been moving about, putting Léone's room straight. The doctor looks at her for a moment; then he says:

You can lie down now and sleep. I'll keep watch!

The nurse continues working with great zeal. The doctor now says to her in a cutting, almost hissing, tone:

Did you hear what I said?

The nurse looks at him in astonishment and encounters a cold stare. She realizes that there is no use in protesting; it would be in vain. She puts aside what she has in her hands, and goes off. The doctor closes the door after her and looks round the room.

In the adjoining room Nikolas has dozed off. He feels very weak. In this weakened condition he feels as if he is fainting, which is curious, because at one and the same time he is both fully conscious and far away. Suddenly he wakes from his doze and stares, open-mouthed, at his bandaged arm. The blood can be seen seeping through the bandage. The wound is throbbing.

Nikolas: *Doctor, doctor!*

From the next room can be heard the doctor's cold, biting voice:

What is it?

Nikolas: *The wound is bleeding!*

Doctor: *Go to sleep!*

Nikolas lets his arm fall into the same position as before, dangling over the arm of the chair. In his semi-conscious state he hears the doctor's voice, which has taken on quite a different tone; he whispers seductively and reassuringly, as if trying to convince a child and overcome its resistance by means of gentleness – or as one talks to somebody one wants to hypnotize. In his drowsy condition Nikolas hears only a few isolated words of this monologue, which in its entirety sounds something like this:

You are suffering . . . you are tired . . . come with me . . . we shall become one . . . bodies, souls, blood . . . there is only one way of escaping from your suffering and finding peace . . . follow me . . . you will not be freed until you have taken your own life . . . come . . . I am waiting for you . . .

Then everything is quiet. In the silence Nikolas hears a sound: drip, drip! He leans forward and looks down. On the floor he sees the lantern which Joseph was carrying when the coachman arrived, apparently dead. The sound of dripping comes from somewhere near the lantern . . . and now he sees what it is: blood running from his wound down onto his fingers and thence to the floor, where a regular pool has already formed. With an expression of bewilderment he looks towards the door into the sick-room and calls:

Doctor! . . .

Again the doctor answers in an ice-cold, hissing voice:

What is it now?

Nikolas (desperately): *I'm losing my blood!*

Doctor: *You're losing your blood?*

Nikolas (urgently): *Yes!*

Doctor (slowly and emphatically): *Nonsense! . . . It's here! . . . Your blood . . .*

Nikolas sits there for a moment – uncomprehending and irresolute – then he leans forward and looks down. The sound of dripping has ceased, the pool of blood and the lantern have disappeared. When he lifts his hand he sees that it is completely white, and that the bandage is in order. With a weary smile he settles himself comfortably in the easy chair. He both sees and does not see the light behind the door of the sick-room moving away and disappearing.

THE DRAWING-ROOM

Here the old manservant is sitting, completely absorbed in the diary. Suddenly he raises his head, as if he has heard a sound. He starts to his feet, with an overwhelming sense of dread and foreboding. He is filled with a presentiment of some horror or other. He goes to the window and sees on the paving stones the shadow of a window on the first floor. There is a light behind the window and the light is *moving*. He goes cautiously into the hall. When he has climbed a few steps of the staircase he can see Marc in the window. In his hand he is holding a lamp which he moves backwards and forwards several times. The manservant stands there motionless and with bated breath . . .

A remarkable change is taking place in Nikolas. His lips open. His breathing becomes more rapid. He is apparently in the throes of a sort of paroxysm, as if some stranger's will is trying to gain control over him.

Now Nikolas wakes with a start, filled with terror, depression, anxiety and despondency. He looks up. The manservant is standing at his side with the glass of water that the nurse brought for him earlier, when he was on the point of fainting. At the same moment he realizes what has happened: it was *his own blood* that spoke to him in his dream, which is therefore nothing but a horrible mirror-image of what has occurred at Léone's bedside. He pushes the glass of water away, and makes his way past the manservant to the sick-room, which is almost completely dark, being lit only by a single small nightlight. He tears the door open.

On entering, he sees Marc coming from the door leading out to the stairs. When he sees Nikolas, Marc's expression becomes hard and malevolent, and he increases his pace. Nikolas, however, reaches the bed first. He turns ice-cold with horror at the sight of Léone. She is lying there almost lifeless. She is whiter even than the bed-linen covering her. Her face is heavy with sleep and relaxed, as if from the caress of a gentle hand. The little medicine bottle with the poison label, which we recognize from earlier scenes, is held in her hand, and with her last remaining strength she is trying to raise it to her mouth. At the very moment when the bottle touches her lips, Nikolas succeeds in snatching it from her. He throws it into a corner of the room, where it smashes. Then he hurries to Léone, and uses his handkerchief to wipe a drop of poison from her lips.

Somewhere in the house a crash is heard, as if somebody has slammed the main door violently to, then another crash, but less violent than before. The manservant seizes Nikolas involuntarily by the arm.

Manservant: *Stay here!*

And he hurries out of the room. From the staircase landing he sees a light at the foot of the stairs. The light is whirling round. The shadow of the handrail flickers nervously on the wall. Nikolas is seized by a new fear: he is uneasy about Gisèle and hurries down. The nurse, who has been woken by the noise, darts into Léone's room. Nikolas rushes through the drawing-room into Gisèle's room. She is not there. He listens for her breathing, but not a sound reaches him. He lights a match. Her bed is empty. The blanket has been thrown back. He hurriedly searches the adjoining rooms, which are lying in darkness behind closed shutters, and returns to the hall.

From the moment he set off down the stairs, a penetrating, continuous howling has been audible outside. He goes to the door, under which at the same moment a white paper appears. He picks it up and reads the inscription: 'Dust thou art, unto dust thou shalt return.' He opens the door just quickly enough to see the shadow of the man with the wooden leg moving off the white paving stones of the courtyard and disappearing into the shadows of the trees. Nikolas hurries off in the same direction.

LÉONE'S ROOM

The nurse stands leaning over Léone. It is evident that the patient's strength is ebbing away. The nurse and the manservant are aware that everything will soon be over. Léone realizes it herself. She moans, sobs and wails. The nurse consoles her as best she can. As for the manservant, he appears to be maturing in his mind some great project or other. Léone, who has great difficulty in getting the words out, says:

I am damned . . . oh God, oh my God!

The manservant's mouth is twitching, which shows clearly that he is faced with an important decision, and he gives a deep sigh, like a man who knows that he is playing with life and death. Then he calls the nurse over to the door and says:

She must not die now . . . you must keep her alive until morning comes . . .

The nurse nods. Then the manservant goes. On the threshold he stops.

Manservant: *God help me!*

He makes the sign of the cross and goes. The nurse returns to Léone's bed. She puts her hands up to her face, presses her fingers hard against her eyes and sobs quietly.

THE WOOD

Nikolas is running in the direction of the factory.

THE CASTLE

The manservant comes pushing a wheelbarrow and stops in front of a tool-shed, from which by the light of a lantern he takes a pick-axe and a shovel; he puts these in the wheelbarrow. He is just about to go when he realizes that he has forgotten something. He goes back into the shed and takes a long crowbar and a wooden mallet. These objects likewise he puts in the wheelbarrow, fastens the lantern on the handle of the wheelbarrow, and sets off.

A FIELD
Nikolas enters at a run and suddenly falls headlong.

OUTSIDE THE CHURCHYARD
The manservant pushes his wheelbarrow along the wall. He makes for the churchyard gate.

A FIELD
Nikolas is lying on the spot where he fell. Suddenly his body divides in two. One part (his 'ego') remains lying unconscious, while the other (his dream) gets up with evident difficulty. He slowly comes to and looks round in amazement. Not far off he notices an object on the ground. It is Gisèle's ring – the ring with the cross which her father gave her. He picks it up and examines it carefully, as if Gisèle has sent him a message by means of the ring; he looks round in the hope of finding a clue which direction to go in order to find her again. Then he discovers some footsteps in the sandy earth, looking as if they have just been made before his very eyes by a pair of invisible feet – Gisèle's feet. He gets up and follows these footsteps. They lead him to

THE BLIND WOMAN'S HOUSE
He goes in at the door, which opens easily, and finds himself in a dark yard at the back of the house. He gropes his way forward in the shadow of the house, until he finds a door without a handle. He opens this in turn. He now finds himself in the old laundry room, which he recognizes from his previous visit. From here he knows the way into the house and goes straight to the door at the other end of the laundry room. He enters the empty room adjoining it. Here everything is as he last saw it. His own footsteps are clearly visible in the dust on the floor; nobody has been here. He listens. Not a sound in the house.

He looks for the door into the room where the coffin stood before. It is locked. So something has happened since his last visit. He tries hard to open the door, but in vain.

He must and shall continue! From the staircase landing he discovers that the door into the consulting-room is open. The moon throws a white beam on the stairs.

Is there someone in there? He steals along on tiptoe, holding on to the handrail, and reaches a point from which he can see most of the room. Inch by inch his view of the room increases, but there is nobody to be seen. On the other hand a large box or something of the kind is standing in the middle of the floor. It is covered by a white cloth. He goes into the room. The door into the adjoining room is open. It was there that he saw the coffin before – and this must be the coffin – surely it must be the coffin under the white cloth. He goes up to it. The cloth is draped over somebody lying in the open coffin. The lid is leaning up against the wall. Merciful God! Gisèle! What has happened? Has he come too late? He looks again at the lid of the coffin standing by the wall. Something is painted on it in large capital letters. He reads: 'Dust thou art, unto dust thou shalt return.'

So these words were intended for her, not for him. He must make certain; he goes back to the coffin and carefully draws aside the cloth covering the corpse's face. But it is not Gisèle that he sees. It is his own face, rigid and open-eyed; his own head that rests wax-pale on the shavings in the black coffin. In bewilderment he bends over his own corpse. How can this be? What can it mean. Tentatively he puts out a hand in the direction of the dead face in order to make sure, but his courage fails and he pulls away his hand. He gets up and stands there motionless, paralysed, petrified. Cold shivers run down his spine.

Then we hear a key turning in a lock and a door opening and closing. Next we hear footsteps and the sound of a stick striking the ground at intervals. The sound at once disappears down to the cellar. He rushes to the staircase landing. There is the door. It is a door with reinforced glass panes. The glass is murky and dusty, but sufficiently transparent for him to see that there is somebody in the room, somebody who has been dumped, hands tied together, on a large iron bed with no bedclothes. *It is Gisèle!* The door is locked and he is just about to look for something with which to break it open when he hears somebody unlocking the main door. Through the murky little pane at the top of the door he can see enough to ascertain that it is Marc coming. There is nothing for it but to return to the consulting-room, and from here he sees Marc approaching the door between him and Gisèle – he is just putting the key in the lock – when we again hear footsteps of somebody with a wooden leg or a stick. The footsteps come down the stairs. Marc abandons his plan and slips the key back in its hiding-place, which is evidently unknown to the new arrival.

The man with the wooden leg comes limping down the stairs. Under his arm he is carrying a small tool box. The two men meet and together make for the consulting-room, from which Nikolas has followed everything through the half-open door. Now he is obliged to retreat further. He has access only to the room where the coffin stood before.

Marc and the man with the wooden leg now stand beside the coffin.

Nikolas has hidden behind the door of the next room, and as he stands there he discovers an open trap-door leading down to the cellar. Standing right beside the trap-door and peeping through the crack of the door, he is able to follow what the two men are up to.

Marc finds the stump of a cigar on the edge of his writing-desk. He looks questioningly at the other: has he any matches? The other shakes the box to show that it is not empty. Marc lights the cigar.

The man with the wooden leg searches for his screwdriver. Obviously it must be with the other tools in the room where Nikolas is. The man goes into this room and makes straight for the wall opposite the door. To avoid being seen as the man returns past him, Nikolas descends the ladder to the cellar, and when he is alone in the room again he is able to stick his head up and see something of what is happening beside the coffin.

There the man is engaged in putting the lid on Nikolas's coffin. Marc stands there, enveloped in tobacco smoke, rocking backwards and forwards on his heels. He has stuck his thumbs in the armholes of his waistcoat, and his watchful, malevolent gaze flits rapidly across the coffin and the dead body.

The lid of the coffin has a square pane of glass just over the dead man's face.

From down in the coffin Nikolas sees the lid dropped into position over him. He hears the dull blows, first of a hand, then of a hammer, before the lid slips into the groove. He sees alternately something of Marc and of the man at work. Both of them peer down at him. Marc is in high spirits, whereas the other man's face reflects only the craftsman taking care that nothing goes wrong.

Now Nikolas hears, as he lies in the coffin, the lid being screwed down, hears the cutting and screeching noises of the screws, as one by one they bore into the wood. It is impossible to imagine a death sentence having a more paralysing effect than this sound. At intervals he sees through the glass the elbow of the arm turning the screw. He hears the men's footsteps on the floor; then everything is quiet.

Now we hear the sound of the blind woman's footsteps and her stick. She is in the room, standing by the coffin. One hand holds a candle over the glass, the other lights it with a match, and now the blind woman's bony hand grasps the light. She bends her hideous face over the glass in the gleam of the candle. Her blind eyes are unable to see the dead man, but he can see her: she is taking her last leave of him. Nikolas sees Marc moistening two fingers with his tongue and putting out the light. The blind woman's footsteps die away from the room, and now various men can be seen coming and stationing themselves on either side of the coffin.

The coffin is to be carried through the adjoining room, where at this moment Nikolas is hiding under the trap-door. To clear the way the man with the wooden leg goes over to the trap-door. With his wooden leg he kicks away the wooden block holding the trap-door open, and the trap-door closes over Nikolas. The man gives the door a push so that it comes directly over the trap-door, which in consequence cannot be opened.

Through the square of glass in his coffin Nikolas sees his surroundings change, and realizes that he is being carried out. Ceilings, damp patches, door frames, cobwebs and more door frames pass rhythmically over his field of vision. Then open sky and branches; he is being carried out of the house, round the church, out of the village, away across the fields.

Marc remains standing in the doorway. He throws away the butt of his cigar and searches in his pocket for his pipe, before going back into the room, from the window of which he takes a last look at the coffin.

THE FIELD

Nikolas (his 'ego') is lying on the ground, as when we last saw him.

He begins to return to consciousness. The dream he has just had enters his semi-consciousness. He opens his eyes a fraction, as if drowned in sleep, and sees the procession from his dream – at first making straight for him, but presently turning away. He turns to watch it, and discovers that he is lying on the ground outside the churchyard. The funeral procession is making for the churchyard.

Suddenly he is awake – and the dream disappears; the strange procession literally vanishes into empty air. He asks himself whether the whole of this dream may not be a message from Gisèle, and if so what she is trying to tell him. He gets up and goes to

THE ENTRANCE TO THE CHURCHYARD

and looks in. There he sees the old manservant, who is pushing away a large flat stone from over a grave. The coffin in the grave is revealed. It is an old, rotten coffin, The manservant now throws away his shovel, and uses his pick-axe to try and get the lid off. Nikolas has caught up with him. The two men exchange meaningful nods. Then Nikolas jumps down in the grave to help the manservant.

LÉONE'S ROOM

The dying Léone wakes up with a start. Her great eyes stare up at the ceiling, and her face expresses unspeakable and speechless astonishment. The nurse bends over her and asks:

What is it you can see?

Léone answers, almost ecstatically:

Now death is coming for me . . . I shall not suffer any more!

THE CHURCHYARD

Nikolas and the manservant have succeeded in getting the lid off the coffin. They look with horror at the sight that meets their eyes.

In the coffin is lying the old blind woman. Her face is completely untouched, as if she is still alive. She is preternaturally pale and sallow.

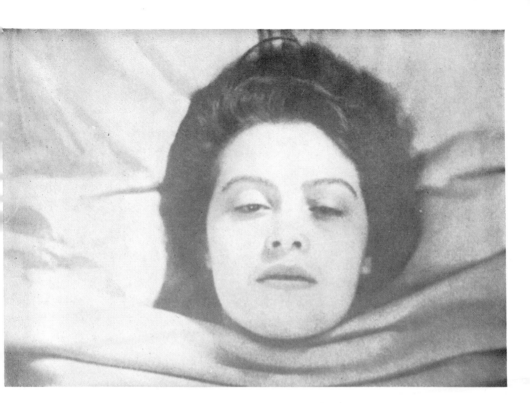

VAMPYR *Léone (Sybille Schmitz) and Gisèle (Rena Mandel) (pp.* 91 *and* 96*)*.

VAMPYR *The vampire and Léone in the castle park p. (*100*)*.

VAMPYR *Marc (Jan Hieronimko) incarcerated in the mill (p. 125).*

Neither her breathing nor her heartbeat can be heard. Nikolas looks at her by the light of the lantern.

LÉONE'S ROOM

Léone looks like somebody waiting and listening. The nurse again bends over her and asks:

What do you hear?

Léone grips the nurse's hand and answers:

My father . . . is calling for me! . . .

Her face still has the same expectant, startled expression.

THE CHURCHYARD

The manservant gives the crowbar to Nikolas and himself takes the mallet. Nikolas lifts the crowbar and directs the point at the blind woman's heart. He raises and lowers the crowbar several times in order to take careful aim. Then he lifts it and, turning his face away, plunges it with all his strength into her heart. Nikolas signals to the manservant, who comes up and hammers the crowbar further and further in with the mallet. They both look very serious. Blow after blow echoes around. As soon as the crowbar is hammered home the two men break off from their work and take a step back. They stare down at the grave in consternation. The blind woman's body has disappeared, and in the place where she lay there is now only a bare white skeleton.

LÉONE'S ROOM

Léone as before. The tension and suffering seem to have gone from her face. Staring straight ahead, she whispers as if in a trance:

Now I feel strong . . . my soul is free!

THE CHURCHYARD

The gravestone is being pushed back into place. In this shot we see only the coffin, the gravestone and the manservant's hands at work.

THE BLIND WOMAN'S HOUSE

There is a fire in the grate. Marc is lighting another cigar. The man with the wooden leg brings him a cup of coffee. Marc brushes some ash from his trousers and takes a gulp of coffee. Suddenly he raises his head and looks towards the window. The man with the wooden leg observes his movements and goes up to him. They both look at the window, where a face now comes into view. It is Bernard, the man who was murdered at the castle earlier in the night under such mysterious circumstances. The face moves and looks in anxiously, while Bernard's hands protect his eyes against the moonlight. The two men in the room are seized with terror. Marc bends forward, and hastily puts out the light, at the same time signalling to the man with the wooden leg to put out the fire in the grate. The latter pours water over the fire, which gives out a hissing cloud of steam.

Marc: *Go and see if the door is properly shut!*

The man with the wooden leg goes, leaving the door of the room open, but it bangs behind him, as if blown by a draught. Above the door is a large window. Marc recalls the man with the wooden leg, as if regretting his order. The man turns back hurriedly, but finds the door closed. In surprise he steps back a pace, and through the window above the door he sees a flickering light moving to and fro in the room. In his bewilderment he remains rooted to the spot. Then he hears a sound resembling that of a mother crooning a gentle lullaby over her child, or of a doctor trying to reassure his patient during an operation. At the same time one senses beneath the ingratiating and affectionate tone something threatening, hard and almost ironic – a threat of revenge. Then we hear Marc's voice:

Oh! Oh! Oh!

On the dirty white pane the shadow of the parrot can be seen in silhouette rocking to and fro, while the silence is suddenly shattered by the parrot's mocking, teasing laughter. The strangely soporific, monotonous voice now begins speaking again; then there is a piercing cry of terror, so frightful and horrifying that the man with the wooden leg rushes in utter panic to the door, tugs at it, hammers on it and throws himself against it with all his strength. Meanwhile scream upon scream resounds, each more frenzied and hair-raising than the last.

Suddenly it is as if an invisible hand seizes the man with the wooden leg and hurls him against the wall opposite the door. The light over the door moves again. The door is opened violently. Marc comes out with every sign of consternation depicted in his face. A sudden gleam of light illumines the room. The parrot, terrified, takes to flight. Marc hurries through the house, rushes out and flees without pausing for a single moment.

But the man with the wooden leg lies motionless on the spot where he was thrown to the ground. His hands grip the handrail convulsively. His face is white, his look bewildered, and his under-jaw hangs down. His eyes are open and have a fixed, vacant expression, as if still seeing the fearful events of the night.

THE CHURCHYARD
The manservant has tidied up the grave and is now putting back the tombstone, on which can be read the following curious inscription: Here lies Marguerite Chopin, born 4 February 1809, died 13 June 1867. Then a catalogue of her virtues.

THE BLIND WOMAN'S HOUSE
We see Nikolas's hand inserting the key in the door guarding Gisèle. He finds it behind the piece of furniture where it is hidden, and inserts it in the lock. The shot is taken in such a way that the spectator is uncertain whether the hand is real or not.

ROLLING COUNTRYSIDE
Marc is running at full speed like a man pursued. He keeps turning round, as if expecting to see his pursuer at every moment.

THE BLIND WOMAN'S HOUSE
Gisèle is lying on her bed, leaning against the wall, with her legs drawn up under her. Her hands are tied behind her back. Nikolas's hands

appear on the screen attempting to loosen her bonds. When the knot refuses to yield, he uses his teeth. Both the hands and Nikolas's profile are taken as in the previous shot, i.e. in such a way that the spectator is uncertain whether they are real or not.

ROLLING COUNTRYSIDE

Marc is running away like a man who has lost his reason. Where he is running there is no road or path.

LÉONE'S ROOM

Léone is at the point of death. She is quite calm. An angelic beauty suffuses her face. She smiles. Then she slowly closes her eyes. She gives a deep sigh, like a child just before it falls asleep. She has expired. A hand lays a little gold crucifix on her closed lips.

[ROLLING COUNTRYSIDE]

Marc has run right across the fields, still pursued by his invisible pursuer. Suddenly he is enveloped in mist. It is like steam rising from the earth. The mist gives everything a ghostly appearance. Marc is seized with terror. He does not know where he is. He can neither see nor hear. He is so confused and agitated that he does not know which way to take. He runs first in one direction, then in another, tries to retrace his steps, but is unable to see them because of the mist. He runs in a more and more random manner. He stops for a moment. Then he sees, a short distance away, a light, which seems to come from a lantern, and the faint outlines of a grey shadow, which might be the shadow of a man. He calls, but instead of answering the shadow merely moves away from him. He runs in pursuit of it; but in spite of all his exertions the distance between them remains the same. Speechless with terror, he pursues his frenzied course with his hands spread out in front of him, as if trying to scatter the mist.

Out of the mist there suddenly looms up a great, dense shadow – the shadow of a house which the doctor recognizes: it must be the mill beside the river. The doctor decides to try and hide in the mill. He will be safe there. Listening intently, he opens the door and ventures in, step by step. He passes the room containing the great mill-wheel, which sets the rest of the mill's machinery in motion. At the moment the mill-wheel is completely at rest. So the doctor continues past it, on into the mill's interior, where the white walls look as if they have been seared by a white-hot fire. Absolute stillness reigns everywhere. The doctor arrives at the little square room where the sacks are filled with the finely ground flour. He enters the room and peers around. The ceiling of this little room consists of a sieve, which can be made to oscillate backwards and forwards, and through which the newly ground flour must pass before it can fall into the open sacks. The doctor is about to leave this room when the grated door behind him bangs to. At the same time the mill-wheel starts turning as if set in motion by an invisible hand. The grinding rhythm of the mill-wheel is transmitted to the many other wheels in the mill and blends with them into a dismal, monotonous drone, which penetrates to the marrow and strikes the doctor as ominous. He becomes still more uneasy on realizing that the sieve above his head is beginning to oscillate backwards and forwards, shaking one load of flour after another over him with clockwork regularity. Suddenly he sees through the sieve the shadow of the old manservant Joseph, to whom he calls, holding his hand over his eyes to protect them. But Joseph remains silent and ignores the doctor, who is caught in his trap. In his frustration the doctor tugs at the grated door, but all in vain. The flour drifts down and down. It is already up to the doctor's knees, and he is almost completely out of breath. He is seized with ungovernable rage, and with clenched fists he threatens the silent and invisible pursuers who are incarcerating him in this white terror. He stares straight ahead, as if hoping to penetrate the flour dust's white darkness with his gaze. The flour rises higher and higher in the cage with its many gratings, and has now reached the doctor's chest. He writhes and struggles desperately, with his one free hand he digs like a madman. All without result. The flour has powdered his hair and eyebrows completely white. He shouts – is silent for a moment – shouts again – but nobody answers. His fate is inexorable. He weeps and screams for help. The flour is up to his face, he closes his mouth and presses his lips together. The flour reaches his mouth. His head slowly disappears. His last expression is a malevolent grimace. A reflection of light gleams in one of his glasses. When it too is extinguished.

THE RIVER

Cross-cutting with the scenes described above recording Marc's death are scenes showing Nikolas and Gisèle on their way down to the river. When they reach the bank, they find it veiled in a white mist so thick as almost to blot out the opposite bank. A boat is lying right at their feet. They jump down in it, and Nikolas seizes the oars and starts rowing. When he has taken a few pulls out into the river, the mist grows thicker; but he continues to row. Now they cannot even see the bank they have just left. Gisèle stares anxiously around, and Nikolas rests on the oars to get his bearings. But they see that they are completely enveloped in mist. They are somewhat uneasy and confused. Nikolas puts his hands up to his mouth as a megaphone and calls:

Hullo!

No answer.
   Nikolas calls again, and Gisèle joins in:

Hullo!

Far away a man's voice can be heard answering:

Hullo!

Nikolas stands up and shouts:

We're completely lost!

After a short pause he adds:

Where are we?

The voice from the other bank:

This way!

Thank you.

He sits down again and begins to row. He rows in silence for a moment without getting any closer to the bank. Gisèle is kneeling in the bow keeping a look-out. The mist is now so thick that Nikolas can only distinguish her as a dark shadow. She says:

Do you think it's that way?

He rests on the oars, and the boat drifts with the gentle current. An eddy catches it, and it starts spinning round and round. Nikolas shouts:

Hullo!

The reply comes from a completely different direction from what he had expected, and is much further away than the first time.

The voice: *Hullo!*

Nikolas and Gisèle shout together: *Hullo!*

The voice: . . . *This way!*

Gisèle: *Where are you?*

The voice (very distinctly, a word at a time): *Wait . . . we . . . will . . . light . . . a . . . fire!*

Nikolas: *Good!*

Nikolas stays where he is, but backs water so as not to be carried further away by the current. On the bank we see the ferryman, whom we recognize from the opening of the film; he is signalling to a number of small boys to collect straw and wood for a bonfire. Presently a strong flame shoots up, but the light from the fire, instead of piercing the blanket of mist, seems able only to make it shine like a white wall.

In the boat Nikolas and Gisèle keep their eyes fixed on the place where they think the bank must be. Nikolas shouts impatiently:

Hullo!

Ferryman: *Can you see the fire?*

Gisèle: *What did you say?*

Ferryman: *Can you see the fire?*

Gisèle: *No!*

The ferryman stands and ponders for a moment. Then he goes to the bonfire himself to throw a bit more straw on it, saying to the boys:

Sing, children!

The boys exchange slightly embarrassed glances; then one of them begins to sing, and the others join in. A number of women, who have arrived on the scene, also join in the singing. The verse which they sing is:

> *Hark, an angel bears its light*
> *Through the gates of heaven.*
> *By God's angel's beams so bright*
> *All the black nocturnal shades are driven.*

During the singing the boat has come close in to the bank. For the two people in the boat the singing sounds curiously muffled, even if they can hear it distinctly. Then it ceases. The ferryman hears the oars on the water. Nikolas and Gisèle now see the fire and the ferryman, who is walking along the bank, following the rhythmical sound of the oars and the creaking of the rowlocks. Now the boat pulls into the bank, and the ferryman wades out into the water in order to catch hold of the prow and pull the boat ashore.

Nikolas and Gisèle jump ashore. When they reach the top of the bank, the mist melts away. The path leads them into a little cluster of birches. The sun breaks through the clouds. They have left the night and the shadows behind them. In front of them are mountain ranges and light. They still hear, as if proclaimed by heavenly bells:

Hark, an angel bears its light . . .

VREDENS DAG

Day of Wrath

By way of introduction we are shown the opening verses of the illuminated text of the *Dies Irae*.

This text dissolves into a shot of a legal document. The document, which is lying on a table top, is drawn forward into the picture. A heavy male hand holding a quill pen appears in the picture and signs the document, which reads as follows: 'And in as much as the said Herlof's Marte is named as a witch by three upright and honourable men, we order her to be seized and brought before the law.'

Dissolve from the document into Herlof's Marte's living-room. The sequence opens with a close-up of Herlof's Marte, a wrinkled old peasant woman. She is standing with her back to the camera but with her face turned towards it, and is engaged in pouring out 'medicine' into a bottle.

By means of a track back – or of a new shot – we realize that Herlof's Marte is not alone. Sidse Skraedder, an old woman with lined features, is sitting on a three-legged stool. She has come to get medicine for her sick husband.

SIDSE SKRAEDDER: I only hope it will help.

HERLOF'S MARTE: It will help all right. It's herbs from under the gallows.

SIDSE SKRAEDDER (*opens her mouth in silent terror. Then she says*): It's strange to think they can have so much power.

HERLOF'S MARTE (*lingering over the words, as if to give them added weight*): There is power in evil.

Faintly at first, but growing in volume, we hear a violent clanging of the town bell. Simultaneously, and in rhythm with the bell, we hear a mounting chorus of voices chanting in unison:

> Swing her up,
> Swing her up,
> Swing her up,
> Swing her up.
> Roast her, toast her,
> Scorch her, torture her.
> Swing her up,
> etc.

Herlof's Marte's eyes take on a dog-like expression. Sidse Skraedder also strains to hear.

SIDSE SKRAEDDER (*in a whisper*): Who do you suppose they're hunting now?

Herlof's Marte does not reply, but listens to the chanting chorus, while keeping her eye fixed on the door. The chorus is by now not far away, and the town bell is ringing more furiously than ever. The two women look at each other in consternation. Without a word Sidse Skraedder bustles over to the door and wrenches it open.

4   The din outside increases in volume. Sidse Skraedder rushes out into the alley. Through the open door we see her looking to the right, the direction from which the chanting voices can be heard. Then she turns abruptly round and runs off in the opposite direction.

5   Herlof's Marte remains standing in the middle of the room, frozen and irresolute. All at once the chanting chorus breaks off.

Sudden silence.

This silence seems to bring Herlof's Marte back to life. She hurries over to the door and bolts it. She stays by the door, ear cocked, and hears

A crescendo of murmurs.

There is something threatening in their tone; she keeps hoping that it is not her they are after. But now there is a thundering at the door.

Herlof's Marte starts. So it is her after all.

More thundering.

Herlof's Marte is stricken with terror. She looks around frantically. Her limbs fail her, and she collapses on a bench.

She sits with her hands on her knees, gazing in front of her, glassy-eyed. Not a muscle in her face moves, although they are hammering like mad at the door.

VOICE OF THE SHERIFF: Open up.

Fresh uproar.

A VOICE: Come out and have your hot bath.

Herlof's Marte sits silent and motionless, as if turned to stone. Then suddenly she collects her wits and realizes the peril she is in. She jerks out of the lethargy to which her terror has reduced her. A twisted smile passes across her face, as if something is amusing her. She gets up and puts on her cloak.

Outside there is a sudden silence.

A VOICE: All right, we'll break the door in.

Herlof's Marte has heard the voice. With a calm that contrasts strongly with her situation she leaves the room. All this time the shouting outside has continued.

VOICE OF THE SHERIFF: Give me the axe.

Just as Herlof's Marte is leaving the room we hear the crash of the axe on the door.

Herlof's Marte has left the room through a door out to a narrow passage, leading past the brewery and the sheep-pen to the pig-stall. We follow Herlof's Marte along this passage. When she reaches the pig-stall, she bends down and opens a square hatch at ground level which leads out into the open. It is through this hatch that the pigs are let out into the pigsty behind the house. The hole is just big enough for Herlof's Marte, by bending double, to squeeze through. First she puts her head out, looking round and listening as she does so, then she makes a rapid decision and edges out through the hole.

Throughout this scene we have heard the sound of the axe, followed by a crash announcing that the door has been broken in.

9 THE LIVING-ROOM

The Sheriff and two messenger boys have entered through the broken-in door. They find the room empty, but the Sheriff has already realized which way Herlof's Marte has gone. Followed by the messenger boys he hurries out into the narrow passage.

10   The Sheriff and the messenger boys arrive at the pig-stall. They find the hatch out to the pigsty open, and the Sheriff realizes that Herlof's Marte has got away. One of the messenger boys is already crawling out through the hole.

11 A STONE WALL NEAR A PARK

Herlof's Marte is climbing over it. In her fear of being caught she scrapes her hands, drawing blood. Fade out.

12   Fade in to

THE VICARAGE LIVING-ROOM

Anne is day-dreaming as she dusts. At this moment she is standing and wiping a silver tankard. Her mother-in-law, Merete, comes in from the entrance hall. From her belt, and over her starched apron, a bunch of keys is hanging on a chain – the symbol of authority which denotes the mistress of the house. Her cold, searching gaze fixes for a moment on Anne. Then she crosses to the door of the bedroom. On the way she hands Anne some spoons which she has brought in from the kitchen.

MERETE: Put them on the table!

13 The door to the bedroom.

Merete knocks on the door and calls. Absalon's voice is heard from within.

MERETE: Absalon ...

ABSALON'S VOICE: Yes, Mother ...

MERETE: Martin may be here any moment ...

ABSALON'S VOICE: Already?

MERETE: Yes, the ship has just come in.

ABSALON'S VOICE: I'm coming right away ...

Merete moves away from the door.

Merete returns to the table. She prepares Absalon's place for his lunch. As she does so her stern gaze fastens once more on Anne.

Closer shot of the two women, who are now standing close together. Merete is about to move away from the table when a thought suddenly occurs to her. She turns abruptly towards Anne.

MERETE: Have you got the key to the loft?

ANNE: Yes.

MERETE (*curt and imperious*): May I have it?

Merete holds out her hand towards Anne, who slowly produces the key from the depths of her dress pocket and hands it to Merete. Merete adds the key to the bunch and glances sharply at Anne.

MERETE: In this vicarage it is I who carry the keys . . .

ANNE (*quietly*): But I am Absalon's wife.

MERETE (*scathingly*): Yes, and I am his mother.

Merete's answer is given in a tone which precludes all further discussion. Anne feels humiliated. She is almost in tears and to conceal this she goes over to the window.

The window.

Anne looks out. Absalon goes past. Close-up of Merete, looking towards the door of the bedroom.

By the table.

Merete's stony gaze has followed Anne – the gaze which Anne feels as an animal feels its tether. At this moment Absalon comes in wearing his cap and goes over to the table. He looks from one to the other. He understands immediately that there has been yet another of the almost daily disagreements between his wife and his mother. He looks seriously and reproachfully at Merete, whose gaze, however, does not falter. He gives in and goes over to

Anne by the window. He puts a protective arm round her shoulders.

Close-up.

Merete's expression and attitude are unchanged; she feels hurt at her son taking Anne's side.

MERETE: It's not easy for an old dog to learn new tricks.

20 By the window.

Absalon has taken Anne in his arms – but more like a father embracing his daughter than a husband his wife. He answers Merete, but turns towards Anne as he speaks.

ABSALON: And it's not easy for a young wife to come to an old house either.

He tries to look into Anne's eyes, but she turns her face away, wriggles out of his arms and runs out of the room into the bedroom. The door bangs. Absalon has taken a few involuntary paces after her as if to hold her back.

21 By the table. Merete and Absalon still have their eyes fixed on the bedroom door as Absalon comes over to her. Mother and son look each other in the eye.

ABSALON: You are too hard on her.

MERETE: I want her to be a good wife to you.

Panning shot.

Absalon shakes his head silently and sits down. He knows from experience that a further letting-off of steam is to follow, and he knows beforehand what his mother will say. In the following dialogue he speaks with a faint indulgent smile, and also with a hint of good-humoured teasing which is in no way inconsistent with filial respect for his mother.

MERETE: When your first wife was alive . . .

ABSALON (interrupting): Yes, but she is no longer alive.

MERETE: No, but your son is . . .

ABSALON: And?

MERETE: He is coming home now.

ABSALON: And?

MERETE: He is coming home to a new mother . . .

Absalon gives a grunt of interrogation.

MERETE: . . . who is many years younger than himself.

ABSALON: And what of it?

MERETE: What of it? Why, I think it is . . . scandalous.

Absalon looks at his mother as she breaks off in the middle of this
sentence.

There is silence in the room.

Then Absalon gets up. Merete looks at him and shakes her head in
silence.

She grieves for her son, grieves to see an old man besotted with love
for a chit of a girl, whom he has more or less picked up off the street.
Absalon goes over to his mother and puts his arm round her in filial
affection.

ABSALON: I'm going to meet Martin.

He goes. Merete goes – still shaking her head – out into the kitchen.
The camera pans over to the door.

The door to the bedroom.

At the same moment as Merete leaves the room, the door to the bedroom is opened an inch or two. As soon as Anne has made sure that the
room is empty, she comes in. In her hand she has a wide, lace-edged,
white collar, with which she intends to adorn herself.

She goes to a mirror and places the collar on her slender shoulders. Just
as she has fastened it to her satisfaction, there is a knock at the door.
She turns, and we hear the sound of the latch being raised. She takes a
few steps towards the door.

ANNE (*without coquettishness*): Come in.

The door to the entrance hall opens.

Enter Martin. In his hand he has a travelling-bag, which he puts down.
He catches sight of

Anne, who comes towards him.

Martin is overcome by embarrassment for a moment before pulling
himself together.

MARTIN: Is Master Absalon at home?

ANNE (*going nearer*): No, he has just gone to meet his son.

28   They meet.
MARTIN (*smiling*): I am his son.

29 ANNE (*alone; a broad happy smile passes over her face*): Are you his son?

30   Two-shot.
MARTIN (*in apparent astonishment*): Are you his wife?

31   Big close-up of Anne, who nods.

32   Two-shot. Light seems to dawn on Martin.
MARTIN: So you are my mother.

33   Big close-up of Anne, who nods.

34   They stand facing each other in embarrassment. Then Anne breaks the
silence.
ANNE: Won't you sit down?
MARTIN: Thank you.
They move to sit down.

35   They sit down. Their mutual embarrassment has now disappeared.
They sit for a little and look at each other without speaking. Once they
both open their mouths to speak, but end by saying nothing. Then
Anne breaks the silence again.
ANNE: I think I've seen your face before.
MARTIN (*surprised*): Where could that have been?
ANNE (*is living in a dream world. She nods in an absent-minded, mysterious
way, and smiles*): Perhaps in my thoughts.

36   Big close-up of Martin, looking at Anne with an expression of curiosity
and wonder.

37 ANNE: I've thought of you many, many times.

Big close-up of Martin. A joyful smile flits across his face.

Two-shot.

ANNE: And wondered what you would say to such a young mother.

MARTIN (*touched, taking her hand*): I promise to be a good son to you.

ANNE (*gives him a long look of great warmth*): Yes, now you are my son.

Martin strokes her hand. She allows this to happen.

MARTIN: My young mother.

ANNE (*smiling at him*): My great big son.

They look at each other for a long time. Then she slowly takes her hand away.

(*This scene and the next are both coloured by an incipient love which springs up in each of them without their realizing it. This incipient love will reveal itself less in the words that are spoken than in the tone of voice.*)

New focus. Two-shot.

When Anne draws her hand away, Martin gets up, shot through with a new and, for the moment, inexplicable feeling. He looks round the room, as if embracing it with his glance.

MARTIN: Everything here is just the same.

Martin walks around, looking at various things. Anne follows him.

For a moment, while both Martin and Anne have their backs to the window, Herlof's Marte can be seen taking a quick look through one of the panes before disappearing.

Martin is still wandering around, looking at all the objects in his childhood home. He glances inside the books lying on the table. These include *Our Lord's Sufferings*, *The Home Treasury of Sermons* and *The Psalms of David*. Martin opens a book.

MARTIN: This must be my old song-book.

At this moment Anne's attention is caught by the hall door opening.

It is the maid Bente who comes in, carrying a pile of linen, which she puts down. Anne turns towards her.

BENTE: I was to say to put these things in the proper place.

ANNE: All right . . .

Anne is eager to get Bente out of the room. (*Martin is invisible to Bente.*) When Bente has gone, Anne turns to Martin.

ANNE (*anxiously*): What's the matter? (*She hurries over to him.*)

45 MARTIN (*standing and shaking his head*): I've got something in my eye . . .

ANNE (*already at his side*): I'll get it out . . . that's something I'm good at.

46 She guides him to a chair by the table and makes him sit down. Martin, who has kept his song-book in his hand, puts it down on the table. Meanwhile Anne has prepared a tongue of handkerchief and is ready to proceed.

47 Anne and Martin. Closer shot.

ANNE (*directing him*): Put your head back.

Martin puts his head back.

ANNE: And look down.

Martin looks down.

ANNE: Are you looking down?

MARTIN: Yes, I can see your feet.

ANNE: Can't you find anything else to look at?

MARTIN: Yes, my own feet.

ANNE: Now just keep still . . .

She lifts his eyelid and removes the painful speck of dust. Martin blinks his eye.

48 Close-up.

Anne is still standing bent over him with a calm, maternal expression.

ANNE (*tenderly*): Why, you're crying . . .

49 Close-up.

MARTIN (*looking up at her with tears in his eyes*): Yes, I'm seeing you through tears . . .

Close-up.

ANNE (*speaking to Martin in the same gentle voice, but this time without dissimulation*): . . . tears which I am wiping away. (*Drying his eye like a mother with her child.*)

Longer shot.

MARTIN (*rising with a sense of liberation, going to the window and looking out*): There's Father . . . (*Has an idea.*) Anne, shall we give him a surprise?

ANNE (*happily*): Let's.

MARTIN: I'll hide in here.

He points to the study area and goes there. Meanwhile Anne hastily adjusts the chair and prepares to play her part.

ANNE (*hearing Absalon in the hall, opening the door and pretending surprise*): Haven't you brought Martin home with you?

ABSALON: No, hasn't he come?

ANNE: No.

ABSALON: In that case he'll soon be here.

ANNE: Yes, indeed.

Absalon, not noticing the false note in Anne's voice, puts an affectionate arm round her waist and walks her over to the table.

Martin peeps through the lattice surrounding the study area.

At the table.

ABSALON (*finding the song-book*): What's this? Why, it's Martin's song-book . . .

He sits down heavily in a chair with his back to the study area, and thumbs through the book. For a moment he sits with a smile on his face, lost in happy memories. Anne gets secret amusement from watching him and beams at Martin.

ABSALON: Ah yes, here is the rhyme about the maiden in the apple tree. That's a song we often sang together. (*Clears his throat.*) First I would sing . . .

55   Close-up.
      ABSALON (*singing with an expression of delight*): A maiden sat, etc.

56   Close-up.
      Anne is bubbling with mirth.

57   Close-up.
      ABSALON (*enjoying Anne's happiness*): Then he would sing . . .
      Absalon is about to sing when Martin, still hiding in the study area,
      chimes in unexpectedly.
      MARTIN'S VOICE: She reached and she stretched – and she landed in his lap.
          Absalon listens in astonishment; but he immediately puts two and
      two together and joins in the joke. Now Martin comes out of his hiding-
      place and approaches his father, who remains sitting with his back to
      his son, but with his hand stretched out towards him. Martin takes the
      hand; father and son embrace each other warmly. Without releasing
      Martin, Absalon puts his free arm round Anne's waist and looks from
      one to the other, happy and proud. He is radiant with joy.
      ABSALON (*to Martin*): Yes, and this is Anne . . . (*After a short pause*):
      Aren't you going to give your mother a kiss?
      Awkwardly and bashfully Martin kisses his young mother.
      Meanwhile Absalon has got up.
      ABSALON: Shall we go into my room, my boy?
      He and Martin go into Absalon's room.

58   When they have left the room, Anne sets to work arranging the linen
      which Bente brought.
      She stands by the table with her back to the windows.

59   Herlof's Marte's head is seen bobbing up and peeping in through one
      of the window panes before immediately disappearing again. The sun
      goes in.

60   Anne takes the pile of linen which she has sorted out over to the linen
      cupboard in the corner. As she goes, the door from the hall is opened
      cautiously.

The door to the hall.

Herlof's Marte comes into view. Her face is white and terror-stricken. After first making sure that Anne is alone, she shuts the door carefully and advances a pace or two with a silent, gliding movement.

HERLOF'S MARTE (*in a whisper*): Anne...

Anne, who is busy at the linen cupboard and is therefore standing with her back to the room, turns round in amazement. An unaccountable, indefinable fear creeps over her.

ANNE (*tonelessly*): Herlof's Marte.

She puts down on a chair the linen which she was about to put in the cupboard, and advances towards Herlof's Marte.

Anne and Herlof's Marte meet somewhere near the table. When Anne has come right up to Herlof's Marte she notices

Close-up.

... that blood is dripping from one of Herlof's Marte's hands.

Anne and Herlof's Marte.

ANNE (*commiserating*): You're bleeding...

Herlof's Marte makes light of it. She is so abject, so wretched, that Anne feels pity for her.

Herlof's Marte's eyes are fixed on Anne.

HERLOF'S MARTE: Anne, you must help me. You must hide me.

Anne doesn't answer.

Herlof's Marte leans forward towards Anne to give added weight to her words.

HERLOF'S MARTE: They will burn me, if they catch me.

Anne looks at Herlof's Marte in terror.

ANNE (*quietly*): Have you been denounced as a witch?

70   Close-up.
      Herlof's Marte nods and whimpers.

71   Anne breathes heavily.

72   Herlof's Marte's eyes are boring into Anne's. She speaks earnestly and
      persuasively:
      HERLOF'S MARTE: The time may come when you too need help . . .

73 ANNE (*almost to herself*): No, I can't. I daren't.

74   Herlof's Marte tries to take Anne's hand, but with the revulsion of the
      clean and healthy against the unclean and unhealthy Anne pulls her
      hand away as if the plague had touched it.
      Panning shot.
      Herlof's Marte notices the movement, and her tone changes.
      HERLOF'S MARTE: I helped your mother.

75   Anne nods as if to say: Yes, that's true enough, but what you are asking
      me is impossible.

76   Herlof's Marte's voice takes on a hard edge.
      HERLOF'S MARTE: Your mother too was denounced as a witch!

77   Big close-up.
      ANNE (*terrified and incredulous*): Mother? No, it's not true . . .

78 HERLOF'S MARTE (*heavily underlining every word*): It's true all right, and
      she only escaped because you were her daughter . . .

79   Big close-up.
      Anne gazes in front of her with a distant expression, without speaking.

80   Herlof's Marte senses that she should not have said this. She strokes
      Anne's arm, and her voice resumes its whining tone.
      HERLOF'S MARTE: Anne, you couldn't send me to my death, could you?

Anne takes a few steps away from her as if to make up her mind inde-
pendently and at leisure. At this moment Merete's voice is heard from
the hall.

MERETE'S VOICE

Anne starts and on a sudden impulse directs Herlof's Marte to

The staircase to the loft.
Herlof's Marte hurries over to it. On the first step she turns round, but
Anne pushes her impatiently up the winding staircase. Herlof's Marte
disappears up above. Anne struggles to regain her composure. She goes
over to the table where the song-book is lying.

The door out to the hall opens, and Merete comes in briskly. She stops
abruptly, several paces inside the room. Her cold glance glides round
the room. She feels instinctively that something has happened. There
is something about the room and about Anne which was not there
before.
(*The following scene must suggest Merete's implacable determination to oust,
indeed to destroy, the woman who has come between her and her son.*)

Anne, aware of Merete's look resting on her, becomes more and more
ill at ease. In an attempt to shake off her disquiet she turns suddenly and
takes a few steps into the room. Then she stops. She wants to say something but changes her mind and instead goes over to the door into the
hall.

Merete follows her with her eyes.

The door out to the hall.
Anne approaches it.

MERETE: Where are you off to?
Anne stops at the door and turns towards Merete, but does not answer.

Merete, whose eyes have not left Anne for one second, asks again.

MERETE: Did you not hear my question?

ANNE: Yes.

88   By the hall door.
Anne is still standing with her face towards Merete.
MERETE: Where are you off to then?
ANNE (*opening the door*): Nowhere.

89 MERETE (*with a toss of her head in the direction of the linen cupboard*): Aren't
you going to shut that cupboard?
ANNE: Yes.
We hear the hall door closing again, and from Merete's gaze we realize
that Anne is going over to the linen cupboard.

90   By the linen cupboard. Anne is hurriedly putting the linen away.

91   Close-up of Merete.

92   By the linen cupboard, which Anne is now closing. All the time she
senses Merete's burning gaze, and in her nervousness she strains so hard
to appear natural that she achieves exactly the opposite effect. With her
hands behind her back and an affectation of indifference she saunters
across the room.

93   Close-up of Merete following her with her eyes.

94   Anne comes over to the window. Peeping out gives her a pretext to
turn her back on the room and on Merete.

95   Close-up of Merete, who continues to keep her eyes fixed on Anne.
Now, however, she turns her head, and the cold, hard expression is
wiped out by a bright and cordial smile.
The door from Absalon's room has just opened and Absalon and
Martin are entering. Merete has seen Martin, and the smile is for him.
He is her own flesh and blood. She goes to meet him.
Merete's and Martin's voices.
Exclamations of surprise and the joy of recognition.

)6 By the window.

Anne has turned back towards the room. Her heart is beating feverishly. She advances a few steps into the room.

)7 Here Absalon joins her. She is pale with fear and tension. Absalon looks at her, anxious and solicitous.

ABSALON: You are so quiet, Anne . . .

Anne forces a smile, and Absalon is reassured. Now Martin and Marete come over to them. Absalon feels like a man whose cup of joy is full. He puts his arms round the shoulders of Anne and Martin and draws the deep breath of a liberated man. Voices are heard from out in the hall. Involuntarily all eyes turn to the door.

)8 The door out to the hall. Bente hurries in. She is in a state of violent agitation over something or other. She turns to Absalon.

BENTE: The Sheriff is out there . . .

)9 Absalon gives an irritated sign for the Sheriff to be allowed in and prepares to receive him. Anne's face reflects anxiety and uneasiness. She sinks into a chair. Martin gazes at her anxiously, meeting her expression of helplessness with one of wonder.

)0 The door to the hall.

The Sheriff enters and stands facing Absalon.

SHERIFF: We're searching for Herlof's Marte.

ABSALON: Here?

SHERIFF: Yes.

)1 Absalon alone. He shakes his head uncomprehendingly.

ABSALON: Here in the vicarage?

)2 Absalon and the Sheriff.

SHERIFF: Yes, some children saw her coming in here.

ABSALON (*incredulously*): It's impossible, you must . . .

)3 Absalon alone. He turns towards Anne.

ABSALON: Have you seen anything of Herlof's Marte?

104   Anne shakes her head, but her expression as she does so is such that

105   Absalon keeps his eye on her a little longer than he would otherwise
        have done.

106   Close-up of Anne, irresolute and ashamed.

107   Then Absalon turns to the Sheriff and explains.
        ABSALON: If she is in this house she must have sneaked in here; by all
        means look for her.
        And with a gesture of the hand he gives the Sheriff permission to
        search the house. The Sheriff looks round and moves away from
        Absalon, who returns to the group consisting of Merete and Martin.

108   Close-up of Anne, who follows his movements, tense and anxious.

109   The Sheriff goes over to the winding staircase and squints up.

110   In the door out to the hall stands the old servant Bente. Her face
        expresses fear and tension.

111   The Sheriff by the winding staircase. His glance falls on the steps.
        Something or other catches his attention. He looks more closely. Then
        he turns to the room and speaks in emphatic tones.
        SHERIFF: There are bloodstains here . . .
        A cry is heard. It is Anne, unable to restrain this expression of her fear.

112   Anne, beside herself with terror at the discovery. Martin comforts her.

113   By the winding staircase. The Sheriff summons Bente with a gesture
        and examines her quietly.
        SHERIFF: Is there another way up to the loft?
        BENTE: Yes, by the other staircase.
        SHERIFF: Go out then and tell Hans and Henrick to go up that way.
        Bente obeys, confused and perplexed. The Sheriff himself tiptoes up
        the stairs.

4   Close-up of Anne.
The group. Merete moves away.

5   By the winding staircase.
Merete comes to have a good look at the bloodstain. She bends over
to see better.

6   Close-up of Anne.

7   By the winding staircase.
Merete straightens up again. She remembers Anne's remarkable behaviour a moment ago; she looks at Anne, and her gaze assaults her
like a silent accusation. She goes slowly over to Anne.

8   Close-up of Anne, who with terror in her eyes sees Merete approaching.
But now Anne turns her head in the other direction, from which
Absalon is approaching. He bends over her and speaks to her quietly
and earnestly.
ABSALON: Do you know if she is here?
Anne can hardly get a word out. Finally she stammers out a few
incoherent syllables.
ANNE: No . . . I don't know . . . no . . . no . . .
Absalon sees that she is lying but pretends not to notice. As he straightens up he sees, on the other side of Anne, Merete, who is practically
impaling the young woman with her gaze. Absalon looks sternly and
steadily at his mother – for such a long time that she finally removes her
gaze. Martin is so completely fascinated by Anne that he notices
nothing of all this. Now we hear from up in the loft the sound of a chest
being pushed aside and the thud of a piece of furniture falling over.
Everybody listens in extreme tension, with their eyes turned towards
the loft.
Suddenly a ghastly, long-drawn-out scream is heard. It is Herlof's
Marte, as they seize her. Anne turns away and sobs.
A shudder runs through all of them. Anne is wailing audibly, so intensely does she experience Herlof's Marte's fate. Martin looks at her
anxiously and sympathetically. Absalon folds his hands.

ABSALON: May God look down in pity on us!

A few more hoarse, animal screams are heard from Herlof's Marte who is being dragged through the vestibule leading to the outer staircase.

119   By the hall door.

The servants withdraw to the hall. One of them opens the door out into the open, and they all hurry out to catch a glimpse of Herlof's Marte as she is taken away.

120   The group by the table.

A final heart-rending wail is heard from Herlof's Marte – followed by complete silence, in which only Anne's sobbing can be heard. Absalon speaks wearily as if to himself.

ABSALON: And this day was to have been a day of rejoicing!

Anne gets up in violent agitation and throws herself, sobbing, on Absalon's breast.

Fade out.

121   Fade in.

THE CHURCH

One of the long walls. On the left, windows through which a light is coming. On the right, pillars. In the foreground a stone staircase with a single iron handrail. The staircase, of about ten steps, leads up to the sacristy. In the background a small door out into the open. Through this little door Anne comes into the church. She looks round cautiously to make sure that no one shall surprise her in her plan. Then she lifts her heavy dress and half runs, half floats across to the stairs, which she climbs with a last glance back over the church.

122   On the staircase. Anne opens the sacristy door a few inches.

123   The same door, seen from inside the sacristy. It opens slowly, Anne's head comes into view in the doorway, and we now see what Anne sees, namely . . .

124   Through a little door at the opposite end of the sacristy the parish clerk

leads in Herlof's Marte. She advances into the room as the parish clerk goes out by the same door.

Absalon is sitting centrally at a great oak table which serves him as a desk. He sits with his back to Anne. Herlof's Marte has advanced as far as the end of the table, where she remains standing humbly. Absalon is busy writing in a ledger and refuses to let himself be interrupted by her entry.

Absalon reads through the lines which he has entered in the ledger.

HERLOF'S MARTE (*uncertain and bewildered, summoning up her courage and speaking imploringly*): Help me, Absalon . . . save me from the flames.
ABSALON (*in his priest's voice*): Only God can help you.
HERLOF'S MARTE (*a little more boldly*): Yes, you can, if you want to . . .
Absalon, who has kept his pen in his hand, now puts it down and closes the ledger. He takes another ledger and – standing now – thumbs through it. That is all the attention he pays to Herlof's Marte.

Anne has followed him with her eyes.

Herlof's Marte. From the expression on her face it is clear that her mind is hard at work. It is as if she is saying to herself that now it is a case of kill or cure. Then she plucks up courage.
HERLOF'S MARTE: I am only asking you to do the same for me as you did for Anne's mother.

ABSALON (*looking up from the book he is thumbing through*): What did you say?

HERLOF'S MARTE (*meeting his gaze; sharply*): You spared *her*.

Absalon remains completely silent for a moment. His expression and bearing must make it clear that these words have touched on some nerve which he thought had been killed forever.
ABSALON: Do not say any more than you can justify.

133 HERLOF'S MARTE (*impertinent rather than fearless*): I am only saying what I know . . . (*after a short silence*) you knew that she was a witch . . . in the service of the Evil One?

134   Absalon gives her a sharp look of admonition.

135 HERLOF'S MARTE (*stubbornly, and without yielding to Absalon's gaze*): But you kept quiet about it.

136 ABSALON (*indignantly*): You are lying.

137 HERLOF'S MARTE (*doggedly and callously*): You kept quiet . . . (*with added emphasis*) for Anne's sake.

138   Absalon stands as if petrified. This thought has never occurred to him before. He closes his eyes as if to collect his thoughts more effectively. Then he speaks in a resolute voice.
ABSALON: It is not true.

139   Herlof's Marte's tongue is now loosened and not to be halted.
HERLOF'S MARTE: Yes, it is. Because if the mother had been condemned the daughter would have been burnt as well, and then she could not have become your wife.
She has said what was in her mind, and now she is silent.

140   Anne has followed this scene with an expression of tense anxiety.

141   The silence in the room is broken by Absalon, who has managed to defeat the past. He is once again back in the present. He sits again in the arm-chair – and is once again a priest, with a priest's authority. He makes a sign to Herlof's Marte to come nearer, and speaks to her in a tone of command.
ABSALON: Kneel.

142 HERLOF'S MARTE (*kneeling*): I am asking for my life.

ABSALON (*unapproachable, speaking in his priest's voice*): It is not your life that you should be asking for, but your soul.

He gives her a sign to fold her hands and does likewise.

He bends forward over her and speaks to her earnestly.

ABSALON: Now confess the truth.

HERLOF'S MARTE (*snivelling*): What am I to confess?

ABSALON: That you are a witch.

With the palm of her hand Herlof's Marte wipes away the tears from her cheeks.

HERLOF'S MARTE: A witch? . . . (*changing to an embittered tone*) I know somebody who was one, and that's Anne's mother, and you let her escape . . .

ABSALON (*seriously angry; springing up and striking the table*): Be quiet . . .

HERLOF'S MARTE (*defeated*): All right.

Absalon looks at her keenly and rings a bell.

Absalon goes over to the door through which the parish clerk admitted Herlof's Marte.

ABSALON (*shouting*): Nils! Parish clerk! . . .

Anne in the doorway.

Absalon returns to the table. His look conveys an order to Herlof's Marte to take herself off.

Herlof's Marte, after getting up from her kneeling position, gives Absalon the customary deep bow and goes, dispirited, to the door. On the way she turns and says to Absalon, with the fawning gaze of a dog –

HERLOF'S MARTE: I am so dreadfully afraid of death.

Absalon does not answer.

Herlof's Marte resumes her shuffling progress to the door, through which the parish clerk Nils has entered. He conducts her out of the sacristy and follows her out.

152   The chink of the door, through which Anne has seen and heard all that
       has taken place, is slowly and carefully narrowed and the door closed.

153 THE CHURCH
       Anne, having closed the sacristy door, makes her way to the little
       staircase joining the church and the sacristy. She treads gingerly on the
       stone steps as she descends the staircase. Halfway down she stops in
       alarm at the sound of the boys' choir singing a hymn. This means that
       both the choirmaster and the boys are in the church. Anne creeps
       cautiously down the last steps. She still hopes to slip across, unseen, to
       the little door by which we saw her enter.

154   In order to reach it she keeps as close as possible to the pillars. A track
       shot along the row of pillars, with the pillars in the foreground, shows
       Anne gliding behind them, one after another.
       The boys sing.
       Suddenly Martin comes into view, listening to the hymn.
       Anne stops abruptly as she meets him. He turns to her, pleasantly
       surprised.
       ANNE (abashed): You here?
       MARTIN: Yes, I came to listen to the hymn.
       He draws her down to a seat beside him. They sit looking across to an
       aisle facing them (or simply the opposite wall of the church).

155   Here the choirmaster stands, surrounded by his choirboys. The hymn
       is interrupted every so often, when they sing it wrongly. Then the
       choirmaster has to break off and sing the preceding strophe, after which
       the hymn is resumed.
       Slates for music. The boys are wearing caps and wooden shoes.
       There has just been a pause. Now the hymn is resumed.

156   Anne and Martin listen, Anne with a distant expression. It is easy to see
       that her thoughts are still in the sacristy. Martin notices that they are
       elsewhere. There is another pause in the hymn, and the choirmaster is
       heard singing on his own. To escape from her feeling of constraint
       Anne breaks the silence.

ANNE: What are they singing?

MARTIN: They are practising the *Dies Irae*.

ANNE (*looking at Martin with an expression of great uneasiness*): *Dies Irae?*

MARTIN (*to himself*): 'Dies irae, dies illa
          Solvet saeclum in favilla.'

7   A sudden thought strikes Anne.

ANNE: Why are they learning that?

MARTIN: To sing when Herlof's Marte is burnt.

8   Anne rises with a convulsive movement and an agonized expression.

ANNE: Oh no!

Martin has taken her hand. Anne allows him to do so, but is unable to break the chain of thoughts which the hymn has started.

ANNE: I keep hearing her screams. Come, let's go.

Martin strokes Anne's hand to comfort her. At the same moment the hymn swells up. Anne rises and again suggests they go. Martin follows her.

9   Back to the long shot, with the sacristy staircase in the foreground. We see Anne and Martin hurrying out, she a pace or two in front of him.

10   Dissolve to

THE TORTURE-CHAMBER

Since Herlof's Marte has refused to confess of her own free will, she is being submitted to 'examination by pain'. This is taking place in an oblong vaulted cellar.

If we think of ourselves as standing in the middle of one long wall, we see on the left the members of the Cathedral Chapter sitting in arm-chairs round a table, on which a single light is burning. Ink, pen and paper. At his place behind the table Absalon sits with an expression of pain and disquiet. To the left of the Cathedral Chapter is an area of bare wall. Then a small table, likewise lit by a single light. Behind this table, with his back to the wall and therefore with his face to us, sits the notary. In front of him is a thick, parchment-bound ledger, pen and ink. To his left (as we look at him) stands a young priest. This is

Master Olaus, who is leaning over the notary and supervising the entries in the ledger.

To the left of the notary are the rack and Herlof's Marte. Master Laurentius is conducting the 'examination by pain', assisted by two executioners. Laurentius is a theological expert.

The first picture in this scene is a track shot parallel with the long wall where we are standing. We first see the group of priests, then the notary and finally the rack. From the moment the picture fades in, a feeling of feverish agitation prevails – as at the end of a thrilling race. The priests are leaning forward or half standing up, in breathless suspense and with shining eyes. The notary's pen races over the paper. The priest, Master Olaus, who is standing at his side, corrects him in a whisper.

And at the rack Master Laurentius and the executioners are 'working' under the influence of a tremendous tension resembling that which is found in a hospital during a difficult operation. The whole scene, and especially the opening, must be characterized by a hectic, forced, ecstatic note.

While the camera is still on the group of priests we hear a heart-rending wail. It is Herlof's Marte crying out. One of the priests leans towards his neighbour.

PRIEST: She is weakening, the old . . .

We hear Master Laurentius shouting at Herlof's Marte in a furious voice.

LAURENTIUS'S VOICE: Will you confess then?

Herlof's Marte gives out a wail.

HERLOF'S MARTE'S VOICE: Yes.

There is a stir among the priests.

PRIEST: At last.

We hear Master Laurentius giving orders to the executioners.

LAURENTIUS'S VOICE: Release her.

During this last dialogue the panning movement of the camera has begun. The camera reaches the notary's table.

The music becomes a mere hammering.

MASTER OLAUS (dictating): . . . her limbs were stretched by the executioner whereupon she undertook to make confession.

The panning movement of the camera continues and the rack comes into view.

A rope attached to a hook is floating up through the air, to the creaking of the winch. Master Laurentius bends over Herlof's Marte, who is lying face downward on the rack like a corpse.

The priests watch this scene with intense interest.

The rack. With difficulty Herlof's Marte lifts her naked trunk. At a sign from Master Laurentius the executioners withdraw from the rack.

LAURENTIUS (*bending over Herlof's Marte*): Tell me then: how did you come into the Devil's service?

Herlof's Marte doesn't answer.

LAURENTIUS: Answer now . . .

Herlof's Marte still doesn't answer.

LAURENTIUS (*giving the executioners a sign*): Oh, so you still won't confess . . . (*To the executioners*) She has not yet had enough.

Shadow on the wall.

The executioners take a step forward.

Herlof's Marte is terrified.

HERLOF'S MARTE: Yes, yes.

The following questions come like whiplashes, without a pause, at breakneck speed. The notary settles himself comfortably.

LAURENTIUS: Answer then: where did you first meet the Devil?

Herlof's Marte doesn't answer.

LAURENTIUS: Was it under the gallows?

HERLOF'S MARTE: Yes.

LAURENTIUS: You had to trample on the Cross?

HERLOF'S MARTE: Yes.

LAURENTIUS: And he forbade you to go to Communion?

HERLOF'S MARTE: Yes.

LAURENTIUS: You had to renounce God and Christ?

HERLOF'S MARTE: Yes.

LAURENTIUS: And sign a contract with the Devil for all eternity?

HERLOF'S MARTE: Yes.

Close-up of the notary.

LAURENTIUS: Have you anything more to confess?
HERLOF'S MARTE: No.

163   The notary's table.
       The notary is working with feverish haste, eagerly assisted by Master
       Olaus who helps him get each word down almost as fast as it is spoken.
       Laurentius hurries over to the notary to see that he has got everything
       down.
       MASTER OLAUS (*nodding appreciatively at Master Laurentius*): That was a
       beautiful confession.
       LAURENTIUS (*wiping the sweat from his forehead*): She's a tough nut . . .

164   Another member of the Cathedral Chapter, Master Jørgen, hurries
       over to the notary's table. He whispers a few words in Laurentius's ear.
       Laurentius nods approval and hurries back to the rack.

165   The rack. Laurentius again bombards Herlof's Marte.
       LAURENTIUS: We have not quite finished. Tell me: do you know any
       other witches?
       HERLOF'S MARTE: No.
       LAURENTIUS: Have you *known* any?
       HERLOF'S MARTE (*hesitating*): Known?
       LAURENTIUS: Yes, have you known any? Is there anybody you can
       denounce?
       HERLOF'S MARTE: She's dead now!
       LAURENTIUS: Who was she?
       Herlof's Marte remains silent.

166   Absalon listens uneasily. A priest passes behind him.

167   The rack.
       Herlof's Marte is still silent.
       LAURENTIUS: Come on, who was she? What was her name?
       HERLOF'S MARTE: That I don't remember . . .
       In the anger and bitterness aroused by her maltreatment she suddenly
       loses her self-control.

HERLOF'S MARTE: But I shall remember *you* . . .

LAURENTIUS: What was that?

HERLOF'S MARTE: If you send me to my death, you will follow me there.

LAURENTIUS: Your threats leave me cold. You had better tell me her name, the one you knew. Come on, tell me now.

HERLOF'S MARTE: I'm not saying anything. I've said enough . . .

Laurentius loses patience and gives a sign to the executioner, who advances to the rack. Absalon gets up. The creaking of the winch is heard. The rope descends. The executioner reaches for the hook as he bends over Herlof's Marte and speaks to her.

EXECUTIONER: We'll soon loosen your tongue for you.

The camera goes behind the rack. In the foreground the executioner, as he seizes Herlof's Marte, who lets out a shriek. Behind her Laurentius – and behind him Absalon, who is just coming into view. With a movement of his hand he stops the excutioner, who falls back. Absalon speaks to Laurentius.

ABSALON: That will do. I shall speak to her myself . . .

Laurentius bows obediently and goes.

Panning shot. Laurentius joins the notary (with the ledger) and Master Olaus, and all three go over to the other priests, who are discussing Herlof's Marte's confession with some animation. This shot is very short, only a few feet of film.

The camera returns to the rack. The executioners have withdrawn. Throughout the following scene between Absalon and Herlof's Marte we hear the muttering of the priests.

Close-up. Herlof's Marte looks up at Absalon with an expression half of suffering, half of cunning, and smiles an ambiguous smile.

HERLOF'S MARTE: You thought it was hard on me?

Absalon looks at her seriously, without anger, concerned only for the salvation of her soul.

172   Herlof's Marte pursues her train of thought. Her words have a sarcastic, venomous edge.

HERLOF'S MARTE: Or was it Anne you were thinking about?

173   Absalon's forehead furrows.

174   Herlof's Marte observes this, veers suddenly round and looks imploringly at Absalon as if hoping to extract a promise from him by her gaze, as she begs him in a whisper to help her.

HERLOF'S MARTE: Save me from the flames.

175   Absalon looks sorrowfully and seriously at her.

176   Herlof's Marte thinks only of how to extract a promise from him.

HERLOF'S MARTE: I know you won't fail me.

177   Absalon says neither no nor yes. He does not refuse, but neither does he make any promises. He says absolutely nothing. Instead he folds his hands and offers a prayer.

ABSALON (praying): I beseech thee, oh God, that this woman may feel a sincere repentance, may turn unto Thee, may let Thy mercy enter her heart, and may take good heed to her salvation. Amen.

178   Herlof's Marte gives him a look of disappointment.

The priests in the torture-chamber are discussing theological problems in connection with the burning of witches. One advances as an argument Matthew 3:10: therefore every tree which bringeth not forth good fruit is hewn down, and cast into the fire. Meaning that the woman in question shall first be beheaded and then cast into the fire. Another advances John 15:6: If a man abide not in me, he is cast forth as a branch.

Close-up: Herlof's Marte.

179 ABSALON (looking at her with compassion): Take heart, be strong.

180   Herlof's Marte takes new heart, for surely his words can be interpreted as a promise. She clings to him with her eyes.

Meanwhile Absalon has given a sign to the executioners who are approaching Herlof's Marte, and now turns away. The executioners lead her away.

Absalon goes over to the priests. He takes his place at the table.

Absalon at the table. The notary places the ledger in front of him for his signature. Absalon dips the pen in the ink in order to sign. Laurentius and Olaus come close to him.

LAURENTIUS (*respectfully*): Did she denounce anybody?

ABSALON (*curtly*): No.

OLAUS: If we had tortured her, we might have got her to speak.

ABSALON (*signing*): All things are revealed in God's good time.

He pushes the ledger over to one of the other priests and hands him the pen. We are to understand that all the priests will sign their names one after the other.

Dissolve into a shot of the parchment page of the legal ledger, where we read the final lines:

> After the aforesaid Herlof's Marte had been tortured by the executioner to the glory of God, she made a voluntary confession as stated above, and witnessed by us assembled priests.
>
> Absalon Pedersøn.

A hand is in the act of signing another name.

Dissolve to a shot of

A meadow with scattered groups of trees and bushes. Anne and Martin are following a path up a hillside.

On a slope of the hill, waving corn, which they stop to admire.

Anne breathes in the scent.

They walk on.

188   Dissolve to a new shot.
       THE MEADOW
       They wander off together, happy at being alone with each other,
       although they are not yet conscious of the true nature of their feelings[1]

189   Dissolve to a new shot.
       THE MEADOW
       Anne and Martin stand still, listening. They hear the bleat of a lamb.
       Martin turns and points to the edge of the wood.

190 THE EDGE OF THE WOOD
       We see a lamb approaching its mother in order to suck.

191   Anne and Martin are warmed by the sight. Then they hear the whimper
       of a tiny child. The sound seems to come from behind a bush some-
       where near them.
            They stand and listen. We hear again the bleating of the lamb alter-
       nating with the whimpering of the child.

192   Anne goes over to the bush, quickly and carefully, so as not to be
       discovered.

193   The bush seen from the other side. Anne pushes the branches aside to
       see better – and sees

194   A young mother with her child at the breast.

195   Close-up of Anne (*fading out*).
       ANNE: Bodil . . .

196   Close-up of the mother, surprised and happy.
       BODIL: Anne . . .

197   The young mother takes the child from the breast and adjusts her
       bodice. Anne has called to Martin, and stands there for a moment.

       [1] Scenes 189 to 209 were omitted during shooting.

8 ANNE (*kneeling beside Bodil and bending over the child*): Isn't she sweet? May I hold her?
Panning shot from the mother to Anne. The mother hands the child to Anne.

9 Anne takes the child, gets up and holds it jubilantly in the air. Then she takes it in her arms and looks at it tenderly. Martin looks over her shoulder at the child. They exchange smiles – Anne turns to the mother.
ANNE: What is her name?

0 BODIL (*smiling*): Anne . . . like you.

1 ANNE (*joyfully*): Anne?

2 BODIL (*after a moment's silence*): Yes, I only hope she will be as happy as you are.

3 ANNE (*suddenly serious*): Do you think I am happy?

4 BODIL (*surprised*): Aren't you happy then?

5 ANNE (*hesitating*): Ye-es . . . (*quickly changing her tone*) Yes, of course I am . . .
Panning shot from Anne down to the mother. She gives the child back to the mother.
ANNE: Here is your Anne back again . . .

6 MARTIN (*bending down and picking up something from the ground*): Look what's here.
He has found the child's tiny shoes – which he holds up.

7 The mother makes sure that they are little Anne's shoes.
Panning shot of Anne.
BODIL: Yes, they're Anne's shoes.

208   Martin cups the shoes in his hands, one in each. He looks up at Anne
       who is just bending down to take the shoes from him.
       MARTIN: Your feet must have been just as small once.
       He hands the shoes to Anne, who looks at them for a moment before
       standing up.

209 ANNE (*giving the shoes to the mother*): May Anne have many happy days.
       Then Anne and Martin say goodbye and go.

210   Anne and Martin run down a steep slope, at the foot of which there is
       a road.

211   When they are almost at the road they see (*fading in*)

212   A peasant driving a load of firewood on a low, sledge-like cart. The
       peasant is walking beside the cart and leading the horses.

213 MARTIN (*calling to the peasant*): Are you taking home firewood already?

214 PEASANT (*in reply*): No, it's firewood for the bonfire. Herlof's Marte
       isn't going to freeze.

215   Anne clutches her heart involuntarily. Martin, concerned on her behalf,
       takes her hand; she allows him to do this as she turns her head away
       from him and her eyes follow

216   The cart as it moves off.
       Fade out.

217   Fade in to
       A CELL FOR PRISONERS IN THE TOWN HALL
       Herlof's Marte is sitting on a stone bench and leaning against a pillar,
       like a wild beast on the run, a grim figure with staring, burning
       eyes.

218   The door opens. The jailer admits Absalon.

Enter Absalon to Herlof's Marte. The jailer has gone, and Absalon is alone with the prisoner. Herlof's Marte fixes her eyes on him and never releases him from their burning gaze.

ABSALON (*speaking to her now in a mild and human manner*): I have come to prepare you for death, Marte.

Herlof's Marte does not answer or change her position, and she continues to keep Absalon transfixed. But presently she speaks.

HERLOF'S MARTE: So you have failed me after all . . .

ABSALON (*shaking his head indulgently*): No, I have not failed you. My thoughts have been with you all these days . . . how I might win eternal life for you.

HERLOF'S MARTE (*with a sneer*): Oh, you can leave off your sermon. I'm not afraid of Heaven or Hell. I'm only afraid of dying.

Her bitterness and disappointment over Absalon's failure to help her seem to have taken away her self-control, and suddenly she turns right round and faces him. Her eyes shining with hate, she continues.

HERLOF'S MARTE: I spared Anne . . . and you failed me . . . (*She smooths back her hair from her forehead.*) But it's still not too late: Anne shall suffer as I am suffering. If I am burnt she shall burn too.

Absalon looks at Herlof's Marte with an uneasy expression.

Herlof's Marte veers suddenly from defiance to despair. She looks round her in terror and confusion and bursts into wails of grief.

HERLOF'S MARTE: Oh no, oh no, they're going to burn me, oh no . . . (*Her voice rises suddenly into a scream.*) I don't want to burn, I don't *want* to, I don't *want* . . .

She hides her face in her hands and groans like an injured animal.

Absalon pats her compassionately.

Now Herlof's Marte raises her face to Absalon's with an expression suggesting surprise at finding him still there, and shouts at him with a mad gleam in her eyes.

HERLOF'S MARTE: Go, go, go . . .

226   Absalon, in consternation, leaves her.
        Fade out.

227   The room in the loft at the vicarage.
        Anne comes up into the room. She approaches the window, which
        faces onto the square by the church where the witch-burning is to take
        place. She looks out and sees the executioner and his assistants occupied
        in constructing a ladder. The executioner, on the point of hammering
        in the last nail, straightens up when he hears the street rhyme:

                    Swing her up,
                    Swing her up,
                    Swing her up,
                    Roast her, toast her,
                    Scorch her, torture her.

        The executioner summons one of his assistants and gives him an order.
        EXECUTIONER: Light the fire.
        The executioner's assistant hurries over to the bonfire. We see the
        choirboys headed by the choirmaster coming into the square and taking
        up their positions. Two of the executioner's assistants are about to
        carry the last faggots to the bonfire. Another climbs up to the bonfire
        and sets it alight. A little white puff of smoke appears. Anne by the
        window, seen from outside. She turns her eyes from the executioner
        towards a little gate in the wall of the churchyard. Herlof's Marte is
        brought to the square. The Sheriff's lads have difficulty in keeping the
        curious crowd at bay. Laurentius, who is escorting her, protects her
        and speaks a few calming words to the crowd. The chorus of chanting
        voices can still be heard, but during the following shots becomes fainter
        and fainter. At the window Anne's eyes follow Herlof's Marte who, as
        she passes the bonfire, is on the point of collapse. Laurentius tries to
        support her, but Herlof's Marte refuses his help with a gesture express-
        ing anger and embitterment. One of the executioner's assistants comes
        forward and helps her on her way. Anne, at the window, follows her
        with her gaze. Herlof's Marte arrives at the ladder, where the execu-
        tioner and his assistants seize hold of her and place her on the ladder.
        Herlof's Marte lets them do what they like with her. Anne, at the

VREDENS DAG 1943. Scene 227: *Anne Pedersdotter (Lisbeth Movin) sees Herlof's Marte being burnt.*

VREDENS DAG Scene 160: *Members of the Cathedral Chapter.*

Scene 162: *Herlof's Marte (Anna Svierkier) on the rack. Master Laurentius (Olaf Ussing).*

VREDENS DAG Scene 212: *Faggots being brought for the witch-burning.*

VREDENS DAG Scene 227: *Herlof's Marte being prepared for the stake; Absalon (Thorkild Roose) in prayer.*

Scene 326: *Absalon and Anne.*

window, watches this scene with an expression of horror and dread. As if following an impulse from within, she turns her gaze on the platform where the priests are sitting. Martin is sitting at Absalon's side. With an expression of pain and disgust he sees the executioner starting to lash Herlof's Marte securely to the ladder.

Martin rises. Absalon looks up at him in surprise.

ABSALON: Are you going?

MARTIN: Yes – I can't bear it out here.

Absalon nods to him and Martin hurries away. Anne at the window. Her eyes follow Martin, who, as he passes the bonfire, turns away to avoid seeing the flames. By the wall behind him we see one of the Sheriff's lads chasing away some inquisitive person who has climbed up on the wall. Anne, at the window, turns her gaze back to Herlof's Marte, who is now lying tied to the ladder. One of the executioner's assistants is under the ladder, making sure that all the fastenings are in order. Now the executioner and his assistants lift the ladder in order to carry it nearer to the bonfire. Laurentius is still at Herlof's Marte's side. Anne, at the window, follows the dismal pageant with her eyes. The ladder bearing Herlof's Marte is now ready to be cast into the flames. The ladder is placed for the time being on trestles. Anne by the window. She cannot bear to see any more and hides her face in her hands. Sobbing loudly, she leaves the window and collapses on a bench in the darkest corner of the room. She is still sitting like this when Martin comes cautiously up the steps and into the loft. He touches her shoulder lightly. She breathes more freely again when she sees that it is Martin. She stretches out her hand to Martin and makes room for him.

ANNE (imploringly): Stay with me . . .

He sits down beside her. They listen to the noise which reaches them from the bonfire in the square. Herlof's Marte has realized that there is no longer any hope for her, and her defiance and will to live seem to flare up for the last time and to break through her torpor. The glow returns to her eyes, and she gestures with her head to Laurentius, who approaches the ladder, while simultaneously the executioner and his assistants move away.

HERLOF'S MARTE (shouting in a hoarse, grating voice): I want to speak to Master Absalon . . .

LAURENTIUS: What do you want with him?

HERLOF'S MARTE (*stubbornly*): I want to speak to Master Absalon.

LAURENTIUS: Do you want to denounce somebody?

HERLOF'S MARTE: I want to speak to Master Absalon . . .

Laurentius shakes his head, but nevertheless decides to fetch Absalon. He goes, the executioner and his assistants return. When Laurentius reaches the platform Absalon leans forward.

LAURENTIUS: She is asking to speak to you.

Absalon rises and goes. Laurentius sits down among the other priests. When Absalon reaches Herlof's Marte the executioner and his assistants move away, so that Absalon is alone with her.

HERLOF'S MARTE: Let me escape the flames, do you hear? If not, then . . .

As soon as Absalon perceives Herlof's Marte's aim in summoning him, he begins rattling off prayers with the clear intention of stopping her mouth.

ABSALON: Have no fear. The Lord is merciful. He wants to open your eyes that they may see and to turn your soul from sin . . .

Absalon makes a pause, of which Herlof's Marte takes advantage.

HERLOF'S MARTE: . . . if not, I shall denounce Anne's mother as a witch.

ABSALON (*again resorting to prayers*): The glory of the Lord is infinite; blessed is he whom the Lord punishes, for the hand that smites also heals . . .

He again makes a pause, of which Herlof's Marte takes advantage.

HERLOF'S MARTE: I shall denounce Anne . . . do you hear . . . I shall get even with you . . .

ABSALON (*resorting again to prayers, his only weapon in this duel*): I will pray to God that He may spare you from the everlasting fire, which burns night and day through all eternity without ceasing . . .

Absalon turns and gives a sign to the executioners.

The priests on the platform crane their necks. One of the older priests speaks to Laurentius.

A PRIEST: Go and ask Master Absalon if she has denounced anybody.

Laurentius goes. The executioners are on the point of raising the ladder. Herlof's Marte pours out screams and curses, and is about to shout her denunciation of Anne to the whole square, when Absalon gives the sign to the choirmaster to strike up. The choirmaster sees the sign from

Master Absalon and begins the *Dies Irae*. The boys break into full-throated song. The hymn rises louder and louder. Under the ladder, which is now being lifted, Absalon stands. He is singing lustily. Laurentius comes over to him. He tries to make himself understood to Absalon, but the latter is completely absorbed in the hymn and waves him away with his hand.

THE VICARAGE
Anne and Martin in the room in the loft. They are sitting close together, but only in the way that two children huddle together during a storm. Anne listens as the hymn mounts higher and higher . . . a shock of pain passes over her face.

THE BONFIRE
Tall flames shoot up into the sky, and the bonfire emits rumbling and crackling noises. Herlof's Marte is poised in the air on the top of the swaying ladder, which is enveloped in smoke. The hymn grows louder and louder. The executioner and his assistants stand ready at the foot of the ladder, awaiting a sign from Absalon. Now Absalon gives the sign and the executioner and his assistants let the ladder topple forwards. The top of the ladder, with Herlof's Marte on it, falls forward towards the bonfire.

THE ROOM IN THE VICARAGE
Anne and Martin are sitting as before. From out in the square we hear a long, piercing scream from Herlof's Marte as she falls into the flames. In her agitation Anne throws herself against Martin, with her head on his breast as if seeking strength from him. Unconsciously he puts his arm round her as if to protect her.
ANNE: Oh God, oh God . . .
MARTIN: Anne, Anne.
ANNE: Oh my God . . .
MARTIN: Don't cry, Anne.
Anne doesn't answer, but only huddles closer to Martin. The sound of the hymn grows fainter. The picture dissolves to a page of Absalon's journal. We see Absalon's hand writing a few lines as a record of this day.

The page in the journal reads in its entirety as follows: 'On this day, which was an exceedingly fine one, Herlof's Marte descended into eternal fire, being by good fortune burnt – *in majorem gloriam dei.*'

228 Dissolve from the page in the journal to Absalon, sitting at the writing-desk in his study area (which also serves as an oratory). He shuts the book and puts it away in a drawer. An expression of pain and suffering lingers over his features. He rises and kneels on the altar-step. He has become silent and introspective, listening to inner voices.

229 Merete comes in from the hall. Not seeing Absalon, she approaches the oratory without making a sound, but when she sees her son absorbed in his devotions she withdraws and sits quietly on one of the chairs by the table in the middle of the room.

230 New shot of Merete, sitting at the table in the wing chair. Every now and then there is a sigh or a murmur from the oratory. Then we hear Absalon getting up. He emerges from the oratory, and stops in surprise at seeing his mother – with a trace of annoyance, realizing that she must have come in order to pump him. There is a hint of reproach in his voice when he speaks.
ABSALON: Do you want me for something?

231 Merete has turned to face him and stretches out her hand towards him. She speaks with a tenderness and mildness which we have not heard in her voice previously.
MERETE: Absalon ... Yes, I do.

232 Absalon goes to his mother and stands beside her. Their attitude must suggest to the spectator the way in which as a boy he came to his mother when something was weighing on him. Now she takes his hand and looks him in the face. Then she speaks.
MERETE: There is something worrying you.
Absalon does not actually answer, but a slight inclination of his head acknowledges that this is so.

MERETE: What is it? Tell your mother.

Close-up of Absalon.

For a moment silence reigns; Absalon twice sighs deeply before speaking.

ABSALON: Mother, I have sinned ... (*after a pause*) ... sinned against God.

Close-up of Merete, who looks at Absalon questioningly.

ABSALON: I have lied to him.

3 MERETE (*seriously*): How? You tell me.

4 Close-up of Absalon shaking his head.

5 Close-up of Merete.

MERETE (*wheedling*): After all, I'm your mother, aren't I?

6 ABSALON (*rebuffing her*): Yes, but this is a battle I must fight by myself.

7 Absalon sits down.

Merete has been rebuffed, and feels it. But she doesn't give up the attempt to extract her son's secret. If he is not prepared to give her the key to the riddle, she must try to solve it by her own wits.

During the following speeches she begins by taking great care not to venture too far – until suddenly she catches him off guard.

Merete alone, watching him.

She rises and takes one or two paces, then turns, stations herself behind Absalon's chair and talks down at him, in an earnest, maternal way, but also in tones of cool reason.

MERETE: Ever since Herlof's Marte was taken away, you've been a different person ...

Absalon makes no reply but merely leans forward over the table, on which he rests his elbows, supporting his chin in his hand.

MERETE: And now that she's been burnt you go round in such a strange way.

Absalon still makes no reply. Merete stands bolt upright behind his chair, gazes in front of her, ponders. A sudden change in her facial expression tells us that a thought has struck her.

238   Merete leans forward so that she can see his face clearly and watch the
        effect of the question she is about to ask.
        MERETE: Has she denounced somebody, and you've kept quiet about it?

239 ABSALON (*with tell-tale haste*): No, no, she hasn't denounced a living
        soul . . .
        He breaks off abruptly, as if realizing that he has said too much already.

240   Merete straightens up; her surprise attack has succeeded. She smiles the
        contented smile of somebody who feels that a difficult sum is about to
        come out.
        MERETE: A living soul? . . . (*then, after a pause*) . . . a *living* soul?

241   Absalon raises his head, but stops in mid-movement, perhaps from fear
        of giving himself away still further if he speaks. Merete, however, does
        not need to know any more. Her mother's instinct has revealed the
        conflict in her son's life, and her mother's anxiety now impels her to
        speak out to him once and for all. She draws up a chair and sits beside
        him so that she can see right into his eyes. Then she speaks.
            Back view of Absalon.
        MERETE: Have you ever looked into Anne's eyes? Have you seen how
        they burn?
        Lines of anger appear on Absalon's forehead, but Merete does not allow
        this to affect her.
        MERETE: I'm thinking of her mother . . . (*then, with an emphasis on every
        word*) Her eyes burned in just the same way . . .

242   Merete meets her son's gaze steadily, and there is a brief silence. Then
        Absalon speaks – in a low, distressed and reproachful voice.
        ABSALON: Why are you saying this to me?

243 MERETE (*in the same firm tones*): The day may come when you must
        choose . . .
        She pauses.

244 ABSALON (*hesitating, almost as if he dreads the answer*): Choose between what?

MERETE (*sternly*): Between God ... and Anne.

Absalon gazes at his mother with wide-open eyes. Then he shakes his head several times, as if to impress firmly on himself that his mother is in the wrong.

Merete waits for a word from her son.

Absalon has regained his composure. Now he speaks in a serious, commanding voice.

ABSALON: You say that because you hate Anne.

MERETE (*leaning towards her son*): No, because I love you.
She gets up and stands for a moment looking at him with deep feeling and moistened eyes. Then she bends right forward over him, lays her cheek against his and kisses him.
MERETE: Good night, my boy.
Absalon is unhappy and perplexed, but without bitterness or anger.
ABSALON: Good night, Mother.

Merete straightens up and leaves the room.

THE VICARAGE KITCHEN
Here Martin is sitting on the free-standing bench at the long table while Anne puts away the pewter things after the evening meal. They both look enquiringly at Merete as she comes in from the entrance hall. She, however, shows no intention of answering their silent question as she walks straight across the picture

To the corner where her bed stands, The maids Bente and Jørund curtsey good-night to her and go into the room adjoining the kitchen. Merete draws back the curtain round her bed. Martin is heard saying good-night to Merete. The latter turns towards him and bids him good-night in mild, warm tones.
MERETE: Good night, Martin.
Next we hear Anne saying good-night to Merete. The latter answers with her back towards her and in a hard voice.

MERETE: Good night.
Anne and Martin are heard leaving the kitchen.

253 THE VICARAGE LIVING-ROOM
Absalon is sitting in the same spot as when Merete left the room. He is a picture of loneliness and grief. Anne and Martin enter. They close the door carefully and walk with cautious steps. Martin says good-night to Absalon. With infinite tenderness Absalon says good-night to his son. Martin says good-night to Anne also and goes up the staircase to the loft.
   Anne remains standing in perplexity. Absalon stretches out his hand towards her.
ABSALON: Anne.

254   Anne comes over to Absalon. He takes her hand. The angle of the shot and the mood of the picture must recall the earlier, corresponding scene between Absalon and Merete.
ABSALON (*seriously*): There is something the two of us must talk about.

255   Anne nods with an expression of surprise and disquiet.

256 ABSALON (*after a moment's hesitation*): It concerns your mother.

257 ANNE (*with a look of fear*): Mother?

258   Absalon nods.

259   Anne lowers her eyes. It is clearly causing her an effort to speak. When she does so it is almost inaudibly.
ANNE: Is it about mother's being . . .

260   Close-up of Absalon.
ABSALON (*with an expression of surprise*): Did you know that?
ANNE: Yes, but is it true?
ABSALON (*nodding*): Yes, she admitted it.
ANNE (*nods. Presently she asks*): What did she admit?
ABSALON: That she had the power of calling.

ANNE (*with an expression of wonder*): Calling?

ABSALON: Yes, she could call both the living and the dead, and they had to come. And if she wished somebody dead he had to die.

There is a short silence. Then Anne speaks.
(Dolly shot.)
ANNE: Is it true that you spared *her* to save *me*?
ABSALON: Anne! (*stretching out his hand towards her*).

Dolly shot.
Anne withdraws her hand, which Absalon has taken, and goes to the other side of the table, so that the table is between them. It is as if she has suddenly become aware of a strength that she has not known before.

Absalon has been following her movements uneasily.
ABSALON: Do you condemn me for that?

ANNE: For being good to my mother? No ...
The 'No' is said with an intonation which suggests that she might add: No, I don't condemn you for that, but there is something else I do condemn you for.

ABSALON: But?

ANNE: But were you also good to *me*?

ABSALON: Have I not been a good husband to you?

ANNE: Yes, of course ... yes. But did you ever ask me if I loved you?

ABSALON: But you were so young, virtually a child.

ANNE (*obstinately*): Yes, but did I *love* you?

273 Absalon suddenly feels himself confronted with something that puts his relationship with Anne in a completely new light.

ABSALON (*quietly*): It's strange. I've never thought about that . . .

274 ANNE (*lingering over the words, and with a hint of contempt in her voice*): No, I suppose you haven't . . .

It is quiet in the room. Anne looks up at the ceiling reflectively while her fingers play with the back of the chair. Her thoughts are clearly far away.

275 Absalon, who has been looking at her with great seriousness, gets up to go to his room.

276 Absalon cautiously approaches Anne to say goodnight to her. He puts his arms round her.

ABSALON: What are you thinking about?

For a moment Anne looks him in the face. Then she throws herself into his arms, clinging tightly to him, throwing her arms round his neck, all with passionate intensity, as she speaks. Her actions must convey that she is making a last, desperate attempt to transfer to her husband the desire which Martin has aroused.

277 ANNE (*with her arms round his neck*): It's as if there's a fire burning in me . . . ah yes, hold me close to you . . . Absalon, take me and make me happy.

Meanwhile her hands have been occupied in the way that is natural to the hands of a passionate woman – caressing his hair, his neck, his ear.

278 Now one of Anne's hands tries to sneak through the barrier of buttons, and in under the priest's smock. But it is stopped on the way, and it is Absalon who stops it. Gently but firmly Absalon takes her hand and removes it. He feels the ageing man's unease over the ardour which he cannot reciprocate. Her passion confuses and disquiets him. Instead of returning her caresses and her tenderness he preaches at her.

ABSALON: Anne, let us pray to God that the love which proceeds from the source of all goodness may warm us and lighten us. But the lusts of the flesh are sent to us from Hell.

Anne has listened to his sermon as a child listens to a reprimand. Shamed and hurt by her rebuff, she has sunk onto the chair.

Absalon fails to notice the distress he has caused; or rather, he would be incapable of understanding it. He is completely absorbed in his own reflections. For a few moments he paces to and fro across the floor; then he stops.

ABSALON: I'm going to my own room. I have many things to talk about with God.

Absalon approaches Anne to bid her good-night. She gets up and stands before him with head bowed. She is once again the obedient little girl.

ABSALON: Good night. (*Lifts her face up. Then he appears to think of something he has been on the point of forgetting.*) Look into my eyes.

Anne obeys and looks into his eyes.

ABSALON: Your wonderful eyes.

Anne makes no movement. Absalon looks searchingly into her eyes before speaking again.

ABSALON: So innocent. So pure and clear.

He kisses her eyes and goes.

Absalon approaches the door of his private room.

ANNE (*turning quickly towards him*): What happened to Mother?

Absalon turns with his hand on the latch, and looks at her questioningly.

ANNE (*from her place at the table*): She could call the living and the dead, and they had to come. Wasn't that it?

ABSALON (*surprised*): Yes, why do you ask?

288 ANNE (*with an enigmatic smile*): I'm thinking how strange it is, that power that Mother had . . . (*reflectively*) To think that a human being can possess such a power.

289 Absalon looks at her with an expression which suggests that he would like to talk to her, warn her; but evidently he prefers to remain silent. He opens his door quietly.
ABSALON: Goodnight, Anne.
He goes into his room, looks at her once more, and shuts the door.

290 With a peculiar secretive smile Anne begins preparing for the night – putting things away and so on. She does everything with a certain agitation, and breaks off constantly in the middle of a movement. We must feel what is happening to her. Absalon's words have sunk in dangerously deep.

291 The room is lit by two lights. She bends over one to blow it out. Stops in the middle and glances up. Listens. Then puts out the light. Listens again. A roaring noise is heard outside, a remarkably violent noise, such as one sometimes hears at night.

292 Then she goes over to the other light. As she bends over it to blow it out in turn, she says, half aloud and tentatively: 'Martin.'
ANNE: Martin.
She stands quite still. Fear, tension. Puts out the light. The room is now in darkness, but moonlight streams in through the window from the spring night.

293 Anne goes over to the window, where she stands with her back to the room. The moonlight envelops her in a mantle of dreamlike poetry. It is as if she is gathering all her will-power for one single purpose. We hear her whispering tonelessly.
ANNE: Martin.
Her voice is followed by a long pause, in which we hear once more the monotonous roaring noise. Then we hear her whispering again, this time a little louder, but tonelessly as before.

ANNE: Martin.

This time, after she has called, a change comes over her. She puts her head back and whispers, with closed eyes, half in joy, half in terror.

Anne enacts the phenomenon known to sixteenth-century witches as 'calling', and in our time as 'hypnotic suggestion'.

ANNE: I can do it. I can do it.

An expression of joy mixed with fear passes across her face, as she turns and looks in the direction of the built-in staircase.

94 The staircase, which Martin now descends. When he reaches the bottom he remains standing and looking round him with a curiously confused air. In his face and bearing there is nothing of the sleep-walker. He is simply a man overcome by long-restrained passion. He sees Anne and goes over to her.

95 Anne stretches out her arms towards him. He goes up to her and clasps her to him, crushing her fiercely in his arms. She sobs on his breast. With an air of wonder he holds her at arm's length.

MARTIN: Why, you're crying.

96 Anne raises her face to his. Her tears are flowing, but she looks at him with a smile.

ANNE: I'm seeing you through tears . . .

97 Martin remembers the scene at the beginning of the film when *he* saw *her* 'through tears'.

MARTIN: Tears which I am wiping away.

He kisses her eyes and turns her head so that the light shines in her eyes.

MARTIN: Nobody has eyes like yours.

ANNE (*coquettishly*): What are they like?

Martin searches for an answer.

ANNE: Innocent? Pure and clear?

MARTIN (*laughing and shaking his head*): No, deep and mysterious. I see . . .

ANNE: What do you see?

MARTIN: A trembling, quivering flame . . .

ANNE: Which you have lit.

MARTIN: Anne.

They kiss passionately. Everything has been said in a whisper which has merely added to the intensity of the words. Now a sound is heard somewhere in the house – perhaps from Absalon's room – of a chair being pushed back or something similar. Martin and Anne hurriedly break free from their embrace and listen tensely. When nothing further happens Martin points out of the window and whispers to Anne.

MARTIN: Come out to the birches.

She nods and pledges herself with a glance.

298 Martin steals over to the door into the entrance hall, which he opens with great care.

299 Anne stands still until he has gone. Then she goes to her room, whence she returns immediately with a hooded cape which she puts over her shoulders.

300 Anne steals over to the door into the hall, which she closes cautiously behind her.

301 IN THE VICARAGE MEADOW

A group of birch trees, standing like pale virgins in the white moonlight. Not a breath is stirring. It is absolutely still. Only the birch leaves are quivering. Martin has already come. Now Anne follows. They fall into each other's arms and stand for a moment locked in an embrace, completely absorbed by their feelings, Martin dreamy, Anne jubilant.

ANNE: Ah, how happy I am . . .

Martin looks lovingly at her.

ANNE: . . . Just saying 'I love you' . . .

Martin lays his cheek against hers.

ANNE: . . . and knowing that you . . . and I . . .

302 MARTIN (*taking her head between his hands and looking earnestly into her eyes*): You were always in my thoughts.

ANNE: ... and you in my dreams.
She presses herself passionately against him.

He puts an arm round her and they walk on in the brilliant moonlit
night.

THE VICARAGE
Absalon's room. It is lit only by a single light. Absalon walks up and
down, struggling with his doubts.

A PATH THROUGH THE SILVER BIRCH WOOD
Anne and Martin are wandering in the moonlit night, their arms round
each other's waists. The camera tracks after them. Between them and
the camera are brushwood and slender birch stems.

When they have gone a little way they stop.
ANNE (listening): How still it is (looking round her). It's just as if the trees
are asleep.

They walk on.

Suddenly Anne stops again. She points up into the sky.
ANNE: Look, a shooting star.
Martin looks in the same direction. They are both quite solemn.
Martin is the first to speak.
MARTIN: Did you wish?
ANNE: Yes, did you?
MARTIN: Yes.
ANNE: What did you wish?
Martin bends over her with a smile. She offers him her mouth to kiss.
He kisses it.
MARTIN: That was my wish.
She squeezes his arm.
MARTIN: And what did you wish?
ANNE (roguishly): I've told you already ... (after a pause) ... but I'll
gladly tell you again.
She offers him her mouth to kiss.

309   They walk on. The camera tracks after them for a while, until they disappear out of the picture.

310 THE VICARAGE
Absalon's room. Absalon, brooding in solitude. He throws himself into an easy chair, exhausted.

311 THE SILVER BIRCH WOOD
Near a spring in the wood. Anne and Martin come into sight, walking.
    The bubbling of the spring can be heard.
When Anne sees the spring she breaks away and runs on ahead.
ANNE: Here's the spring.

312   She cups her hands, fills the cup with water and drinks. As she is re-filling her cupped hands, she calls to Martin.
ANNE: Come here.

313   Martin drinks carefully from her hands.

314   When he has drunk, Anne asks:
ANNE: More?
MARTIN: No more water.
ANNE: What then?

315   Martin looks at her with burning eyes.

316   Anne raises her face to his and offers him her mouth.
ANNE: Drink.

317   He kisses her again. They blaze up in a long, burning kiss.

318   Then Martin lifts Anne's slender form in his arms and goes with her into the wood.

319 A PLACE NEAR THE SPRING
In the foreground low brushwood, with grass and bracken near the

VREDENS DAG Scene 227: *The executioner's assistant at the bonfire.*

Scene 434: *Anne and Martin (Preben Lerdorff Rye).*

VREDENS DAG Scene 576: *Martin and Anne.*

VREDENS DAG Scene 479: *Martin and Merete (Sigrid Neiiendam).*

Scene 655: *Anne, the Bishop (Albert Høeberg) and Martin.*

ground, hiding a grassy sunken path that lies further down. Martin and Anne appear, walking along the sunken path. They stop.

0   With feverish hands Martin takes the cape from Anne's shoulders. She lets him do this. He spreads out the cape on the slope, where it is hidden from us.

1   He kneels and stretches out his hand to her, and she lets herself sink down beside him, so that they both disappear from view, the sunken path being just deep enough for them to be completely hidden as they sit on the slope. Everything is quiet. The camera tracks nearer, though without our seeing Anne or Martin. But their whispering voices come closer.

ANNE: Listen to the whispering.
MARTIN: It's the grass humming.
ANNE: What is it humming?
MARTIN: A song about you and me.
ANNE: A song about your love.
MARTIN: And about yours.
ANNE: Martin, hold me close to you . . . take me and make me happy.
    The last words have been spoken in a husky voice. Now we can only hear a low whispering.
    Fade out.

22   Fade in to
THE VICARAGE LIVING-ROOM
    Morning prayers are in progress, and the inhabitants of the vicarage, including the servants, are sitting round the table with folded hands, listening devoutly to Absalon reading aloud. The servants, Bente and Jørund, reveal their respective natures, one with a vacant, guileless look, the other with an air of austere piety.

23   Merete sits motionless as a pillar of stone. Her eyes are cast down over her folded hands, but her brooding thoughts are taken up with Anne, whose behaviour has altered of late to a remarkable degree. Unconsciously her glance wanders over to

324   Anne and Martin, who are sitting directly opposite her. Nothing in
their faces, however, betrays their feelings.

325 ABSALON (*concluding his prayer and closing the Bible*): Amen.
They all repeat this 'Amen' with a variety of intonations. Bente's
'Amen' comes somewhat after the others'. She looks round in alarm.
Absalon is about to rise when Anne takes one of the books lying on the
table.
ANNE: May I read a passage from the Song of Songs?
ABSALON (*appears surprised, but gives permission*): Yes, with pleasure . . .

326   A delicate, almost imperceptible smile forms on Anne's lips, and her
glance brushes lightly, and as if accidentally, against Martin. Then she
opens the book and reads.
ANNE: Thus spake the Rose of Sharon to her beloved: 'Behold, thou art
fair, my love; behold, thou art fair . . . His left hand is under my head,
and his right hand doth embrace me . . . As the apple tree among the
trees of the wood, so is my beloved among the sons. I sat down under
his shadow with great delight . . .'
Merete, the only person to penetrate Anne's ruse, has followed the
reading with her eyes fixed on Anne and Martin. She now gets up with
complete self-possession.
MERETE: I think we have heard enough for today. We had better be
going about our work.
They all rise. Bente and Jørund hurry out into the kitchen. Martin goes
upstairs to fetch a book. Anne begins winding yarn from a spindle into
a ball. Absalon has gathered up his books, which he takes with him to
his room.

327   Merete follows him with anxious eyes.

328   Absalon shuts himself in his room. He has fallen into a marked decline.

329   Merete turns her gaze on Anne. This gaze constitutes a silent accusation.

330   Anne hums as she winds the yarn. The creaking of the spindle can be
heard.

Merete's air of surprise makes it clear that she regards Anne's humming as a misplaced frivolity. She tries to silence Anne with a look.

Anne, however, is for the moment invulnerable. Her happiness in love has matured her and changed her, given her courage and self-confidence. Unperturbed, she continues to hum.

Merete grows angry. She speaks in a tone of command.

MERETE: Anne!

Anne hears but pretends not to.

Merete repeats Anne's name with an ominous ring in her voice.

MERETE: Anne.

Anne is obliged to hear. She looks enquiringly at Merete, but continues to hum.

Merete looks sharply at Anne.

Anne stops humming and looks at Merete, but with a gaze that does not falter. It is a staring match. Anne meets Merete's eyes with a look of defiance. She feels as if she is obtaining redress now for all her bitter thoughts, all her bitter hours, all the painful pinpricks she has had to endure.

Merete approaches Anne, struggling with her anger. There is a threat in the tone she adopts.

MERETE: Just you take care!

Anne begins humming again.

MERETE (*more and more indignant*): I've said nothing as yet.

Anne goes on humming as if Merete didn't exist. There is a suggestion of concealed laughter behind this humming.

343   Merete, now beside herself with rage, speaks in a voice vibrating with bitterness and strikes the table with her clenched fist.
MERETE: Will you be quiet?

344   Anne pretends to be terrified, and does in fact stop humming now. But now she looks across to

345   The staircase in the corner, where Martin is just coming into view with a book in his hand. He stands in the doorway to the staircase and looks at the two women.

346   Anne, for whom the sight of Martin has restored her sense of security, turns suddenly to Merete with a teasing question.
ANNE: Do you know what that song was?

347   Merete, who is standing with her back to the staircase and has therefore not seen Martin, answers coldly.
MERETE: No.

348 ANNE (*teasing and provoking her*): It's a song about us two . . .
She has now finished winding the yarn, and with a mocking smile she struts out of the room.

349   Merete follows her with a look of hatred.

350   Anne goes into the bedroom and bangs the door behind her.

351 MERETE (*hissing after her*): You detestable bitch . . .

352   Martin, still standing on the stairs, is unable to restrain an expression of reproach.
MARTIN: Really, grandmother . . .

353 MERETE (*turning and speaking weightily, underlining every word with little taps on the table*): Yes, I meant it.

4 Merete goes up to him and turns her strong, piercing gaze on him; this gaze confuses Martin so much that he cannot meet it. She puts her arm round him.

MERETE (*earnestly*): Martin, what is the matter with you?

Martin tries to look up, but at once lowers his eyes again, for fear of her reading in them the secret he must hide.

MERETE: You've become so distant . . . to me and to your father.

Martin has no answer to this, for his grandmother's words are all too true. When he starts to turn away impatiently,

55 Merete turns him towards her in such a way that she can see straight into his eyes, while her words hint at more than they say.

MERETE: You must promise me to think of your father . . . not to bring sorrow upon him.

She looks at him warningly for a moment. Then she lets him go and moves away from him. His eyes follow her, and his face expresses shame.

56 Merete goes to Absalon in his room.

57 Martin's eyes wander from the door of Absalon's room to the door of the bedroom.

58 The bedroom door.

Anne is just emerging from it. Apart from her ball of yarn she is carrying a netting needle and a mesh-pin. As she enters the room she beckons to Martin.

ANNE: Martin, will you . . .

59 Martin, who has not yet overcome the feeling of shame which Merete has awakened in him, goes quietly and picks up an easel standing by the wall opposite the windows, which he brings over to the light for Anne.

60 Martin places the easel in front of Anne.

A netting frame is set up on the easel. On this frame rests a quantity of fine-meshed netting material, with which Anne is engaged in netting a figure, which for the moment we cannot make out. The figure is on the left and forms part of a composition which is to fill the whole frame.

Anne sits down and begins to work.

361   Martin has sat down on the edge of the table some distance away from Anne. He looks at her with an expression of great tenderness.
MARTIN: Grandmother is not good to you . . .

362 ANNE (*with a look of gratitude*): What does it matter? If only you are good to me.
She turns towards him and stretches out a hand.
Panning shot of the hand.
ANNE: If only you love me . . .
She beckons to him with the outstretched hand.

363   But Martin does not respond to her expectant arm. It is not that his love for Anne has become less ardent than before, but Merete's words to him about his father are fresh in his mind. Until now Anne has managed to deaden his conscience, but now it rises to the surface.
MARTIN: Anne, what will become of us?

364   Anne withdraws her hand and looks at him with eyes that blaze with a burning passion. She gets up and goes over to Martin.

365   Anne and Martin. With a tender smile she speaks to him.
ANNE: Kiss me.
Martin looks past her. He has grown up in this room. Everything in it seems to shout his sin aloud. She bends to one side in order to catch his eye.
ANNE: Martin . . .
Martin looks at her with an expression of fear, but she quickly draws him to her breast.
ANNE: Then I shall kiss you.
She kisses him passionately. He surrenders and presses her violently against him.

(This scene must make it clear that the erotic initiative lies with Anne. And from the action we are to understand that this has been the pattern many times before. By virtue of her suddenly kindled passion she is the stronger of the two – strong enough to overcome his resistance when remorse creeps in.)

Suddenly they hear a sound – perhaps an imaginary one. They break free from their embrace with glowing cheeks. Anne sets to work, while Martin begins reading in his book. They are both still breathless from their burning kiss. They sit like this for a few seconds, until the danger is past.

Martin looks up from the book which he has been reading with feigned interest. He looks at her through the netting frame. He smiles at her. The shot is taken through the stretched netting material.

Anne, who is also pretending to be absorbed in her work, abandons it, intercepts his smile and breaks out laughing. The shot of her also is taken through the stretched material, but without the figure on the left being visible. Anne and Martin: hearty laughter – a deep and a high-pitched laugh blending together.

ABSALON'S ROOM

Absalon, old and tired, is sitting at a little table or escritoire. Merete is sitting on a chair by his side. She has evidently had some household matter or other to discuss with her son, and we see Absalon counting out some money for her. Merete gets up to go. As she opens the door leading to the living-room Anne's laughter is heard from within – high-pitched, gay, provocative. Absalon makes a gesture to stop Merete, who stands with the door ajar. The laughter again drifts into the room.

Absalon signals to Merete to close the door. There is something he wants to say to her.

ABSALON: That's the first time I've heard Anne laugh like that.

Merete makes no reply, but merely looks at her son with maternal tenderness.

370 ABSALON (*almost as if talking to himself*): It's as if she has changed. Even her voice is different.

371 MERETE (*shaking her head and speaking with a trace of irony in her voice*): Yes, she has indeed changed . . .
She says this in a tone which suggests that she might add: 'but not exactly for the better'.

372 But the irony is lost on Absalon. He continues to voice the secret thoughts with which he has been preoccupied for some time now.
ABSALON: When I see those two together I really begin to feel how old I am, and how young she is.
He nods as old people do when they sit wrapped in their own thoughts.
ABSALON: It's good that Martin has come home.

373 Merete looks at him with an expression of tenderness and a shake of the head that almost expresses pity.

374 Absalon nods again. Then he gets up abruptly as if to free himself from something unpleasant.
ABSALON: I'll go in to them . . . (*laughing*) and be young with the young.
He opens the door to the living-room and follows his mother in.

375 THE VICARAGE LIVING-ROOM
Anne is sitting humming the same tune as before. Martin is reading – or pretending to read.
Merete passes through the room with an unmistakable expression of aversion which shows that she already has her suspicions about Anne and Martin. Without stopping she goes into the kitchen. Absalon, on the other hand, goes up to the young people and looks at them both with an affectionate, paternal gaze.

376 Anne is sitting in the direct line of the sun, beautiful in the happiness of her love. Absalon's gaze expresses his pride in having so attractive a wife, and he goes joyfully up to her. He gives her a caress – without noticing her discomfort at his touch.

ABSALON (*his voice full of love*): How lovely it is to hear you laugh . . .

He sits down close beside her and looks at her tenderly. Her reaction shows that she feels no pleasure in his proximity, and almost as soon as he sits down she gets up and stretches herself in the sunlight, though without moving away from Absalon.

ANNE (*to Martin*): Come, let's go.

Absalon gives Anne a look of enquiry. He is visibly disappointed.

ABSALON: Where are you going?

ANNE: To the river.

ABSALON (*turning to Martin*): Ah well. I was going to ask you to read through my sermon.

Martin alone.

MARTIN: I'll gladly do that, Father.

Anne and Absalon.

ANNE (*sulking*): Can't it wait? I was so looking forward . . .

ABSALON (*standing and putting an affectionate arm round Anne*): I'd be the last person to take away a pleasure from you, so off you go . . .

Delighted at getting her way, Anne snuggles up to Absalon as affectionately as a kitten and gives him a fleeting kiss on the cheek.

She hurries over to Martin, who looks from one to the other. When he looks at his father he feels guilty. When he meets Anne's dazzling gaze he experiences an enervating joy throughout his being. Then Anne drags him away. Vice has triumphed over virtue.

(*The whole of this very short scene must indicate that, while Martin's scruples about his father are still intact, they are easily overcome when the love which Anne has woken in him takes away his strength. As for Anne, her passion fills her so completely, and is so overwhelming, as to oust all other feelings and destroy all inhibitions. Her love for Martin has become for her a kind of obsession. Hence her recklessness and egoism.*)

When the two young people have left the room Absalon sits down again. An expression of disappointment and grief passes across his face.

His eye is caught by Anne's work on the netting frame and wanders across the frame on to the pattern fastened on the left of the frame.

381   By means of a panning shot of the frame and the pattern we now see the figure on the left of the stretched netting material. The figure represents a little naked child, while the pattern reveals to us the whole composition; a young woman in an antique style of dress, wandering through a meadow thick with flowers. She is holding the little child by the hand. Possibly she is holding a child in each hand or is carrying an infant in the other arm.

382   Absalon nods to himself, as if he understands that Anne's work is really an expression of her unconscious longings.

383 A PATH THROUGH THE MEADOW, BETWEEN TREES
    Anne running. We follow her with a panning shot that concludes with her in close-up, as Martin catches up with her. He takes her in his arms.

384   Close-up of Martin and Anne.
    MARTIN: Why are you running?
    ANNE (*teasing*): Don't you know?
    MARTIN: No.
    ANNE: Because I'm longing . . .
    MARTIN: For whom?
    ANNE (*confidentially*): For someone I'm going to meet.
    MARTIN: Who's that?
    ANNE (*pressing herself against him*): The one I love most.
    She kisses him and gazes at him with love in her eyes.

385   They continue in the direction of the river, half walking, half running.

386 THE VICARAGE LIVING-ROOM
    Absalon is sitting as we last left him. Merete comes in from the entrance hall, followed by the parish clerk.

Merete goes up to Absalon.

MERETE (*seriously*): Nils the parish clerk is here . . .

The parish clerk comes and stands beside Merete.

PARISH CLERK: Master Laurentius has sent for you . . . He's dying.

Absalon is terrified.

ABSALON: Laurentius?

The parish clerk and Merete.

PARISH CLERK: Yes, and he wants you to come and prepare him . . . (*indicating a leather carpet-bag he is carrying*). I've brought the holy vessel with me, in case . . .

ABSALON (*getting up*): All right, I'll come at once. I must just . . . He goes over to the door of his room.

Merete and the parish clerk follow him with their eyes.

Absalon goes into his room.

When he has left the room the parish clerk looks at Merete and shakes his head.

PARISH CLERK: How is he?

MERETE: Not well. It's his heart . . .

PARISH CLERK: There must be a lot of wear and tear on it.

MERETE (*emphatically*): There certainly is.

Absalon now returns with his hat and coat and some sacred books under his arm.

ABSALON: Here I am.

He and the parish clerk leave.

BY THE RIVER

A landing-place, with a couple of moored boats. The sun is shining and there is a gentle breeze; the river is flowing slowly and peacefully, without a ripple on the surface. The shot is taken from out in the river or from the other bank. Anne and Martin come down to the landing-place.

396   Shot taken from the near-side bank.
      Anne jumps down in one of the boats, flourishing Martin's hat in her hand.

397   Shot taken from out in the river. Martin unfastens the moorings. He straightens up with the moorings in his hand and speaks to Anne.
      MARTIN: Who's going to steer and who's going to row?

398   Anne in the boat, high-spirited and wanton, waving Martin's hat. She answers.
      ANNE: Nobody's going to steer, and nobody's going to row. We'll just be two lovers drifting with the stream.
      She sits down.

399   Shot taken from out in the river. Martin laughs as he jumps in the boat and pushes off.

400   Shot of Anne, who has sat down in the stern. We have the sensation of the boat swinging round in midstream and being caught by the current.

401   Long shot, taken from the bank, of the boat, which is now drifting with the stream. Anne beckons to Martin. Martin goes over to her cautiously and sits at her feet.

402   The boat drifts on between green meadows.

403   The stern. Anne is gazing in front of her with a happy smile. Martin's face is also, at this moment, without a trace of care. She caresses him. He takes her hand, kisses it and examines it.
      MARTIN: How wonderfully alive your hands are . . .

404   Anne revels in his adoration.

5 The pair in the stern.
MARTIN: ... your fingers ...
He kisses her fingers one by one.
MARTIN: ... your wrists.
He lays his cheek against her wrist.
MARTIN: I can feel your pulse beating.

6 Anne alone, happy.
ANNE: Beating for you.

7 Two-shot. Martin turns and looks up at her.
MARTIN: The sun is colouring your cheeks.
ANNE: It's not the sun. It's happiness.
MARTIN (*suddenly serious*): Happiness – how long will it last?
ANNE (*with complete confidence*): For ever.
But Martin lacks her faith. He is gripped by a feeling of uneasiness.
MARTIN: Anne, where are we going to end?
ANNE (*smiling and making a joke of it*): Wherever the stream takes us.
She talks to him like a mother comforting her child, although she is
well aware of their danger. Martin is not comforted.
MARTIN: The day will come ...
ANNE (*interrupting him*): Don't think about it. So many things can happen.
MARTIN (*in pain*): I keep seeing my father.
ANNE (*leaning forward and looking him in the eye*): I can only see you.
He turns his face away from her, that is, to the front. He gazes ahead
reflectively.

8 Long shot of the boat, with Martin and Anne.
The meadow gives way to a wood coming right down to the river.
The leaves of the trees overhang their heads like a canopy of many
colours.

9 IN THE BOAT
Anne ponders over how to free Martin from the dark thoughts
weighing on his mind.

ANNE: You don't say anything?
Martin merely shakes his head.
ANNE: Are you thinking?
Martin nods.
ANNE: What about?
After a pause Martin turns and faces her.
MARTIN: But how could we bring ourselves to do it?
Anne answers in a tone reflecting confidence that she has found the word that cannot fail to convince him.
ANNE: Because we two are destined for each other.
Martin, however, is not convinced.
MARTIN: So you think it was God's will?
ANNE: I think . . . (*after a pause*) I know that I love you. Isn't that enough for you?
MARTIN: Anne . . .
He lays his head in her lap. A quivering, transient gleam of sunlight falls on them.

410 MASTER LAURENTIUS'S ROOM
Laurentius is lying in his broad bed. The light falls on his pillow but not on his face. Apart from him there is only an elderly servant, who throughout the following scene stays at a respectful distance from the main characters. Absalon, who has just arrived, puts down his hat and coat and approaches the bed. He speaks to Laurentius with the assumed calm which doctors and pastors display towards dying men to avoid making the hour of departure harder than necessary.

411 As Absalon reaches the bed, Laurentius opens his eyes. He smiles to Absalon in greeting – the bright, almost boyish smile of a face already transfigured by death.
LAURENTIUS (*jokingly*): Yes, here I am.

412 Absalon's manner is confidential and cordial.
ABSALON: As soft and snug as in your mother's arms.
Absalon sits down beside the invalid.

3   A brief interval. Then Laurentius speaks again, in jerky, broken
     phrases.
     LAURENTIUS: Herlof's Marte didn't forget me.

4 ABSALON (*uncomprehending*): How do you mean?

5 LAURENTIUS (*with a shy smile*): Why, she promised that I would die.

6 ABSALON (*nodding to show that now it all comes back to him*): She got the
     punishment she deserved.
     LAURENTIUS: I suppose she did . . .
     ABSALON (*with conviction*): Every tree that bringeth not forth good fruit
     is hewn down, and cast into the fire . . . saith the Lord.

7   Laurentius lies for a moment absolutely still. His gaze is distant, as if
     his thoughts are far away. Then he lifts his eyes to Absalon.
     LAURENTIUS: Will you stay with me till it's over?
     ABSALON (*from the heart*): Of course I will.
     Laurentius closes his eyes again.

8 THE RIVER
     The boat drifts almost imperceptibly ashore, where it is held firmly.
     Only the purling of the water is heard as it glides past. Suddenly Martin
     sits up and speaks with a force that shows he has brooded long over the
     thought to which he now gives vent.
     MARTIN: Anne. Let me travel.

9   Anne's expression freezes.
     ANNE: Travel?

10 MARTIN (*standing*): Yes, let us separate for a time.

11 ANNE (*sitting facing him*): Separate?
     For a moment she sits in silence. Then she smiles, as if she thinks Martin
     only said it to frighten her.

ANNE (*repeating her question with a smile*): Separate?
Her look has not escaped Martin. She feels with the sure instinct of a
woman in love that Martin is already beginning to weaken.

422   Anne draws Martin down beside her and makes him put his arm round
       her.
       ANNE: How could you and I separate?
       Martin's face reflects the battle being fought out inside him.
       ANNE: Think of everything we have given each other . . .
       Martin nods, but looks away.
       Anne searches for a new point of attack. She finds one.
       ANNE: Look at that tree.
       She points in the direction of a birch.

423   The tree is shown. It is a weeping birch which hangs aslant the slope
       and is mirrored in the still water.

424   Anne and Martin in the boat.
       MARTIN: Yes, it is bowed down in sorrow.
       ANNE (*triumphantly*): No, in longing.
       MARTIN: In sorrow for us.
       ANNE: No, in longing for its own reflection in the water. And we can
       no more be separated than they can.
       Martin turns on her a face in which pain and love, grief and happiness
       are all present.

425   She gets up and stretches out her hand to him.
       ANNE: Come.
       He gets up, precedes her ashore and helps her out of the boat.

426   In the room of Master Laurentius, who is still lying with closed eyes.
       Absalon is sitting beside him. The parish clerk is walking up and down,
       quietly, in a corner of the room. The servant is sitting on her own,
       frightened and moist-eyed.

7   The dying man opens his eyes and speaks as if to himself.
  LAURENTIUS: My body I have of this world, and to the world I return it.
  My soul I have from God, and to God I return it.

8   Absalon alone.
  ABSALON: Amen.

9 LAURENTIUS (*with an imploring look up at Absalon*): Will you give me
     your hands?
  The two pairs of hands meet over the counterpane.
  ABSALON: Here they are.
  LAURENTIUS: Now I can hold them when my own grow cold.

10 ABSALON (*presses the dying man's hands. Speaks warmly and consolingly*): It
     will not be long before I follow.

11 LAURENTIUS (*with a feeble smile*): Are you trying to comfort me?

12 ABSALON (*shaking his head*): No, I often feel death tugging at my coat.
     But I go to meet him with courage and hope (*pause*). 'Though he were
     dead, yet shall he live' – as it is written . . .

13   Anne and Martin throw themselves down in the wood, somewhere
     near the river. A few leaves fall near them.

14   Both sitting on the grass. Martin catches a leaf in the air.
  MARTIN: Look, the leaves are falling – dying . . .
     Neither of them speaks for a moment. Then suddenly it is as if Martin
     has at last found the solution to the problem which he is continually
     mulling over.
  MARTIN (*earnestly, persuasively*): Anne, if we could die together now . . .

15 ANNE (*terrified*): Die?

16   Martin nods.

437 ANNE: Die? . . . (*she is almost paralysed*) Die? Why?

438 MARTIN: To atone for our sin.

439 ANNE (*who is incapable of following his train of thought*): Sin? Is it a sin to love?

440   Martin looks at her with a feeling of impotence; she is stronger than he, because she has no sense of sin.
       MARTIN: Anne . . .

441 ANNE (*with indescribable tenderness*): Hush, don't speak or think – of anything except that we two belong to each other.

442   She throws her arms round him and rests against him with her cheek touching his. They sit like this for a while.
       ANNE (*as if joking – ingratiatingly*): As the apple tree among the trees of the wood, so is my beloved among the sons . . .
       Martin is held more and more spellbound by the enchantment she exudes.
       ANNE (*in the same tone*): . . . I sat down under his shadow with great delight . . .

443   Anne gazes at him with hungry eyes – rejoicing in the victory which is already in sight. She offers him her mouth.
       ANNE: Kiss me.

444 MARTIN (*embracing her wildly and kissing her passionately*): How your lips burn.
       ANNE (*huskily*): Kiss me.
       They kiss. She holds his head away from her and looks at him.
       ANNE: I want to see your eyes become wild.
       He bends over her. She lets herself fall back. He follows, covering her face with kisses as he does so.
       Fade out.

THE VICARAGE LIVING-ROOM

Late the same evening. Merete and Anne are alone in the room. Merete is sitting in a high-backed chair, engaged in knitting or darning. Anne is sitting at the table, working on two new patterns for her netting work. She appears cheerful and light-hearted, in strong contrast to the uneasy atmosphere which otherwise prevails in the room. Outside, a fearful storm is raging, hammering on the doors and windows of the house and howling in the chimney. In the intervals of the storm the pounding of waves on the shore can be heard in the distance.

It is deathly quiet in the room which is lit only by a few tallow candles. We hear a door opening – the outside door of the entrance hall – and somebody struggling to get it closed. Finally she succeeds and a moment later Bente comes into the room dishevelled by the wind. In her hand she has a few keys.

BENTE: Ugh, what weather!

She goes up to Merete to hand her the keys according to custom. Merete adds the keys to her bunch. Meanwhile Bente speaks.

BENTE: We shall hear of disasters after this storm.

MERETE (*drily*): Do we ever hear of anything else nowadays?

The keys being now securely on their bunch, she nods to Bente as a sign that she is not needed any more and can go to bed. Bente goes.

5   Merete looks at the stove and then at Anne.

MERETE (*sharply*): Did you remember Absalon's ale?

7   ANNE (*unperturbed; completely absorbed in her drawing*): No, I forgot.

8   MERETE (*nodding*): Hm hm.

She gets up and goes over to the stove.

9   Anne follows her movements with an air of indifference.

0   By the stove.

Merete pours ale into a bowl which she puts to warm. She goes back to her place and continues knitting.

Fade out.

451   Fade in.
 In the room of Master Laurentius, whose end has come. The parish clerk has placed a little table by the bed and covered it with a clean cloth on which he has put a lighted candle. Apart from the storm which can be heard here also, the stillness of death reigns in the little room.

452   Absalon holds the Body of Christ before the dying man, with the customary words: 'the Body of our Lord Jesus Christ, which was given for thee, preserve thy body and soul unto everlasting life.'
 After which Absalon takes the cup and holds it out to the dying man with the words: 'the Blood of our Lord Jesus Christ, which was shed for thee, preserve thy body and soul unto everlasting life.'

453   Laurentius drinks from the cup which Absalon holds out to him.
 Fade out.

454   Fade in.
 THE VICARAGE LIVING-ROOM
 Martin comes down the stairs.

455   He goes behind Anne's chair to see what she is working at, but Anne puts her arm over the drawings to prevent him from seeing them, doing so, however, in a way which makes it clear that she is really itching to show them to him.
 ANNE (*coquettishly*): You're not allowed to see . . .
 MARTIN (*pleading*): Please let me see . . .
 He takes hold of her arms and draws them gently away from the drawings, which are now revealed to his gaze.

456   A drawing is shown, of an apple tree, on a finely reticulated background. The drawing is very graceful and feminine.

457   Anne takes the drawing and holds it out at arm's length, so that both she and Martin can see it.
 ANNE: Can you see what it is?

MARTIN (*with a teasing smile*): Yes, a pear tree.

ANNE (*pretending to be hurt*): A pear tree? Anyone can see it's an apple tree. (*She points with her pen at one of the highest branches.*) And up there is an apple blossom.

MARTIN (*pretending surprise*): Only one?

ANNE (*coquettishly*): Yes, on *my* apple tree there's only one apple blossom. Gust of wind. Martin goes to the window.

Merete has followed this by-play with watchful, suspicious eyes. At this moment a violent gust of wind is heard. Merete listens anxiously to the storm.

MERETE: I hope Absalon doesn't go across the marsh.

MARTIN (*looking out of the window*): If I knew which way he would come, I'd go to meet him.

ANNE: Yes, but if you go across the marsh he may go round it.

Merete knits with pursed lips.

MERETE (*scathingly*): Yes, and if you go round he will go across the marsh. You see, Anne wants you to stay at home.

MARTIN (*trying to assuage his grandmother's anger against Anne*): Anne is right. There's no sense in wandering about the paths in the dark. It's better to wait for him here.

Merete doesn't answer at once, but merely snorts contemptuously. Then she adjusts her position, folds her hands and stares straight in front of her. And now she speaks.

MERETE: In that case we'll all wait.

It is clear that she is only sitting up to prevent the two of them being alone together.

467   Anne steals a glance at Merete, gathers up her drawings and gets up.
ANNE: Are you sitting up?

468 MERETE (*ironically*): Yes.

469 ANNE (*with assumed calm and indifference*): Then I'm going to bed. (*Nods goodnight.*)
A violent gust of wind makes the house shake.
ANNE: God have mercy on those at sea.

470 MERETE (*sharply*): Yes, and on those who are not.

471 ANNE: Are you thinking of Absalon?

472 MERETE: Yes . . . (*she looks at Anne as if she has read her innermost thoughts*) . . . and of you.
Her eyes flash.

473   Anne is unmoved by Merete's anger. She has quite ceased to be afraid of her. With perfect composure she says good-night.
MARTIN: Good night, Anne.
Merete mutters a peevish good-night.
      Anne goes into the bedroom. There is an interval while Merete listens to her footsteps. After the door has closed behind Anne, Merete gets up and takes a few steps across the floor, perhaps to the stove to have a look at the ale which she has put to warm.
      Fade out.

474   Fade in.
      In the room of Master Laurentius, who has just breathed his last.
      Absalon draws the linen sheet over his face. He stands for a few moments in silent prayer, interrupted only by the howling of the storm. Then he turns back into the room.
ABSALON: There is nothing so peaceful as a heart which has ceased to beat.

5 The servant, who has been standing sunk in prayer, nods and dries her eyes.

6 Absalon and the parish clerk get ready to go home.
Fade out.

7 THE VICARAGE LIVING-ROOM
Martin and Merete alone. Martin is thumbing through a book. Merete goes behind his chair. It is clear that she is anxious to have it out with him but uncertain how to begin.
MERETE (*casually*): Martin . . .
Martin looks up in surprise.
MERETE: You ought to find yourself a wife.
MARTIN (*lightly*): There's no hurry.
Merete is dissatisfied with this answer, and attacks Martin from a new angle.
MERETE (*leaning forward*): There's nobody in the world who means so much to me as your father . . . (*Her voice takes on an almost solemn tone.*) In him God gave me the son I wanted. (*Then, with a new note in her voice, less mild, more threatening*) And I will protect him till I lie in my grave.
She moves away from Martin.

8 Merete goes over to the table in order to gather up her darning or knitting materials.

9 Martin remains sitting for a moment in a state of perplexity. He has understood the hidden meaning of her words and the threatening note. But how much does Merete know? He hits on a way of getting at the truth of the matter. He gets up, then sits down again directly opposite his grandmother. He looks at her with an open, earnest gaze.
MARTIN: Grandmother . . .

10 Merete looks up.

11 Martin tries to catch her off guard.
MARTIN: Why is it that you can't stand Anne?

482   Merete realizes she is under attack and tries to escape with a show of
       indifference.
       MERETE: I have never done her any harm that I know of . . .

483 MARTIN (*stubbornly*): But you can't stand her?

484   Merete straightens up and looks intently at Martin. Her face takes on a
       hard expression. If Martin really wants to know what she feels about
       Anne, he shall do so. She speaks to him in a subdued voice, which
       trembles with a hatred that she is now able to ventilate with the most
       impeccable intentions.
       MERETE: No, Martin, I can't stand her. I *hate* her.

485   Martin is appalled. He knew that his grandmother was a stern old
       woman, but her *hating* Anne fills him with dismay.
       MARTIN: Father's wife?

486 MERETE: The only sorrow your father ever caused me was when he took
       her into the house . . .

487   Martin is indignant. Now he understands. The old woman has been
       driven frantic by her impotence in the face of Anne's youth. He would
       like to speak severely to her, but all he can manage is a reproachful
       question.
       MARTIN: But how can you talk like that?

488 MERETE: I *have* to talk like that, because it's the truth.

489 MARTIN: An innocent woman.

490 MERETE: Innocent? – (*snorting contemptuously*) that . . .

491   Martin shakes his head.

492   Merete, panning over to Martin.
       MERETE: Ah well, I've said what I had to say, and now I'm going to bed.

She goes up to him and speaks to him gently.

MERETE: Goodnight, Martin. May the hand of the Lord be upon you.
She goes out through the door into the hall. Martin remains sitting,
deep in thought.

A BRIDGE ACROSS THE RIVER
Absalon and the parish clerk, on their way home, are battling with the
storm.

Straw blowing away from a rick.

Absalon stops in the middle of the bridge and looks up at the sky. The
parish clerk looks at him in surprise.
ABSALON: Look at the sky, the clouds ... they're like some strange
writing on the wall ...

Close-up of the parish clerk.
PARISH CLERK (*naïvely*): It is the Lord's hand that writes.

ABSALON (*nodding*): But where is he who can read the writing?
They continue to fight their way forward against the wind.

THE VICARAGE LIVING-ROOM
Martin, pacing the floor with a brooding air, stops suddenly. He hears
his name being whispered, turns in the direction of the sound and sees –

The door of the bedroom opening stealthily, and Anne appearing in
the doorway. She has taken off her cap, but is otherwise fully dressed.

Martin is about to speak.

Anne hushes him. She takes a few steps into the room and listens.

Martin's eyes follow her.

504 Moving more gently than we have hitherto seen her, she crosses to the door out to the entrance hall. She gives a sly smile and with the utmost caution bolts the door.

505 Then she comes over to Martin and embraces him wildly. They stand for a long time in a silent embrace. Then she speaks.
ANNE: Did she say anything?
MARTIN (*hesitating*): No-o . . .
ANNE: Did she speak evil of me?
A violent gust of wind.
Anne presses herself hard against Martin. Then she leads him over to

506 The large easy chair.
She makes him sit down and seats herself on the footstool at his feet – smiling all the time. From time to time she can be heard laughing quietly.

507 Closer shot. She looks at him happily.
MARTIN: My Anne . . .
ANNE: Yes, yours . . .
MARTIN: Mine . . . but my father's wife.
ANNE: His wife, yes. But I have never loved him . . . (*after a pause*) and he has never loved me.
MARTIN: Do you never think about him?

508 Anne sits quietly for a moment, as if weighing her words. Then she speaks, almost to herself.
ANNE: Yes, I often think that *if* he was dead . . .
MARTIN (*frightened*): Do you *wish* he was dead?
ANNE (*quickly*): No, no. I only think that if he was dead . . .

509 She sits for a little, then turns abruptly towards him.
ANNE (*vehemently*): Ah, Martin, I'll never let you go.
She presses herself against him. He strokes her hair. Presently she becomes calmer. She speaks again, but now her voice has a dreamy quality.

ANNE: If only we were far, far away, you and I . . . just the two of us . . .
  He continues stroking her hair.

  Absalon and the parish clerk on the way home. They are now at a gate.
  The storm is raging and the clouds are hurtling across the sky. Absalon
  stops, as if frightened by something or other in the dark. The parish
  clerk looks at him anxiously.
PARISH CLERK (*sympathetically*): Are you unwell, Master Absalon?
ABSALON: No, no. Only I had a strange feeling of fear. It was as if death
  brushed against my sleeve.
PARISH CLERK (*alarmed*): Death?
  Absalon nods. The parish clerk shakes his head in compassion. Absalon
  has got his breath back. They walk on slowly.

THE VICARAGE LIVING-ROOM
  Martin and Anne are sitting in the same position as before.
ANNE (*sentimentally*): . . . We shall live right out by the sea, in a little
  house. Every morning I shall wake with my head on your shoulder. I
  shall wake you with a kiss. We shall lie like that for a long time. Then
  we shall hear a little Martin, lying in his cradle and yelling. I shall take
  him up, and just as I found life on your breast he shall find it at mine.
  All the tenderness that you gave me, I shall pass on to him, as I sing for
  him . . . the song about you and me.

  Anne closes her eyes and after a short silence continues.
ANNE: Isn't it lovely to think about?
MARTIN: Yes, but it's only a dream.
ANNE (*with a happy smile*): What does that matter? If only the dream is
  nice . . .

  They sit in silence, wrapped in their shared happiness. Then voices are
  heard. Absalon is returning home and taking leave of the parish clerk
  outside the house.
ANNE (*getting up hurriedly*): There he is.
  She points at the table and the book. Martin goes across, sits down and
  reads.
    Close-up of Martin at the table.

514   Meanwhile Anne goes to the door leading out to the hall and cautiously
        unbolts it. She goes out into the hall. Through the door, which she
        leaves open, her voice and that of Absalon can be heard.
        ABSALON: Haven't you gone to bed yet?
        ANNE: No, we sat up for you, Martin and I.
        Absalon comes in, followed by Anne. He is pale and tired, and looks
        very old. Martin gets up from his book, goes to meet his father, and
        takes his books.
        MARTIN: Good evening, Father.

515   Anne has gone to the stove to fetch the ale which Merete put to warm.

516   Martin accompanies his father to the table.
        MARTIN: You were out for a long time. How is Master Laurentius?
        ABSALON: God granted him a gentle death.
        He sits down heavily at the table. He is evidently exhausted by his
        visit and deadly tired. Anne comes to the table with the ale.
        Panning shot. Close-up of Anne with the ale.
        ANNE: Wouldn't you like a little ale? It's been kept warm . . .
        ABSALON (nodding slowly): Thank you, Anne. And thank you for sitting
        up . . .
        He gives them a searching glance which he takes pains to make look
        casual. Drinks.
          Anne retires to the stove. Martin, however, goes up to his father as
        he drinks.
        MARTIN (affectionately): Father, you're tired. Why don't you go to bed?
        ABSALON (gazing up at him affectionately): I'm tired all right . . . but I
        can't find any rest.
        Anne in close-up.

517   Absalon gazes in front of him with a look of infinite sadness and makes
        a quick movement as if to wipe away a tear from his eye.
        Close-up.
        ABSALON (to himself): I have come from a man who died a good death . . .
          After a short silence he continues with what sounds like a cry from a
        soul in torment.

ABSALON: But in general . . . when I think of all the deathbeds I have sat by, and all the sighs I have heard, all I can see is sin, sin, sin . . .
Absalon looks across at

8   Anne, who evades his glance and is apparently quite unmoved by his pain.
She sinks back into the shadow.

9   Close-up.
Absalon looks from Anne to

0   Martin, who is deeply moved.

1   Absalon resumes his train of thought.
Close-up.
ABSALON: . . . often a fleeting pleasure, a secret sin . . . (*sighing deeply*) . . . Lord Jesus, what lives people live.
Close-up of Anne.

2   MARTIN (*personally affected by his words*): Father, how strangely you're talking.

3   ABSALON (*with a distant gaze*): It's because I have such a strange feeling of uneasiness.
He sits for a moment, as if wondering whether to speak now about what is on his mind. Martin bends over him and puts his arm round him.
ABSALON: Out there . . . I felt as if death was holding my hand.
Martin, deeply and sincerely shaken, puts his cheek against his father's.

4   Anne, who up till now has sat with averted eyes, now turns towards Absalon and listens with a tense expression.
She moves out of the shadow.

5   ABSALON (*continuing his story*): I heard nothing . . . saw nothing, but in my innermost soul I felt: now my death has been determined.

526   Anne turns away again. A faint smile, as of suppressed joy, forms on her lips.

527   Absalon and Martin.
        Martin speaks to his father in tones of tenderness.
    MARTIN: But Father, you're tired, you're ill.
    Long shot.
    ABSALON: No, I'm not ill, but I'm tired, and now we'll go to bed. Good night, my boy, sleep well.
    MARTIN: Good night, Father. If only I could take away your burdensome thoughts.
    Absalon gives his son a look full of affection and forgiveness. It is as if he is fully aware of the agonies Martin is suffering – but without knowing their precise origin.
    ABSALON: You have your own worries.
    Martin kisses his father in the same way that he used to kiss him good-night as a boy. He goes across to

528   The staircase.
        Here he turns, serious and emotional.
    MARTIN: Anne.

529   Anne gives him a nod and a bright smile.

530   Martin goes up the stairs.
    During the latter part of the preceding scene there has been a lull in the storm. Now it seems as if the storm has been summoning all its strength, and as Martin goes up the stairs we hear a gust of wind more violent than any yet.

531   Absalon sits with an absent expression. Anne comes up to him, quietly and deliberately. Slowly she leans forward over the single light and puts it out. She remains standing and looking at Absalon, that old, worn-out man.

532   Absalon sits lost in his own remote thoughts.

3   Anne, who wants to settle the account, opens her attack.

ANNE: You shouldn't think so much about death.

4 ABSALON (*looking up and nodding wearily*): You are right, Anne, but . . .
I can't help it.
Without conscious thought he repeats to himself, after a moment's
silence:

ABSALON: Now my death has been determined.

5 ANNE (*leaning forward*): Who would wish you dead?

6 ABSALON (*with a look of wonder*): No, who would wish that?
He holds out his hand towards Anne and looks at her seriously. He
expects her to take the outstretched hand, but she does not do so, and
he lets his hand fall back heavily on the table.

ABSALON: Anne, have you never wished me dead?

7   Anne has remained standing, quite imperturbable. With simulated indifference she answers his question.

ANNE: Me? Why should I do that?

38 ABSALON: I don't know. I have so many strange thoughts . . .

39 ANNE (*sitting down, tense and curious*): What sort of thoughts?

40 ABSALON: In the first place, that I have done you a great wrong.

41   Anne gives a faint nod.

42 ABSALON: I never asked you if you wanted to be mine . . . I just took
you . . .

43   Anne confirms this with a nod.

44 ABSALON (*in self-reproach*): I took your best years.

545   Anne turns her flashing eyes on him.

546 ABSALON: And that is a wrong I can never put right again.

547   Anne makes no reply, but looks at him with eyes full of hatred.

548   Absalon seems to flinch before the power of her gaze.
     ABSALON: I have many things to ask your forgiveness for.

549 ANNE (*speaking now with her face turned directly towards Absalon and with her eyes boring into his*): Are you certain I'm going to forgive you? Her long-accumulated hatred, bitterness and desperation are now seething in Anne's mind. She looks up at him, her eyes flashing with anger and hate.

550   Absalon stares at her with the expression of a man who has suddenly seen a gulf opening before his feet.

551 ANNE (*without releasing him from her gaze*): Yes, it's true, you have taken my best years . . . and you have taken my joy . . . (*Her voice rises very gradually. Her tone is one of infinite bitterness.*) I have yearned for somebody I could love . . . (*Her voice becomes husky and for a moment a charming smile breaks through her hard expression.*) I have dreamt of a little child that I could hold in my arms. And you never gave it to me.

552   Absalon tries to answer, but cannot find words. There is a silence, during which the storm can be heard lashing against the vicarage.

553 ANNE (*as if gathering strength for a new attack*): You asked if I had ever wished you dead. Yes, I have wished it hundreds of times.

554   Big close-up of Absalon, dumb with terror.

555 ANNE (*staring into his face and speaking calmly, as if stabbing him to death in cold blood*): I have wished you dead when you were with me – and wished it when you were away from me.

6 Big close-up of Absalon.

7 ANNE (*pausing as if to take aim at his heart*): But I have never wished it so intensely as since Martin . . . since Martin and I . . .
She breaks off abruptly.

8 ABSALON (*white as a sheet and trembling with agitation*): Martin and you?

9 ANNE (*with glowing eyes*): Yes, I and Martin. Now you know. (*Continuing with an expression of savagery*): That's why at this very moment I wish you dead . . . *dead.*

50 It is as if the death-wish suddenly loses its grip on Absalon. A tremendous strength surges up in him. He gets up.

51 Hardly knowing what he is doing, he goes over to the staircase and climbs a few steps. In a strong voice he shouts up the stairs.
ABSALON: Martin, Martin.

52 Anne jumps to her feet and stares after him with an expression which suggests that she is enjoying in anticipation the approaching struggle between the two men who love her. Suddenly her expression freezes. Her eyes open wide. Then we hear a cry from Absalon, followed by the sound of his body falling heavily down the stairs. Rapid footsteps from the floor above. Anne takes a moment or two before she understands what has happened. Then, terror-stricken, she tries to scream. At first the scream seems unable to escape; then the constriction in her throat seems to vanish, and she utters a loud cry of despair, while her eyes remain glued to the stairs.

53 And now for the first time we see what Anne sees, namely Absalon lying lifeless at the foot of the stairs. Martin descends in dismay and kneels beside his father's body.

54 At this moment Merete comes in from the entrance hall. She is in her nightdress. She stands for a moment just inside the door as if to get used to the light.

MERETE: What is it?

MARTIN: Oh, Grandmother.

Merete rushes across from the door.

565   Merete comes up to her son and kneels beside him. She is no longer the hard, cold woman, but an old, despairing granny; she collapses, sobbing, over her son's body. Martin gets up. He feels that his place is beside Anne.

566   Martin comes over to Anne, who clings to him tightly. During this shot we hear Merete's lamentations.

567   Merete by her son's body. She straightens up, turns towards the other two and looks threateningly at them. A violent gust of wind is heard.
      Fade out.

568   Fade in.
      Late evening in the vicarage demesne, where a short time ago Martin and Anne met in the moonlight. But this evening there is no moon. Instead there is a thick mist. A strange, ghost-like atmosphere hangs over the landscape and contrasts with the earlier brilliant, moonlit night.
      Martin has come out here in order to be alone with his heavy thoughts and has settled himself on a grassy slope.
      As he sits there, lost in his brooding thoughts, we hear, far away, Anne calling for him. We hear her distant call, but, preoccupied as he is, he does not answer.

569   Near a group of birches, where Anne and Martin met that moonlit night, Anne enters at a run, anxious and bewildered. She looks helplessly round and hurries on in the direction they went before, every now and then calling plaintively for Martin.

570   Martin sitting in the same spot. At short intervals we hear Anne's plaintive calls, but Martin continues not to hear them. Or perhaps he doesn't want to hear them.

The path through the field, between birches, which Anne and Martin followed in their time. Anne enters, half walking, half running. She stops and looks round her in confusion. She calls and listens for the answer. Walks on. The mist engulfs her.

THE VICARAGE LIVING-ROOM

which is draped with white on the occasion of Absalon's death. Ceiling and walls are hung with white material, draped from the pelmets or stretched out tight. In the middle of the floor Absalon's body is lying on a bier – a bier with four short legs. Absalon is dressed in his priest's robes. The bier is covered with a white cloth. Absalon's face in shadow.

At the head of the bier stands a table with a white cloth and six candles in candlesticks, which are draped with white crêpe or wide paper fringes. Black crosses are disposed here and there.

Close-up.
Under Absalon's chin a psalter. On his breast a pair of scissors lying open.

At the foot of the bier, as well as at the head, stands a chair. Merete is sitting on the chair at the head and keeping watch over her son's body. She is less erect than before. Physically she is broken, but her will-power sustains her; for she still has a mission to complete before she can lie down and die, namely to avenge her son's death. With eyes that blaze like glowing coals she keeps watch like an avenging fury.

THE VICARAGE MEADOW

Anne arrives at the silver birch grove near the spring, the bubbling of which can be heard. Again she calls for Martin. Her call has become a gentle wailing. No answer. In a voice trembling on the verge of tears she calls again, and this time Martin's voice can be heard not far away. Anne hurries after the sound. We follow her as she runs through the mist.

Martin has got up and is standing and listening. He stands with his face to the camera. Then Anne's call is heard again. Martin turns, and at the same moment Anne appears. Still wailing, she approaches him, but refrains from embracing him.

ANNE: Oh, Martin.

Martin's reaction must show that he is reluctant to break his train of thought, but that he hasn't the heart, now she has come, to send her away.

ANNE: I'm so cold.

Martin, who has a cape over his shoulders, opens the cape and shares it with her.

Her behaviour must make it clear that her plea was only a pretext for coming closer to him, so that the power she has, of which she is fully conscious, can work on his senses and thus overcome his coldness towards her.

He speaks to her in a tired voice, but without hostility.

MARTIN: Come . . .

577   And he leads her over to the place where he was sitting. We follow them by means of a panning shot, at the end of which we realize that they are on the same sunken path where they abandoned themselves that moonlit night. Just as then, they disappear from our sight as soon as they sit down, and we are only able to hear their conversation, without seeing them. Although the landscape is wreathed in mist, certain characteristic plants in the foreground show clearly that we are in the same place. There is a short interval during which neither of them speaks. It is Anne who breaks the silence.

ANNE: Why are you so quiet?

Another silence.

ANNE: Come on, say something.

Martin has long been brooding over a question that keeps recurring in his mind. It is evident from the new tone in his voice that he has decided to take the bull by the horns and have it out with Anne.

MARTIN: Did he know?

Anne, who suffers every time she is forced to think about what has happened, answers evasively.

ANNE: What do you mean?

One has the feeling that it pains Martin to be more explicit.

MARTIN: Did he know that you and I . . .

ANNE (*wailing*): Martin . . .

Martin realizes now that his father did indeed know. During the following exchanges he is working himself up into a mood of bitterness and anger.

MARTIN: You told him?

Anne makes no reply.

MARTIN: He knew. That was why he called for me.

ANNE: Oh, I'm cold, warm me.

Martin doesn't hear, lost as he is in his own thoughts.

MARTIN: I can still hear his voice. (*He groans in despair and bursts into sobs.*) Father, Father . . .

ANNE (*wailing helplessly*): Martin, Martin . . .

One feels there is no contact between them.

ANNE (*whimpering*): Don't you love me any more?

Martin doesn't answer. He continues to sob.

8 THE VICARAGE LIVING-ROOM

Shot of Merete, keeping watch with the same frozen expression.

9 THE VICARAGE MEADOW

The same shot as before. Silence, in which Martin's weeping can be heard. Then Anne speaks.

ANNE: Is it for him you're weeping? Or for me?

MARTIN (*in a thick, husky voice*): For myself.

ANNE: Why?

Martin makes no reply. But presently he speaks as if to himself.

MARTIN: Oh God, I wish I was dead.

We hear him sighing deeply, as people do after a fit of weeping. He relapses into despair.

MARTIN: It's all over, it's all over.

ANNE (*indomitable*): No, Martin, it's only just beginning.

MARTIN: Not for me.

ANNE: For *us*.

Another silence, broken this time by Martin.

MARTIN: Why did he have to die?

ANNE: I believe that he died for our sake.

Another silence.

580 THE VICARAGE LIVING-ROOM

Merete keeping watch in the same position and staring straight ahead with her piercing, inscrutable gaze. Bente comes into the room and goes silently up to Merete.

BENTE: Shan't I keep watch?

MERETE (*looking up at her*): No, Martin will keep watch tonight.

Bente snuffs the candles.

581 THE VICARAGE MEADOW

Same shot as before. At first there is silence, then Martin can be heard speaking.

MARTIN: Anne, I'm frightened of you.

ANNE: Of me?

MARTIN: Don't you feel any remorse?

ANNE: For loving?

MARTIN (*sternly*): There are other things in the world.

ANNE (*naturally*): Not for me . . . (*ecstatically*) Ah, it is better to burn in the flames than never to have loved.

MARTIN: Anne, Anne. I'm frightened of you. I'm frightened of the person I love.

Martin has said this with a mixture of tenderness and fear. Now he gets up. Anne remains seated, and we only hear her voice.

ANNE: Are you going?

MARTIN: Yes.

ANNE (*reproaching him feebly*): Can't you think of me?

MARTIN (*seriously*): Now I can only think of . . . *him*.

He goes, and is at once shrouded in mist. Anne gets up. She calls.

ANNE: Martin . . .

The intonation with which she calls to him must recall her voice that moonlit night, when she 'called' Martin to her. She is visibly disappointed when he doesn't come. She moves slowly off. The mist hides her.

2 THE VICARAGE LIVING-ROOM
Bente comes up to Merete, and the two old women exchange a glance before singing in cracked voices.
BENTE and MERETE: God's mercy is unfailing
For those who have deserved it
And, over sin prevailing,
Have faithfully conserved it.
During the last lines Bente has gone to the table at the head of the bier. She continues singing as she snuffs the candles. When she has finished she says good-night to Merete.

3 Tracking shot.
As Bente goes out into the hall, Martin comes in. She holds the door open for him, and he walks past her into the room as if he hasn't seen her – so heavily is his sorrow weighing on him.

4 Martin goes up to Merete.
MARTIN: Grandmother, I'll stay now and keep watch.
She doesn't look at him or say a word, but merely gets up and leaves the room.

5 Close-up.
Merete goes into what was Absalon's room.

6 Martin sits down on the chair vacated by Merete.

7 A moment later Anne comes in, silent as a shadow.

8 Anne comes hesitatingly towards Martin.
(The following dialogue between Martin and Anne is conducted in whispers. Even when they become agitated they continue to whisper.)
ANNE: Shall I keep watch with you?
MARTIN: I want to be alone.

9 Anne goes to the table at the head of the bier, so that she is photographed with the candles in front of her face.
ANNE: Are you avoiding me?

590 MARTIN (*in a subdued voice*): I'm avoiding myself most of all. (*He turns abruptly towards her.*) Do you know, Anne, we ought to go down on our knees and ask *him* for forgiveness.

591 ANNE (*pointing at Absalon*): I have nothing to ask him to forgive me.

592 MARTIN (*reproachfully*): Anne . . .

593 ANNE (*with complete calm*): But I know that *he* would have forgiven us.

594 MARTIN (*remorsefully*): Now he is standing before God and accusing us.

595 ANNE: No, Martin. He is pleading for us, because he sees how we suffer.
     Then there is quiet in the room. Anne, head bowed, moves away from the coffin.

596 Anne goes to the high-backed chair and sits down in it. She tilts her head back and closes her eyes.

597 Martin has remained seated, deep in thought. His expression shows that he is brooding over a doubt, a suspicion, that is tormenting him. This uncertainty, combined with his gnawing conscience and remorse, and the fearful tension of the last few days, has reduced his nerves to breaking point.

598 Martin's eyes take on an expression which we have not previously seen. He turns and looks in Anne's direction. She is the only person who can resolve his doubts. He gets up and goes across to

599 The easy chair in which Anne is sitting. She starts as she opens her eyes and sees him gazing intently at her. There is something strange about him which fills her heart with fear, so that she involuntarily shrinks back in her chair.
     Close-up.
     (*The following critical exchange is conducted in a whisper, which in itself adds power to the words.*)

MARTIN: Do you remember saying: 'If he was dead' . . . (*pointing at his father*).

Close-up.
　Anne, filled with fear at the savage expression in his eyes.

Martin and Anne.
MARTIN: You *wished* him dead.
ANNE (*trying to justify herself*): I only thought that *if* . . .
　Close-up.
MARTIN (*cutting her short*): You *did* wish him dead . . . but did you wish it so that he *had* to die?
ANNE (*with a break in her voice*): Mart . . .
　She tries to jump up; but he seizes her by the wrist, holds her firmly and forces her back into the chair on one knee, while he stands leaning over her.

MARTIN: Did you have the *power* to wish him dead?

Anne, in big close-up, just looks at him with eyes dilated in terror.

Big close-up. Panning shot.
MARTIN (*gripping her hard*): Answer me.

Close-up.
ANNE (*in terror*): Martin, you're sending me to the flames . . .

Panning shot. Full face. Closer.
MARTIN (*in growing excitement*): Did you have the power to wish him dead? I'm asking you.

ANNE (*forcing herself to be calm and speaking to him as if remonstrating with an unreasonable child*): Do be reasonable. Look at me. I love you, love you. That is my only crime.
MARTIN: Did you *wish* him dead?

ANNE (*feverishly*): Don't drive me mad . . . do you hear? You must believe me, Martin. I wasn't responsible for his death.
Martin gazes at her, still incredulous.

609   Martin, in close-up, looks searchingly in her eyes, as if hoping to find the truth in their depths.

610   Anne, in close-up, meets his gaze steadily.

611   Then Martin has an inspiration.
      Close-up.
      MARTIN: Come and kneel by his bier, and then say it.
      He has seized her by the arm, and without releasing her he takes her over to

612   The bier.
      She kneels. He releases her. She places her hand on the bier as she looks up at Martin. Close-up.
      ANNE: Martin, I wasn't responsible for his death.
      Martin is apparently convinced at last.
      ANNE (*getting up and facing him*): Do you believe me now?
      MARTIN: Yes.
      Martin sits down on the chair at the foot of the bier. Anne stands beside him.

613   Martin and Anne. Closer shot.
      MARTIN (*turning to Anne with an expression of melancholy*): I wonder, Anne, if we will ever find each other again.
      ANNE: Who is to prevent it?
      MARTIN (*pointing at the bier and whispering*): The dead.
      ANNE: It's not the dead we need fear . . .
      MARTIN: You're thinking of Merete.
      ANNE: Yes.

614   There is a pause. Then Anne bends abruptly over Martin. The self-confidence which she displayed during the previous scene has suddenly

evaporated. At this moment there is something infinitely helpless about her.

ANNE: Martin, I love you, and you love me. If we have sinned together we must also stay together in misfortune.

Martin nods.

ANNE: If Merete accuses me, will you still stand at my side?

MARTIN: Yes, I promise you that.

ANNE: You won't let me go?

MARTIN (*with a bitter smile*): We are bound together so tightly, I think, that we can never let each other go.

Martin's assurances fill Anne with new courage, and she faces the future with confidence again. She speaks to him gently and affectionately. Her face lights up with a joyful smile.

ANNE: You'll see, happy days will come again, even if we can't see it now.

With infinite tenderness she lays her cheek against his, but doesn't kiss him. Then she goes over to the door into her room.

At the door she turns and nods to him with a smile intended to reassure him and give him new courage.

Martin gives a feeble, melancholy smile as he sits at the head of the bier. Fade out.

Fade in.

In the sacristy on the day of Absalon's burial. The room has been cleared for the solemn ceremony which is about to take place in the presence of the Cathedral Chapter. The bier for the deceased has been placed on a dais in the middle of one wall, standing a little out from the wall. The bier has been draped with a silver brocade pall belonging to the church, which at the sides reaches right down to the steps. Directly opposite the coffin, armchairs have been put out for the Bishop and members of the Cathedral Chapter.

The bier stands with its head facing out into the room. Left and right of the bier are two chairs, for Anne and Merete respectively. On either side of the bier, by the wall, candles burning in candlesticks as high as a man. At the foot of the dais the choirboys are stationed, wearing their long, black surplices which resemble those of priests. There are twelve of them, each holding a burning torch in his hand. They are singing a hymn. With vacant faces.

To the right of the bier (as seen by the Cathedral Chapter) sits Merete, a in long black cape, with a long black veil and headband. Some distance away from her, but on the same side of the bier, stand Bente and Jørund.

To the left of the bier sits Anne, in a cape coming down to her feet, and over her head a white veil, which also comes down to her feet, but instead of hanging freely like a bridal veil it is gathered round the neck with a band of the same material.

Martin stands close beside her.

The scene opens with a close-up of one of the boys singing. Then the camera tracks back, and the whole scene around the bier is gradually revealed.

At some point in this back-tracking movement the choirboys move away from the bier one by one, and go in single file, still singing, out through the little door into the church. It is timed so that the last line is being sung as the last boy leaves the sacristy.

618   As the hymn dies away Martin comes up to the bier in order to express the customary thanks of the family. He is deeply moved, and his speech, which begins stiffly and formally, gradually develops into a personal confession before the dead man.

As Martin approaches the bier, we hear in the distance the sound of the church bell, which continues throughout his speech. Now Martin speaks:

MARTIN: As the son and heir of the dear departed I stand by his bier and offer you his mother's, his wife's and my own thanks for coming here today. My heart is so full of sorrow that . . .

He pauses, unable to speak for tears.

619   Anne sits with her head deeply bowed.

20   Martin resumes his speech, though with tears in his voice.
    MARTIN: God gave me a father who was greater and better than most
    men . . .

21   Merete sits staring straight in front of her.

22   Martin turns towards the body. He is struggling with his tears.
    MARTIN: . . . Father, you were so good to me that all my days should
    be an expression of thanks to you in word and deed. And now that you
    are gone I bitterly regret the sorrows I have caused you. If you were
    still alive – ah, how much better a son I should be to you . . .
    He stops; his emotions are threatening to master him.

23   Anne, sitting with her head deeply bowed as before. It is as if every
    single one of his words has burnt into her heart.

24   Martin draws a deep breath. He is ashamed of being overpowered by
    his feelings.

25   Merete staring blankly in front of her.

26   Martin ends his speech with a quiet and touching plea for forgiveness.
    MARTIN: Forgive me for being carried away by my . . .
    Awkwardly and with some embarrassment he leaves the bier – after a
    last look at his father – and goes over to Anne.

27   But at this moment Merete gets up and looks at Martin – merely looks
    at him, but with so compelling a force in her look that

28   Martin involuntarily turns towards her. He knows the meaning of
    Merete's look and he turns once more towards the gathering.

29   Panning shot of the priests as they listen to him with serious expressions.

30   On his way to Anne, Martin has thought of something that he has
    forgotten.
    MARTIN: One word more . . . on behalf of the family . . .

631   Anne follows his words in breathless suspense.

632   Martin goes back to the coffin.
MARTIN: In accordance with custom, I witness before God that my
father's sudden death is not to be laid at any person's door . . .

633   Merete, who has fixed her powerful gaze on him, takes a step towards
him.

634   Anne breathes heavily and looks nervously from Merete to

635   Martin, whose whole bearing shows that he intends his words to erect
a wall round Anne to protect her against Merete. He continues, raising
his voice.
MARTIN: His wife was with him when death came to him, and his
mother and I were with him when he passed over.
Martin has concluded his proclamation and turns to go back to Anne.

636   The priests. The Bishop gets up.

637   The Bishop comes forward to the dais. In silence he takes Martin's
hand and advances to the bier. Here he stops and turns towards the
gathering.
BISHOP: Let us then illumine with the Church's peace the man who lies
here . . .

638   Merete has stood up and now stops him with an imperious movement
of the hand.
MERETE: Wait, now *I* am going to speak.

639   The Bishop is about to remonstrate with her but

640   Merete's look shows so much strength of will that he is compelled into
silence.

641   Disturbance among the priests.

2 Merete turns towards them and points at Absalon as she speaks.
   Close-up.
   MERETE: If his son won't tell the truth, his mother must do so.
   Turns towards Anne.

3 Anne looks at her, white with terror.

4 Merete turns her gaze on her, comes forward to the bier as the dis-
   turbance grows, and speaks.
   MERETE: The witness his son gave is a pack of lies.
   She breaks off and looks hard at Anne.

5 Anne, as if hypnotized.

6 The silence adds to the tension. But now Merete speaks again.
   MERETE: My son lies murdered on his bier. (*She continues to hold Anne in
   her terrible gaze as she proceeds with her accusation.*) And his murderer is
   sitting there . . .
   She points at

7 Anne, who is speechless with terror.

8 Merete turns to the Bishop.

9 The Bishop, whose anger at Merete's presumptuousness has not yet
   died down.

50 MERETE (*fearlessly*): I demand life for life, blood for blood . . .
   She lets her hand fall.
   The Bishop looks enquiringly at Martin.

51 To the left of the bier Martin comes up to Anne, who takes his hand in
   a strong grip, as if seeking support from him.
   MARTIN (*shouting . . . to the Bishop*): Don't believe her. (*Raising his voice
   and turning to the Bishop, he continues*): I declare his wife innocent. She
   had no part in his death . . . (*pointing at Absalon*).
   The Bishop looks across at Merete.

652 MERETE (*addressing the Bishop again*): Every word I have spoken is true.

653 MARTIN (*addressing the Bishop*): Do you think I would let my father lie
unavenged . . .

The Bishop looks from Martin to Merete.

MERETE (*staring Martin in the eyes*): Yes, you would. Because you yourself are under her spell . . . (*she turns her stare on Anne*). With the Evil
One's help she has lured you into her power. With the Evil One's help
she murdered her husband. (*Turning to the Bishop, but pointing at Anne*)
I denounce her as a witch. Let her deny it if she dare.

654 Deadly silence reigns, in which the only sound is the Bishop's voice
muttering a prayer.

THE BISHOP'S MUTTERING VOICE: Lord, Lord.

Merete returns calmly to her place. Then she turns round to see the
effect of her words.

654a The priests whisper. Shake their heads.

655 Martin and Anne stare at each other. Then he moves slowly away from
her. She stretches out her hand to him imploringly, but he doesn't
take it.

He looks at her as if she had caught the plague.

MARTIN: With the *Evil One's* help?

Step by step he draws away from her.

656 Anne is a picture of speechless despair.

It is as if she is paralysed. In amazement she looks at

657 Martin, as he removes himself further and further.

658 Anne tries to call to him, but her voice refuses to obey her. Only a few
tiny muscular movements in her face reveal the explosion taking place
in her mind.

9   Martin approaches Merete, who has advanced to meet him. She takes his arm and draws him close to her. He permits this.

0   Anne stares at him as if petrified and sees

1   Merete putting her arm protectively round him.

1a   The priests. Some of them get up and look intently at Anne. One gets up, another holds him back.

2   It seems suddenly to dawn on Anne that she is alone – utterly alone.
     The Bishop approaches her, looking at her seriously.
  BISHOP: You have heard the accusation. What do you have to say in reply?
     Anne doesn't look at the Bishop. Her eyes are still fixed on Martin.

3   The Bishop looks uncertainly from her to Martin and Merete. Then he seems to settle accounts with his conscience and decide how best to handle this case. He speaks to her now with authority, but also with a friendly air.
  BISHOP: In order that the real truth may come to light, I order you to place your hand on the dead man and take the oath.

4   As Anne sits there before the Bishop in all his authority, she is no longer Master Absalon's obedient wife, still less Martin's triumphant, ardent mistress, but only a young woman, bereft of all her illusions. It is as if everything has come to a standstill for her. She shakes her head, as if over something she is unable to understand. She feels alone and crushed to the ground; but it is not the awareness of danger, nor even fear of being burnt, that is crushing her – only the thought that Martin has failed her, betrayed her. This is more than she can bear. Her love for Martin has become the most important thing in her life, and now it has been snatched away. Thus, at one blow, her life has ceased to have any meaning for her. Even survival has become a matter of indifference. She shakes her head again.

665   The Bishop, who clearly feels something approaching sympathy for
       her, addresses her again.
       BISHOP: Are you ready and willing to undergo this test?

666   Anne sits as if glued to her chair. She nods in answer, but it is not clear
       whether she has understood the question or not.

667   The Bishop regards her with a mild, compassionate expression. He
       gives a sign to the priests.

668   Anne. There is something infinitely touching about her. It is as if
       something has snapped inside her.

669   The Bishop takes her by the hand and leads her over to the bier. She
       follows him mechanically; all her movements are mechanical.

670   By the bier. At the signal from the Bishop two of the younger priests
       have removed the shroud from Absalon's face and breast. They go back
       to their places. Anne mounts the steps of the dais, supported and guided
       by the Bishop.

671   The group of priests. Some of them get up. Their eyes are fixed
       intently on Anne.

672   By the bier. Anne, standing, puts her hand on the dead man's breast.
       ANNE: Absalon, I have . . . I give witness . . . I give witness . . .
       She looks feverishly round her. Then she sits on the edge of the bier,
       supports her hand on the pillow and looks the dead man straight in the
       face.

673   Close-up of Absalon.

674   Anne speaks to him. Her voice is intimate and conversational.
       ANNE: So you got your revenge after all . . . Yes, I *did* murder you with
       the Evil One's help . . . and with the Evil One's help I have lured your
       son into my power. Now you know, now you know . . .
       She straightens up abruptly, then relaxes again and sits there smiling.

The priests stand up. Their faces express horror and bewilderment. They huddle together. Turn away.

Anne, whose facial expression is transfigured by madness, in a manner found otherwise only in dying men. The tears begin to trickle from her eyes and run down her cheeks. There is a tinge of sadness in her face when she speaks.

ANNE: I am seeing you through tears . . . but nobody is coming to wipe them away.

She sits with folded hands, looking up at the ceiling. The sad smile still irradiates her features, and the tears continue to pour down her cheeks. At this moment she has the purity of an angel. Suddenly her eyes take on a listening expression, though the smile remains. And now we hear what she hears in her imagination, namely the *Dies Irae*, sung by the boys' choir, beginning as a gentle humming, then gradually mounting to the volume of a storm.

Dissolve into the manuscript words of the *Dies Irae*.

ORDET

The Word

Introductory music.

THE OUTSKIRTS OF THE VILLAGE

1   It is a moonlit, stormy night. A clock is heard striking. Panning shot into a large farm, the largest in the parish. Milk-cans are standing outside. Dissolve into the name of the farm, which is painted over the entrance: Borgensgård.

2   The name dissolves to the interior of

A BEDROOM AT THE FARM

occupied by Johannes and his brother Anders. The scene opens with a close-up of Anders, asleep in bed. He is woken by the sound of a door shutting. He sits up hurriedly in bed and at once turns to look at his brother Johannes's bed. The camera tracks to the bed, which is empty. Apparently Johannes has just left it. The camera tracks back to the window. Meanwhile Anders has put on his trousers. As he pulls on a jacket he goes to the window and sees

3   Johannes walking away from the farm in his billowing, loose-hanging clothes.

4   Anders quickly gets ready and hurries into the adjacent living-room. The camera tracks after him to another door leading from this room into the bedroom of his father, old Borgen. Anders opens the door, and without raising his voice too much, for fear of waking other people on the farm, he calls his father and informs him of Johannes's disappearance.

ANDERS: Father . . .

BORGEN (*drowned in sleep*): Yes, what is it?

ANDERS: Johannes is out on the dunes again.

BORGEN (*irritably*): Is he? Oh no.

ANDERS: I'm going out to keep an eye on him.

BORGEN: All right, I'll come with you . . . I'll come with you.

Anders leaves his father. Borgen is already getting out of bed.

5 MIKKEL AND INGER'S BEDROOM

Inger, who is far advanced in pregnancy, is woken by the sound of footsteps outside. She gets out of bed, goes to the window, pulls up the blind and looks out. She catches sight of

6 Anders outside, buttoning up his jacket. His eyes scour the landscape.

7 By now Mikkel also is awake and asks Inger:

MIKKEL: What's going on?

INGER: It's your brother.

MIKKEL: Johannes?

INGER: No, Anders.

MIKKEL: Anders? Then there must be something wrong with Johannes again.

INGER: Yes.

MIKKEL: I'd better go with him.

INGER: Yes, you'd better. The poor, pitiable man!

MIKKEL: You mean Johannes?

INGER: Yes, don't you feel he needs our pity? Twenty-one and incurably insane.

MIKKEL: Oh, I don't know. Perhaps he's happy as he is.

INGER: You can't mean that! . . . Remember to put something warm on.

MIKKEL: Yes, yes.

INGER (*at the window*): Your father's coming too.

MIKKEL: Right. I'm ready now.

INGER: I'll have some hot coffee waiting for you.

MIKKEL: Yes, I expect we'll need it.

Inger goes back to the window.

8   Outside shot of old Borgen and Anders moving off. Shortly after Mikkel comes too; he has to run to catch up with the others.

9   IN THE SAND DUNES

Old Borgen and his two sons, Mikkel and Anders, are struggling with the gale, searching in all directions.

10   Old Borgen and his two sons come from behind a dune and catch sight of Johannes, who is working his way up another dune directly opposite them. They watch him with startled, anxious eyes.

When he reaches the top of the dune he turns and in a prophetic voice addresses an imaginary crowd standing and lying in groups on the slope of the dune in front of him.

His father and two brothers listen to his words with sad faces and shakings of the head.

JOHANNES: Woe unto you, ye hypocrites, thee . . . and thee . . . and thee, woe unto you, because ye believe not in me, the risen Christ, who has come unto you at the bidding of Him who made the heavens and the earth. Verily, I say unto you: the day of judgement is at hand. God has called me to be His prophet before His face. Woe unto each one who believeth not, for only they who have faith shall enter into the Kingdom of Heaven. Amen.

His 'amen' echoes among the dunes, so that it sounds like an answer from the imaginary crowd on the slope of the dune.

Johannes raises his hands as if in blessing over the supposed crowd of listeners, after which he strolls down the slope with dignified, measured steps.

Old Borgen, Mikkel and Anders retreat so that they are hidden from Johannes, who maintains a Christ-like bearing as he makes his way back to the farm. When he has gone a short distance, his father and brothers follow in his wake.

11   THE LIVING-ROOM

On the wall a picture of Grundtvig.[1] Enter Inger from the kitchen. At the same moment old Borgen, Mikkel and Anders enter from the

[1] Translator's note: N. F. S. Grundtvig (1783–1872), Danish poet, statesman, divine and educationalist, originator of the Danish folk high school movement.

garden door, Mikkel with his collar still up over his ears. Borgen looks enquiringly at Inger.

BORGEN: Is Johannes . . .

INGER: Yes.

Inger nods and makes a sign to indicate that Johannes is out in the kitchen.

Shivering with cold, the three men sit round the table, which Inger has laid in advance. On the table a lighted lamp. Inger pours coffee. Old Borgen has taken a pipe from the pipe rack and begins filling it.

A moment later Johannes enters. He strides through the room as if the others were not there. On his way to the bedroom which he shares with Anders, he stops in front of a chest of drawers, on which two three-branched candlesticks have been placed by way of ornament. He begins lighting the candles, one by one. Inger and the three men watch him in amazement.

BORGEN: What's that for, Johannes?

A brief silence.

JOHANNES (*in the tones of a preacher*): I am the light of the world, but the darkness comprehendeth it not. I came unto my own, and my own received me not.

He has finished lighting the six candles and now picks up the candlesticks, one in each hand, and carries them over to the window, where he puts them down on the window ledge.

MIKKEL: What are the candlesticks doing there?

JOHANNES (*drawing back the little curtains as he answers*): That my light may shine in the darkness.

Then he leaves the room and goes into the bedroom which he shares with his younger brother.

After he has left the room, Inger very quietly goes and takes the candlesticks, puts out the candles and puts the candlesticks back.

INGER: It's so sad about him.

MIKKEL (*shaking his head*): He's as mad as a hatter.

INGER (*remonstrating*): Mikkel.

MIKKEL: I mean, going round thinking he's Jesus.

ANDERS (*anxiously*): I wonder if he'll ever recover his reason.

INGER: It's all that reading that's made his head spin round and round.

Mikkel, like his two brothers, has always suffered from the effect of his father's dominating personality. In his case the subjugation expresses itself in a kind of petulance towards his father. This petulance is clearly apparent in his sullen remarks.

MIKKEL: No, he should never have been encouraged to study.

Old Borgen senses the implied reproach, and there is a touch of acid in his answer.

BORGEN: I did so because of his gifts.

MIKKEL: Yes . . . and because you'd set your heart on having a priest in the family.

BORGEN: No, I hadn't, there are priests in plenty. What is needed is a man who can stir the people up. And when I saw Johannes's gifts I believed he was the spark, here on this farm, that should once more set Christianity ablaze. I prayed with all my heart that he might be the man – the man with the voice of a prophet!

MIKKEL (*with a touch of irony*): The reformer?

BORGEN: The renovator – yes. That was what I prayed for so earnestly. (*With a gesture of despair*) And now see what has come of it.

Inger puts her hand on his arm in a gesture of sympathy and comfort.

There is silence for a moment. Inger, Anders and even Mikkel feel deeply sorry for old Borgen. The silence is broken by Mikkel.

MIKKEL: But we'd better be thinking about going back to bed. Good night, Father.

BORGEN: Good night.

ANDERS: Good night, Father.

BORGEN: Good night, Anders.

Inger, who during the preceding dialogue has collected the cups on a tray, carries the tray out into the kitchen. Now Anders gets up.

ANDERS: I think I'll go and have a look at the sow.

Anders and Mikkel leave the room. Old Borgen sits by himself for a moment. Then Inger returns. She stops by the table and bends over old Borgen – or sits down beside him.

INGER: Johannes will be his old self again.

BORGEN (*shaking his head*): I've hoped and hoped he'd get better; but he never will.

INGER: Why do you say that?

BORGEN (*with a tired smile*): Miracles don't happen any more.

INGER: Nothing is impossible for God, if we pray to Him for it.

BORGEN: Inger, I've prayed and prayed and prayed.

INGER (*with a smile that evidently owes its radiance to an inner conviction*): You must pray again. Because Jesus Himself has said that He will grant us our prayers.

BORGEN: I know, Inger – I know – but what use have all my prayers been?

INGER: How do you know what your prayers may not have set in motion?

He smiles gratefully, but his expression shows that he – although a believer – still has his doubts.

INGER (*straightening up and admonishing him again*): Pray and go on praying, however poor you feel your prayers are . . . Good night, Grandfather dear.

BORGEN: Good night, Inger. I think I'll sit up a little longer.

INGER: You do that. Good night then.

Inger crosses to the door into her bedroom.

12 MIKKEL AND INGER'S BEDROOM

Enter Inger. She goes to the beds and shakes the pillows. Mikkel is sitting on the edge of the bed.

INGER: I feel so sorry for your father.

MIKKEL: I feel sorry for Johannes.

INGER: So do I, but –

MIKKEL: But what?

INGER: Perhaps Johannes is nearer to God than the rest of us. But your father . . .

MIKKEL: Ugh, I can't stand all his godliness.

INGER (*going up to Mikkel and looking into his eyes*): I think you're being unfair to your father.

MIKKEL (*bitterly*): He has also been unfair to me.

INGER: But he's never reproached you with anything.

MIKKEL: No, he's kept silent. But I've known what he was thinking – I saw the look in his eyes when I wouldn't become part of the pious goings-on at this farm.

INGER: But Mikkel, you do believe in God, don't you?

MIKKEL: You know my views on these matters, Inger.

INGER: Then you have no faith?

MIKKEL: Not even faith in faith.

INGER (*with a gentle smile*): But you have something else – something more important.

MIKKEL: And what may that be?

INGER: A heart – and goodness.

MIKKEL (*hesitantly*): Really?

INGER: Yes, because it's not enough to *believe*, if you aren't a good person as well. Which you are.

MIKKEL (*teasing*): But I have no *faith*.

INGER (*confidently*): No, but it will come.

MIKKEL: Are you so sure of that?

INGER: Yes, and just you see how warm you feel then – warm through and through – and how happy you are – and after all, it's nice to be happy, isn't it?

MIKKEL: Yes, Inger girl – and now we must sleep. Good night, lass.

INGER: Good night, my great big boy.

Mikkel kisses her. Inger draws the blind down. Her pregnant form is silhouetted for a moment against the moonlit blind.

13 THE LIVING-ROOM

Old Borgen is busy cleaning his pipe. He gets up, hangs the pipe on the pipe rack, goes back to the table and puts out the lamp.

14 THE KITCHEN AT BORGENSGÅRD

Inger is busy making some special biscuits for which old Borgen will presently praise her. The maid, Karen, is helping in the kitchen; she is a young girl of sixteen or seventeen.

INGER (*pointing at a basket containing crusts and crumbs*): Karen, just go and give that to the hens.

Karen goes. At almost the same moment Anders hurries in. During the following scene Inger goes to and fro between the table, where she is rolling out dough and shaping the biscuits, and the kitchen range, where she is seeing that the biscuits don't get too hot. Anders goes to and fro between Inger and Mikkel, who is sitting making notes in a notebook.

ANDERS: Listen, you two, you must help me.

INGER: What with?

ANDERS: Er – Anne – and me . . . are thinking . . .

INGER (*looking up and pushing back a lock of hair from her forehead*): Anders, you haven't gone and fallen in love with the tailor's daughter Anne?

ANDERS: Why, there's nothing wrong in that, eh, Mikkel?

MIKKEL: No, it's only about the worst thing you could have hit upon.

ANDERS: The worst?

MIKKEL: I don't mean there's anything against *her* – she's a really nice girl . . .

ANDERS: Well, what then?

MIKKEL: What do you imagine *Father* will say?

ANDERS: That's just what I need your help about . . . if you're willing, that is.

INGER: Yes, but what about *her* father – what will *he* say? I mean, you know very well . . . they look differently at religion and all that . . .

ANDERS: If Anne and me love each other, the rest doesn't matter . . .

INGER: Of course, we agree with you there, Mikkel and me, but . . .

ANDERS: But – but what – eh, Mikkel?

MIKKEL (*scratching his chin*): I'm damned if I know –

ANDERS: Listen, will you help me – or won't you?

MIKKEL: Of course we'll help you – why don't you go down yourself and talk to Anne's father?

ANDERS: But he's quite impossible to talk to.

MIKKEL: Go on – you could at least try.

ANDERS: Ye-es, I could try of course – what do you think, Inger?

INGER: That's right, you try, and I'll be having a go at *your* father in the meantime. That'll be the hardest part.

ANDERS: Do you think so?

INGER (*nodding*): Yes, but I'm willing to try anything.

ANDERS: Thanks a lot, Inger. I'm sure you'll manage it all right.

MIKKEL: And you see about managing the tailor.

ANDERS: I'll go straight down. Goodbye for now.

MIKKEL: Goodbye.

INGER: And good luck.

Anders goes out of the door.

MIKKEL: If only Father doesn't get angry now – and obstinate.

INGER: I'm more afraid of his being sad about it. Look, shouldn't you be down cutting the reeds?

MIKKEL: You're right, goodbye, my lass.

INGER: Goodbye, goodbye. Hullo, anyone would think we'd just got engaged.

MIKKEL (*embracing her in a strong grasp*): That we have and all, Inger girl.

INGER: Get along – we've been married for eight years.

A kettle begins to sing. Inger hurries across and takes the kettle off, during the following exchange.

MIKKEL: Well, goodbye then. Don't go and put your foot in it.

INGER: Why, do I usually?

MIKKEL: No, perhaps that wasn't quite fair.

Mikkel disappears from the kitchen. Inger stands thinking.

5 OUTSIDE ONE WING OF THE FARM

A farm wagon is standing, with two horses hitched to it. Mikkel arrives, takes the reins and drives off, standing up in the wagon. The farm hand, who has driven the wagon out, goes with him.

6 THE KITCHEN

Inger has had a bright idea. She hums quietly to herself as she takes out the coffee grinder and starts grinding the beans.

7 PATH THROUGH THE DUNES

Anders on his way to Anne's father, Peter the tailor. He is in good heart. Some people can be seen among the dunes.

8 THE LIVING-ROOM AT BORGENSGÅRD

Enter Inger with the coffee pot, which she puts on the table. She is now ready for the encounter with her father-in-law. She sits down in the middle of the room and looks up at the ceiling.

INGER: Dear God, please help me today also.

Old Borgen enters the room from his bedroom. He is carrying a pair of boots in his hand and is in his stockinged feet, so that Inger doesn't hear him. Borgen approaches her and follows the direction of her eyes.

BORGEN: It's because the rain has been coming through the roof.

INGER: Oh, it's you, Grandfather? You gave me quite a fright.

BORGEN: I did what?

INGER: What were you saying?

BORGEN: I said the damp patch up there (*pointing at the ceiling*) was rain-water. The roof's leaking.

INGER: Well I never – so it is.

BORGEN (*rubbing his thighs*): ... This confounded rheumatism!

Inger has taken the cups and put them on the table. Borgen sits down and begins putting on his boots. Inger pours the coffee.

BORGEN: What – coffee at this time of day?

INGER: It's so cold today, Grandfather.

BORGEN: Well, well – and biscuits. Why – you've made them yourself!

INGER: You like my biscuits, don't you?

Borgen looks round the room with an air of enquiry. Inger brings him his long pipe.

INGER: Tell me, is this what you're looking for?

BORGEN: Ah, thank you, yes, I'd like the long pipe today. Only it needs filling.

INGER: It's filled already.

BORGEN: Can you do that too?

INGER: I can do everything.

BORGEN: Except – having sons.

INGER: Now, now ... There you are ... (*handing him the filled pipe*).

BORGEN: Thank you.

Meanwhile the door into the front parlour opens and Johannes appears in the doorway.

JOHANNES: A body in the parlour, a body in the parlour.

INGER (*in alarm*): *What's he saying?*

BORGEN (*getting up and crossing to the door into the parlour*): Be quiet, Johannes, and shut the door.

JOHANNES: A body in the parlour, and so shall my Father in heaven be glorified.

ORDET 1955. Scene 10: *Johannes (Preben Lerdorff).*

ORDET *Morten Borgen (Henrik Malberg).*

ORDET Scene 9: *Mikkel (Emil Hass-Christensen), Morten and Anders (Cay Kristiansen).*

Scene 11: *Morten Borgen and Johannes.*

BORGEN: There, there, there, Johannes!

Johannes has gone again – but leaving the door open behind him. Borgen shuts it quietly and goes back to Inger.

INGER: Whatever was that he was saying?

BORGEN: Who takes any notice of what *he* says, Inger? (*Sighing.*)

INGER (*after an interval*): Wouldn't you like another cup?

BORGEN: Thank you, Inger ... just a drop – thank you so much. (*Puffing away at his pipe.*)

To get rid of the painful impression Inger goes and begins winding wool. She hears steps outside and peeps out of the window.

19 OUTSIDE

We see – through Inger's eyes – the parish priest walking along the wall of the churchyard and opening the churchyard gate.

20 THE LIVING-ROOM

Inger follows the priest with her eyes.

INGER: That was the new pastor. He went into the church. It's strange he hasn't been here yet.

BORGEN: He'll come one of these days. I suppose Mikkel and Anders are down cutting the reeds.

INGER: Ye-es – Mikkel left just as you came ... (*trying to steer the conversation in another direction*) At all events, he preaches quite a good sermon.

BORGEN: Who? The pastor? ... (*shrugging his shoulders*) Yes – I suppose so – it's just that he takes a bit too long getting to the amen.

INGER: Yes, perhaps.

Inger sits for a moment, wondering how best to introduce Anders's business.

INGER (*plucking up courage*): Grandfather.

BORGEN: Well?

INGER: Do you want to help me?

BORGEN: Certainly, if I can.

INGER: Yes, you can ... like this ... (*She puts the skein of wool over Borgen's hands, and he puts down his pipe.*) You know – Anne – the tailor's daughter?

BORGEN: Yes – what about her?

INGER: Don't you think she might make Anders an excellent wife?

BORGEN: Hm, so that's why we're having coffee?

INGER: Yes – no – not really. But don't you think she would?

BORGEN: That's something I don't intend to go into.

INGER: How can you be so . . .

BORGEN: So what?

INGER: Such a typical proud farmer.

Borgen slips the wool off his hands by way of indicating to his daughter-in-law that the discussion about Anne and Anders is finished. He also turns his back on Inger and goes over to the pipe rack. Inger runs after him.

BORGEN: What I mean is that birds of a feather flock together.

INGER: You know, Grandfather, I think the only thing that matters is that they love each other.

BORGEN: Love comes with years, Inger.

INGER: Grandfather dear, I believe you understand about everything in the world except about love.

BORGEN: Well, indeed . . .

INGER: Tell me, have you ever really been in love yourself?

BORGEN: Have I ever been in love? A dozen times and more.

INGER: Just as I thought.

BORGEN: What did you think?

INGER: That you'd never been in love.

BORGEN (*going up to the portrait of his wife*): Well, I've been married, that I do know.

INGER: Yes, but with you and Maren, surely it was just . . .

BORGEN: Just what?

INGER: Just. . . a farmer's deal . . .

Inger stops abruptly, feeling she has gone too far. And old Borgen is indeed beginning to get angry.

BORGEN: Inger, Maren was a good wife to me – she was exactly the right wife for me.

INGER (*with sham penitence*): I'm sorry.

There is a short interval, during which Borgen puffs steadily at his pipe. Then Inger braces herself for a new attack.

INGER (*making up to him*): Grandfather, if you'll promise to let Anders and Anne marry, I'll promise you something that will really make you happy.

BORGEN: And what may that be?

INGER (*humorously*): You shall have fried eel for dinner on Sunday.

BORGEN: Well, that's an offer, of sorts.

INGER: And Grandfather – I'll promise you it shall be a boy this time. Are you happy now?

BORGEN: Ha, ha, you're all right at making promises.

INGER: Well, do you agree?

BORGEN: Inger, Inger – you're giving yourself a lot of trouble and anxiety. Just you see, Anders will soon get over these fancies of his, and we'll have no trouble finding the right girl, someone . . . (*Sits down.*)

INGER: Well, in that case I must just tell you this: Anders is *not* cutting reeds with Mikkel.

BORGEN: Is he not?

INGER: No.

BORGEN: Where is he, then? Ah, so that's how it is.

INGER: Yes, Grandfather.

BORGEN (*getting up, angrily*): I see, I see. So that *was* the reason for our having coffee.

INGER: Yes, Grandfather, it was. Now listen, when he gets back, we'll both say: 'Congratulations, Anders' – shan't we?

BORGEN: So Peter the tailor is getting himself a son-in-law today.

INGER: And you're getting a daughter-in-law – a good, sweet, capable young girl . . .

BORGEN: I didn't ask for one.

INGER: Do say yes, Grandfather.

BORGEN: After he's gone off without a word to me? And *you*, Inger, you knew about it – and never said anything – a regular conspiracy, a conspiracy by my own children behind my back, no, I'm damned if I will . . . (*Goes towards the door.*)

INGER: Grandfather, where are you going?

BORGEN (*in the doorway*): Why do you ask? . . . You don't any of you tell me where you're going! (*Hurries out.*)

INGER (*calling after him*): Grandfather, Grandfather . . . and in his shirt-sleeves!

Inger hurries into old Borgen's bedroom, from which she returns with his coat. She runs out after him.

21 THE PIG-STALL

Enter old Borgen. Katrine is sitting and keeping watch.

BORGEN: Go in and get yourself a cup of coffee – and tell Hans to give the mare some straw to lie on.

KATRINE: Ay.

Katrine gets up and goes out of the stall. Borgen sits down. He looks sad and tired – a disappointed man.

Inger appears. She goes up to old Borgen.

INGER: So here you are. What's come over you, Grandfather?

BORGEN (*after a silence*): Borgensgård is going to the dogs.

INGER: It's doing nothing of the kind.

BORGEN: Yes, Johannes will never be any different.

INGER: How do you know?

BORGEN: And Mikkel will never be any different.

INGER: How can you think of comparing those two? In any case, what's wrong with Mikkel?

BORGEN (*bitterly*): Only that he's betrayed the faith of his fathers.

INGER: Mikkel's all right. He has God in his heart.

BORGEN (*pursuing his own train of thought*): And now Anders . . .

INGER: There are times when I don't understand you. You go round looking as if you'd been abandoned by God.

BORGEN (*mildly*): Do I? (*After a moment's pause*) You're right, Inger, I've gone to pieces. And you know well enough why . . .

INGER: Because God didn't hear you all those nights you lay and prayed at Johannes's bedside.

BORGEN: No, Inger you're wrong there. It wasn't God's fault but my own. If I'd prayed *with faith* the miracle would have happened. But I prayed because I thought it was worth trying. And when a father can't pray *with faith* for his own child – then miracles don't happen.

INGER: But surely Our Lord might be able to manage it all the same?

BORGEN: No, Inger, I don't believe it any more!

INGER: Do you know what *I* think? I think that many small miracles are taking place in secret all round us. Our Lord hears people's prayers, but He does it on the quiet, like, so as to avoid making a lot of fuss.

BORGEN: Perhaps.

Katrine returns and puts an end to the conversation between Inger and Borgen.

INGER: I think I'll go and meet Maren and little Inger. They must be on their way home from school by now.

BORGEN (*looking at his watch*): Yes, it must be getting on for that.

INGER: Are you coming with me?

BORGEN: Most certainly I am.

INGER: But what about your rheumatism?

BORGEN: Oh, blow my rheumatism. I'm not a cripple yet.

Inger helps Borgen on with his jacket.

They go. Dissolve into the next shot.

22   A sign; Peter Petersen
               Tailor

23 AT PETER THE TAILOR'S

He is sitting cross-legged on the table, as tailors do. He is sewing a pair of trousers, at the same time singing lustily an 'uplifting' hymn.

> The time draws nigh I must away
> At winter's stern compelling.
> I tarry here but for a day,
> And elsewhere have my dwelling.

There is a pause during which we hear a ring at the bell of the shop door, which leads out into the street from a little corridor. Peter stops singing and peers in the direction of the door over his spectacles. It is Anne who enters. She looks sad.

PETER: Hullo, is it you there, little Anne? Did you find anyone in?

ANNE: Yes, Father.

PETER: Did you get the money?

ANNE: Yes. I'll hand it over.

PETER: Do that, my child.

KIRSTINE (*entering*): Ah, you're back, Anne. Can you take the birds out?

ANNE: Yes, and they must need some water.

KIRSTINE: Yes.

PETER (*looking up at his daughter*): Listen to me, Anne. I think you've been crying.

Anne feebly shakes her head.

PETER (*like an inquisitor*): Did you meet anyone on the way?

ANNE (*hesitating*): Yes. I met Anders out on the sand dunes.

PETER: From Borgensgård?

ANNE: Yes.

PETER: Did you talk to him?

ANNE: Yes, they've got fifteen piglets.

PETER: I hope you remembered what I told you?

ANNE: Yes, Father. You know that.

PETER: You know that you must be on your guard?

ANNE: Yes, Father.

PETER: And not let sin prevail over you?

ANNE: No, Father.

PETER: That is good, my child.

KIRSTINE: Anne, can you bring in a bit of firewood as well?

ANNE: Yes, Mother, I'll do that.

She goes out to the kitchen.

Peter resumes his sewing, but suddenly breaks off, lost in thought. Then he takes up his sewing once again.

Kirstine begins getting the room ready for the prayer meeting which is to be held in the afternoon. She brings in chairs from the adjacent room and arranges them in rows.

Peter again stops sewing and says:

PETER: Do you know what I've been sitting here and thinking, Kirstine?

KIRSTINE: No, Peter.

PETER: That being young Borgen's father-in-law might have its advantages after all.

KIRSTINE: Yes, Anne would certainly never want for anything.

PETER (*rebuking her*): Yes, but it wasn't the worldly advantages I was thinking of.

KIRSTINE: No? No, of course not.

PETER: No, no, I was thinking beyond them.

KIRSTINE: What were you thinking, Peter?

PETER: I was thinking like this: what if we humble people down here were to win Borgensgård for God's kingdom?

KIRSTINE: That would indeed be a great joy.

PETER (*rebuking her*): What, does it make your head swim? Ah well, mine did too. But then I came down to earth again.

KIRSTINE: How did you do that, Peter?

PETER: Well, you see, I discovered that I really *was* thinking more about the worldly side than the heavenly.

KIRSTINE: Well, it was good that the Lord opened your eyes.

PETER: Praise and thanks be to Him for that.

Kirstine goes out to the kitchen. Peter is alone. He begins to hum, but presently his humming develops into the singing of a hymn. There is another ring at the shop bell, and Anders appears in the doorway. Peter stops humming.

Peter looks up from his work.

PETER: Well, I never – is it you, Anders?

ANDERS: Yes. Good morning, Peter.

PETER: What brings you here? Is there some sewing you need to have done?

ANDERS: No-o – it's not that.

PETER: What is it then?

ANDERS (*after a pause*): Well, you see – Anne and me, we're fond of each other, and I've come to ask you if I may marry her.

PETER (*emphatically*): I say: no.

Anders is struck dumb by this categorical refusal.

PETER: Quite definitely no.

ANDERS: Couldn't we call Anne in and ask her?

PETER: No.

ANDERS: Why not?

PETER: There's no point.

ANDERS: Aren't I good enough?

PETER: No, Anders, you're not good enough.

ANDERS: What's wrong with me?

PETER: What's wrong with you? You're not a Christian.

ANDERS: I'm not a Christian?

PETER: No, not what *we* down here understand by Christian.

ANDERS: I think I'm every bit as good a believer as you and Kirstine . . .

PETER: That may be, but you're not of our faith, and that's what *I* look for.

During the last lines Peter has put his sewing things away and got down from the table. The bell rings again.

PETER: And now you'd better be going; we're having a meeting. Goodbye.

ANDERS: Goodbye.

PETER: And take my greetings to Borgensgård.

ANDERS: Ay.

The door opens, and the 'faithful' crowd in, greeted 'Welcome in the Lord' by Peter. Kirstine also comes in. Anders makes his way out.

Dissolve into the next shot.

PETER: Please come in and sit down.

24–6 Dune landscape near an inlet, where the reeds are being cut. The scene opens with a panning shot which gradually focuses on Mikkel. He is loading the wagon with reeds. The load is just complete. He jumps up on the wagon and drives off home. We follow him with a panning shot (over the bridge).

Dissolve into the next shot.

27 THE LIVING-ROOM AT BORGENSGÅRD

It is empty. Enter Johannes. He stands and looks round for a moment. Then he goes up to the table, takes one of the biscuits, lifts it in his folded hands and breaks it.

JOHANNES: Gather up the fragments that remain, that nothing be lost . . . (*A knock.*) Come in.

Johannes turns to face the door as the priest comes into view. He sees Johannes.

PRIEST: Ah, good morning, I was just passing, and . . .

JOHANNES (*as he eats*): The Lord be with you.

PRIEST: I beg your pardon?

JOHANNES: The Lord be with you.

PRIEST: Thank you, thank you . . . (*putting down his hat and coat*) Are you . . . perhaps . . .

JOHANNES: Do you not know me?

PRIEST: Are you the son of the house? (*Straightening his tie and smoothing his hair.*)

JOHANNES: I am a mason.

PRIEST: Really?

JOHANNES: I build houses . . .

PRIEST: Hm . . .

JOHANNES: . . . but people refuse to live in them.

PRIEST (*in surprise*): Do they?

JOHANNES: They want to build for themselves. They want to, but they cannot. And so they live, some in unfinished shacks, others in ruins; while the greatest number wander about without a home at all. Are you one of those who needs a house?

PRIEST: I am the new pastor, my name is Pastor . . .

JOHANNES (*interrupting*): *My* name is Jesus of Nazareth.

PRIEST: Jesus? How can you prove that?

JOHANNES: Thou man of faith, who himself lacks faith. People believe in the dead Christ, but not in the living. They believe in my miracles of two thousand years ago, but they do not believe in me now. I am come again to witness for my Father in heaven – and to work miracles.

PRIEST: Miracles don't happen any more.

Johannes, who was on the way to his room, stops at the door and turns in his prophetic manner to the priest, who has given up arguing with this mental case.

JOHANNES: And thus speaks my Church on earth . . . the Church that has betrayed me, murdered me in my own name. Here I stand, and again ye cast me out. But if ye nail me to the cross a second time – woe unto you!

PRIEST (*alone in the room, deeply shaken*): But this is simply dreadful!
He takes his coat and begins to put it on.

28 THE COURTYARD

The rumbling of the wagon is heard. Mikkel drives up with the wagon, which is loaded with reeds. He jumps down, hands the reins to a farm hand who comes forward, and makes for the house.

29 THE LIVING-ROOM AT BORGENSGÅRD

The priest is buttoning his coat when Mikkel appears in the doorway.

MIKKEL: Good morning, pastor. I'm the eldest son, you know, Mikkel Borgen.

PRIEST: Ah, I see. Good morning.

MIKKEL (*shaking hands with the priest*): And welcome to Borgensgård.

PRIEST: Thank you so much.

MIKKEL: Do please sit down.

PRIEST: Thank you.

The priest unbuttons his coat again and sits down. Mikkel fetches a cigar box.

MIKKEL: I don't suppose there's anyone else in. Would you care for a cigar?

PRIEST: No, thank you.

MIKKEL: Have you met anyone else?

PRIEST: Yes – ye-es . . . (*cautiously*) I met – I think it must have been your brother?

MIKKEL: Have you been talking to Johannes? I hope he hasn't been dis-agreeable to you?

PRIEST: No-o, but has he always been like – like – a bit –

MIKKEL: We don't like talking about it up here, but I don't mind telling you – no, it's something that happened.

PRIEST: Was it – love?

MIKKEL: No, no, it was Sören Kierkegaard.

PRIEST: Why, how could that be?

MIKKEL: Well, he was studying theology – Johannes, I mean.

PRIEST: Indeed?

MIKKEL: Yes, and it all went well enough to begin with . . . but then he got bogged down in thoughts and doubts, you know . . .

PRIEST: And so – it was too much for him?

MIKKEL: Yes.

PRIEST: It must have been a bitter blow for the family

MIKKEL: Yes, you're so powerless – you want so desperately to help, but there's nothing you can do . . . (*listening and making a sign to the priest*) Shh, that must be Father coming, we'd better not . . . talk about it any more.

Borgen, Inger and the two little girls, Maren and little Inger, make their entry into the room.

BORGEN: Good morning, pastor, welcome to Borgensgård.

PRIEST: Thank you so much.

INGER: Good morning, and welcome . . . (*signalling to the little girls to curtsey*).

MIKKEL: This is Maren, and this is little Inger.

PRIEST: Have you more than just the two?

MIKKEL (*humorously*): No – not yet. But we shall have.

INGER: Mikkel, dear . . . May I offer the pastor a cup of coffee?

PRIEST: Ah, thank you – perhaps I may save it for next time. I've got an appointment now.

The priest picks up his hat and starts saying goodbye.

BORGEN: Goodbye – and thank you for calling.

PRIEST: The pleasure is mine. Goodbye.

THE OTHERS: Goodbye.

MIKKEL: I'll just . . .

Mikkel accompanies the priest to the door.

Inger meanwhile goes with her two little girls to the door leading to the kitchen.

INGER: Go and have your lunch then.

MIKKEL: He's quite a pleasant fellow, that priest!

BORGEN: Yes, that's what he's paid for . . . (*pause*) Is Anders back yet?

MIKKEL (*to Inger*): Have you told Father? . . .

INGER: Yes, and you may as well know straight away what your father has decided to –

BORGEN: Naturally Anders must find a wife – but a wife of our faith.

MIKKEL: Oh, so Father's afraid.

BORGEN: Afraid?

MIKKEL: Afraid of Anne's faith being stronger than Anders's – that would really be a triumph for Peter the tailor.

BORGEN (*looking hard at Mikkel, then turning to Inger*): Inger, I think you understand me. When I took over this farm, there was not one grain of *living* Christianity in the whole parish. I began on my own, they thundered against me in church – there was nobody on my side. From this farm the battle was fought all those years, until the faith of this farm won the day. And now – now I'm expected to open my door to those sour, sanctimonious people down by the marsh, who fought against me – no, I'm damned if I will. You understand me, Inger?

INGER: Yes, Grandfather, yes – but I'm thinking of Anders, you see . . .

BORGEN: (*interrupting her*): I know Anders, he's a good boy – but weak and easily influenced. That's why he needs a wife of his own faith.

MIKKEL: And is *bullied* into giving up the girl he's fond of.

BORGEN: Watch your tongue, Mikkel.

INGER: You've got your father all wrong, Mikkel . . . ah God, here he is.
Anders enters the room – much dejected.

BORGEN: Well, Anders, have you just come from cutting reeds?

ANDERS: No, Father, I've come from . . .

BORGEN: Ah, yes – from – ah, yes – congratulations then.
Anders bursts into sobs.

BORGEN: What – are you *blubbing*?

ANDERS: He said no, Father, he said no.

MIKKEL: What's that you're saying?

ANDERS: He said no.

BORGEN: Who said no?

ANDERS: Peter the tailor –

INGER (*consoling him*): Anders, dear . . .

BORGEN: Peter the tailor said no?

ANDERS: Yes, quite definitely no – and he ended by throwing me out.

BORGEN: My son was refused Peter the tailor's daughter?

ANDERS: Yes.

BORGEN: And *why*, may I ask –

ANDERS: Because – because I wasn't good enough.

BORGEN: And why weren't you good enough?

ANDERS: Because I wasn't of *their* faith.

BORGEN: I see. I see. So that's why. So up here at Borgensgård we're not good enough for Peter the tailor. Well, I'll be damned. So we're heathens up here? I'd like to know if Peter the tailor has the courage to say that to my face. Anders, you *are* serious about Anne?

ANDERS: Do you think I'd have let him throw me out otherwise?

BORGEN: Well, at least that was a sensible answer at last. Inger, my coat – and you get ready, Anders. Listen, Mikkel . . .

MIKKEL: Yes?

BORGEN: Tell Hans to harness the carriage!

MIKKEL: He's done it already. You wanted to go to the mill, you remember.

BORGEN: What – yes, yes, you're quite right.

Mikkel hurries out.

ANDERS: You're the best father I've ever had.

BORGEN: Yes, yes, only do hurry now. I'll – I'll jolly well . . .

INGER: Here you are!

She has fetched her father-in-law's jacket and now helps him on with it.

BORGEN: Thanks. The Lord knows what he's thinking of. Wait, have you got a clean handkerchief? What, you've got one, you think of everything.

Anders has returned, wearing his overcoat. He and Borgen make for the door.

BORGEN (to Inger): And remember to keep an eye on the sow.

Meanwhile Mikkel has returned, and he and Inger are left alone in the room. Inger slumps into a chair.

INGER: And yet people say that the age of miracles is past.

We hear the rumbling of the carriage and the clatter of horses' hooves over the cobbles leading to the farm.

MIKKEL: Well, I must go and unload.

INGER: And I must go and wash up.

Mikkel leaves the room. Inger begins collecting the cups but leaves the biscuit-dish.

Dissolve into the next shot.

30 Panning shot over the dune landscape. The panning movement overtakes Borgen and Anders in the carriage – and continues past them until, when the carriage is off screen, the empty landscape dissolves into the next shot.

31 Peter the tailor's low-ceilinged living-room. The chairs are arranged for the prayer meeting, and the doors between the rooms thrown open.

A few men and rather more women are present. Some of the men are wearing earrings. A child is holding its mother's hand convulsively.

Peter is standing by the door, addressing them. As he speaks the camera pans over the company.

PETER: ... We who are washed in the blood of the Lamb, we know that the Lord works His wonders among us from day to day. Is it not a miracle, Jensigne, that you can sit there, with the assurance of salvation? Is it not a miracle, Kristen, that the Lord has so guided you that you have renounced your former ways and surrendered all your will to Him? Is it not a miracle that I, miserable sinner that I am, can stand here and give witness before you? Is it not glorious? Is it not beautiful? Is it not blessed?

(*The panning movement has stopped at Peter.*)

PETER: Praise and thanks and glory to such a God. (*Folding his hands.*) During the final sentences we hear the rumbling of the carriage, the crack of a whip and the clattering of horses' hooves. Some of those at the prayer meeting are unable to resist craning their necks and peering out of the windows. Now there is a knock at the door.

PETER: Come in ...

BORGEN (*entering*): Good evening.

PETER: Well, well. Good evening.

THE OTHERS: Good evening ... good evening.

PETER: Welcome to our meeting.

BORGEN: As it happens, I haven't come to your meeting – I've come for a talk with you.

PETER: You are welcome just the same. Please come in.

BORGEN: Thank you.

PETER: Are you alone?

BORGEN: No, Anders is with me.

Anne glances shyly in the direction of her mother, who responds with a stern look.

PETER (*turning to Borgen*): We were just going to hear a little testimony by Mette Maren. Yes, Mette Maren, now we are all ready ...

METTE: Well, I only want to say that I wish for each one of you that you may find the Lord as I have found Him. While I still went in sin, I was truly weighed down and crushed by it ...

Anders cautiously opens and closes the door, takes off his cap, goes across to Borgen and sits down as carefully as possible to avoid making a disturbance. Meanwhile we hear Mette Maren's voice.

METTE: ... but then I was converted, and now I am the happiest creature on earth, and I praise and thank the Lord, and that was all I wanted to say.

PETER: Yes, that was a good confession. (*To Anders*) Please – sit down! (*To the gathering*) Shall we sing Number 13?

Peter, like the other participants in the meeting, opens his hymn book, and they all sing:

Sinner, turn no more a deaf ear,
  Harken to the Lamb, 'twere best.
Listen to the words of mercy:
  Come, and I will give you rest.
Thy steps retrace
And run God's race,
Fear His wrath, accept His grace.

At the end of the first verse, dissolve into the next shot, as the singing dies away.

32 THE LIVING-ROOM AT BORGENSGÅRD

Mikkel comes out of the bedroom in nervous haste, hurries to the telephone standing on the writing-desk, and makes a call. Johannes stands leaning up against the wall, lost in thought.

MIKKEL (*on the telephone*): Yes. Number 82.

While he is waiting for the connection, Johannes walks across the room with dignified steps, pausing for an instant behind Mikkel.

JOHANNES: The Lord be with you.

Mikkel turns irritably towards his brother, but the latter has already left the room.

MIKKEL (*on the telephone*): Hullo – yes, it's Mikkel Borgen again. Hasn't the doctor come in yet? ... What, you *have* ... He said so? ... Hm, in that case he must be here soon ... Who? ... The midwife, yes, she's here, but she daren't do anything before the doctor arrives – yes, she's asked us to bring a large table in – here, wait a bit, there's a car

coming now . . . (*looking out of the window*) Yes, it's him, thank God
. . . All right, goodbye . . . I beg your pardon? . . . Ah yes, thank you.
Goodbye . . .

During the preceding lines the doctor's car is heard.

A car door slams. Mikkel dashes towards the hall door to receive
the doctor, who enters the room at the same moment. As Mikkel is
helping him off with his coat, the following words are exchanged:

MIKKEL: Things aren't going well with Inger, doctor.

DOCTOR: Really – who says so?

MIKKEL: The midwife.

DOCTOR: Hm . . . well, well . . . let's go and see how bad it is.

Mikkel and the doctor cross together to the door into the bedroom.
Slow dissolve into the following shot.

33 PETER THE TAILOR'S LIVING-ROOM

We see and hear the little gathering singing the last verse of the hymn:

> Then cease to stray,
> Make haste, away,
> That God may spare thee on that day.

Peter closes his hymn book and puts it away on the shelf. The prayer
meeting is over. Peter turns and faces the assembly.

PETER: Well, good night then, brothers and sisters. Our next meeting
in Jesus' name will be today week, God willing, at the Home. Good
night, my friends, good night.

The members of the little congregation exchange greetings and stream
out. Peter stands by the door and takes leave of each individually.

Meanwhile Anders tries to approach Anne, but her mother, Kirstine,
anticipates him.

KIRSTINE: Good evening, Anders, and welcome.

ANDERS: Thank you, good evening.

KIRSTINE (*to Anne*): Can you go out and put the kettle on, little Anne?

ANNE: Yes . . . (*She goes obediently out to the kitchen.*)

KIRSTINE (*to Anders, in friendly tones*): Sit down by your father.

When Kirstine shakes Anders's hand, she retains it and in this way
leads him over to Borgen and away from the door out to the kitchen.

ORDET Scene 18: *Inger (Birgitte Federspiel) and Morten Borgen.*

ORDET Scene 11: *Anders, Morten, Inger and Mikkel.*

Scene 35: *Anders, Morten, Peter the tailor (Ejnar Federspiel), Anne (Gerda Nielsen) and Kirstine (Sylvia Eckhausen).*

ORDET Scene 45: *Johannes and Maren.*

ORDET Scene 62: *Anders and Morten Borgen by Inger's coffin.*

Scene 69: *The doctor (Henry Skjaer) and the priest (Ove Rud).*

Anders, who would much rather have been out in the kitchen with
  Anne, has to sit down.
KIRSTINE *(to Borgen)*: Good evening – and welcome.
BORGEN: Thank you, Kirstine.
  Meanwhile the last members of the congregation have left the room,
  and Peter comes up to the group.
PETER: You'll have a cup of coffee?
BORGEN: Don't bother about that.
  Peter nods to his wife, who disappears out to the kitchen.
PETER *(to Borgen)*: Would you like to fill your pipe? *(Offering him
  tobacco.)*
BORGEN: Don't bother about that either.
PETER: What about Anders?
ANDERS: No, thank you, not yet.
  It is hard work getting a conversation going. It is Borgen who breaks
  the silence.
BORGEN: Bacon's going up, Peter.
PETER: Yes, but eggs came down yesterday.
BORGEN: Do you have many hens, Peter?
PETER: About as many as you have pigs, I should think.
  Kirstine comes in from the kitchen with coffee.
PETER: Ah, here's the coffee.
BORGEN: Isn't Anne coming?
PETER: I think not.
BORGEN: Really? Why not?
PETER: She had much better not. In my opinion it will make it a little
  easier for her to walk in the paths of the Lord.
ANDERS: Do you hear that, Father?
BORGEN: Well, in that case *you* can drink your coffee out in the kitchen.
ANDERS: Well, yes – I could, couldn't I, if . . . *(turning to Peter and
  Kirstine)* if you agree, that is?
BORGEN: You can in any case.
KIRSTINE *(with a sour expression)*: In that case the three of us can drink
  coffee out there . . . *(looking grimly at Borgen)* since you're going to be
  in charge here now . . . *(She goes out with Anders.)*
  There is a short interval. Then Borgen breaks the silence.

BORGEN: Look, Peter, on my way here I was trying to look at things from *your* point of view.

PETER: Well, and what conclusions did you come to?

BORGEN: That you and I having different views on religious matters ought not to come between our children.

PETER (*interrupting*): Anne is to marry one of our faith.

BORGEN: Well, we've no intention of taking Our Lord away from her.

PETER: Look, there's no point in our talking, because you never understand me.

BORGEN: And *you* – do you understand *me*?

PETER: Yes, indeed – I understand you perfectly well. I was just like you once.

BORGEN: And that wasn't enough for you?

PETER: You're right, Morten, it wasn't enough for me.

BORGEN: I don't wish to speak evil of you or any of the others . . . but I'm damned if I can put up with you.

PETER: What is it about us that you can't put up with?

BORGEN: First and foremost all that blather about conversion.

PETER: And what else have you got against us?

BORGEN: I can't stand your undertaker's faces.

PETER: No, so I've heard. I know – you have the bright, joyful kind of Christianity, while we – *we* are undertakers and kill-joys. But if you're one of the joyful Christians – why do you look so sad and weary whenever we meet you? Whereas I feel myself light and free, because I know that there is a place waiting for me in heaven.

BORGEN: And the rest of us, all the rest of us? We go straight down to hell and everlasting torment, I suppose? That's what you believe, isn't it?

PETER: Yes – the very words – you've taken the very words out of my mouth.

34 PETER THE TAILOR'S KITCHEN

Anne and Anders are seated at opposite ends of the kitchen table. Kirstine is sitting between them.

Kirstine is reading aloud from the New Testament. It is an illustrated edition, grease-marked and worn from constant use. After she has read several sentences, the book is shown in close-up – a picture of Jesus healing the widow's son from Nain.

Anne cranes her neck to see the picture in the book. Kirstine pauses in her reading and pushes the book in front of Anne to enable her to see better.

KIRSTINE: Yes, it's a beautiful picture . . .

Anders has got up, and now goes behind Kirstine to Anne, over whom he bends in order to see the book. Kirstine closes the book in alarm and pushes it across to the other end of the table.

KIRSTINE: I think you will see better over here, Anders.

Anders has to shuffle back to his place, but he is now much less interested in the picture than when he was bending so far forward over Anne that her hair was tickling his cheek. So Kirstine resumes her reading aloud. When she has read a few more sentences, Peter appears in the doorway.

PETER: Can we have a bit more coffee?

Kirstine turns round and nods by way of answer. Peter closes the door again. Kirstine finishes reading the sentence she was in the middle of. Then she gets up and takes the coffee pot from the kitchen range. She stands irresolutely for a moment, then she hands the pot to Anne.

KIRSTINE: You take it in, Anne.

Anne obediently takes the pot and goes into the living-room.

35 THE LIVING-ROOM

Enter Anne with the coffee pot.

PETER: Ah, little Anne, so it's you coming with the coffee?

Anne goes to the table and looks enquiringly at Borgen as she fills his cup.

BORGEN: Do you think I ought to, Anne?

ANNE (*smiling*): I think so.

BORGEN: Just half, then. Isn't your mother in the kitchen?

ANNE: Yes, but Anders is there too.

BORGEN: I see.

PETER: Thank you, my child, thank you.

Anne goes back to the kitchen. There is a moment's silence, during which Borgen is furtively watching Peter. The silence is broken by Borgen.

BORGEN: Well, Peter, have you had second thoughts?

PETER: And what do you mean by that?

BORGEN: I mean about Anne and Anders.

PETER: No, I have not. Not yet at least.

BORGEN (*surprised*): Not yet at least?

PETER: Tell me, Morten – do you still feel completely satisfied with your God?

BORGEN: I most certainly do.

PETER: You really still do?

BORGEN: What are you getting at?

PETER: Morten, you are *not* satisfied. (*He folds his hands in order to give greater weight to the following sentences.*) Come over to us, Morten.

BORGEN: Have you taken leave of your senses?

PETER: You would get peace in your soul.

BORGEN: Never.

PETER: Morten, Morten . . . don't say that. When you return, earth to earth, then it will be too late. Come over to us.

BORGEN: I'm damned if I will.

PETER (*admonishingly*): Morten, Morten – the Lord is the God of miracles. Borgen looks questioningly at Peter.

PETER: He has the power to lead you out of your unbelief and error.

BORGEN (*getting up indignantly*): Unbelief and . . .

PETER (*sticking to Borgen like a leech*): Unbelief and error.

BORGEN: And you say that about *my* faith? Do you know what the difference is between my faith and yours? You believe that Christianity means pulling a long face and torturing yourself. I believe that Christianity means the enhancement of life. My faith makes me rejoice in life from one end of the day to the other. Whereas *your* faith merely makes you long for death. *My* faith is the warmth of life, your faith is the coldness of death. One of these days it will dawn on you, Peter, that *we* were seeking the true light.

PETER: What are you really seeking?

BORGEN: We are seeking God – and nothing else.

PETER: Hm – that sounds very good – nevertheless we regard you as being neither believers nor converted, and in my judgement . . .

BORGEN: In your judgement?

PETER: . . . you are lost souls.

BORGEN: In Peter the tailor's judgement we are all going to hell . . . (*going to the kitchen door and calling*) Anders, Anders . . .

Anders enters from the kitchen, followed by Kirstine and Anne.

ANDERS: Yes, Father?

BORGEN: We're going home.

ANDERS: Yes, but . . . shan't I have Anne then?

PETER (*decisively*): No.

BORGEN (*just as decisively*): And I say yes – you shall have her, deuce take it, if I have to come and drag her out of this penitentiary with my own two hands. Come on, Anders!

ANDERS (*with a look of desperation*): Father . . .

BORGEN: Off we go – good night then, Peter the tailor.

PETER: Morten, Morten. Can't you see that you are incurring God's wrath?

BORGEN: I'm not going to listen to your twittering.

PETER: Not to me – but the Lord you will have to listen to, Morten. You must be tried still further.

The telephone rings.

PETER (*going to the phone*): Hullo, hullo – Yes, that's right – Yes – No, not yet – Yes, they're just going – What? – No, really – Indeed? – Yes – Good night then, and I hope she'll be all right.

BORGEN: What was that? Who were you hoping would be all right?

PETER: Verily, verily, we live in a world of miracles . . .

BORGEN: What do you mean by that?

PETER: Just as I am telling you that you must be tried still further, Mikkel rings up . . . your son.

BORGEN: Well, and what . . .

PETER: . . . and tells me that Inger is seriously ill.

BORGEN: Inger? But it must be – it must be the child . . .

PETER: No, it was something out of the ordinary, as I understood it.

BORGEN: I'd better hurry then.

PETER (*with a meek, sincere air*): And now I truly hope that this time the Lord may reach your heart, however hard He has to smite.

BORGEN: What's that you're saying? God help me, I believe you're standing there wanting my daughter-in-law to die.

PETER: Yes, if there's no other way, then yes, I wish it in Jesus' name.

BORGEN (*seizing Peter by the throat and shaking him*): You do, do you? You do, do you?

PETER: Let go, Morten. Let go, Morten, do you hear!

BORGEN (*continuing to shake Peter*): You know the answer to that?

PETER: No, let go, do you hear!

BORGEN: There's only one answer... (*He gives Peter a regular box on the ear.*)

ANNE: Oh no, oh no!

ANDERS (*entering and intervening*): Control yourself, Father.

PETER: I've got witnesses! Just because you're the great Morten, I suppose other people still have the right to exist.

BORGEN: Go to hell.

PETER: No, thank you, I wouldn't want to get in your way.

ANDERS (*tugging at his father*): Do come, Father.

BORGEN: All right ... (*putting his hat on his head*).

Anders and Borgen leave. The latter slams the door violently. Peter opens the door again and shouts after Morten.

PETER: You landed lout!

A few whiplashes are heard. Peter has closed the door again. The carriage is heard driving off.

Dissolve into the next shot.

36 THE DUNE LANDSCAPE

Anders and his father in the carriage on their way home to Borgens-gård. The horses are allowed to gallop for all they are worth. Panning shot across the landscape up to the carriage and past it, until it is off screen, whereupon dissolve to the next shot.

37 INGER AND MIKKEL'S BEDROOM AT BORGENSGÅRD

It has been converted into a sick-room. Mikkel's bed has been taken out, likewise the children's bed, which has been moved into old Borgen's bedroom.

Inger is lying on a table which has been fitted up under the operating light. We hear a loud wailing from her. The doctor and the midwife are busily engaged in completing the final preparations for the birth. The doctor rolls up his shirtsleeves.

Mikkel is standing at the head of the bed, holding one of Inger's hands in both of his. Close-up, panning from her face with its tear-filled eyes and expression of fear and pain, and following her desperate, imploring gaze up to Mikkel's somewhat forced smile of encouragement. A moment later we see Inger's other hand reaching for Mikkel's hands and encircling his wrist, while her wailing grows louder.

Dissolve to the next shot.

38   Another panning shot of the dune landscape. The camera overtakes old Borgen and Anders in the carriage, continues past them and ends in the empty landscape, whereupon dissolve to the next shot.

39 THE SICK-ROOM AT BORGENSGÅRD

Mikkel in close-up as before. His two hands enclose one of Inger's, while her other hand still encircles his wrist. We hear the doctor and the midwife exchanging brief, prosaic questions and answers.

MIDWIFE: Yes, definitely.

MIKKEL: Inger!

DOCTOR: In that case you can begin gently with the anaesthetic.

MIDWIFE: Yes, doctor.

DOCTOR: Borgen, can you hold the lamp?

The doctor points at a lighted paraffin lamp standing on a table behind Mikkel, who takes the lamp and holds it up so that the light falls as the doctor wants. The expressions on the three faces show that the birth is in progress.

40   Inger's wailing grows louder still. The pangs come faster and more violently. The wails culminate in a terrible scream, followed by a deadly silence.

41   Inger's free hand falls limply. Mikkel notices that the hand enclosed in his has also become lifeless. He places it cautiously on the counterpane. He looks at the doctor with an expression of fear and uneasiness.

MIKKEL: What is it? What's happened?

DOCTOR: It's nothing – she'll come round presently . . .

42 DOCTOR (*looking at the midwife*): How's her pulse?

MIDWIFE: It's not too good.

DOCTOR: Take your mask off and give me a hand – let's have her heartbeat . . .

With a stethoscope against the patient's abdomen the midwife listens
to the child's heartbeat and then catches the doctor's eye.

MIDWIFE: It's rather rapid!

The misgivings on the doctor's face cause the anxious and impatient
Mikkel to ask again:

MIKKEL: Is the child still alive?

DOCTOR: Yes, so far, but we haven't finished the job yet.

43   After another pause, during which it is clear that the doctor and the
midwife are working feverishly, Mikkel breaks in with a new question:

MIKKEL: Do you think my wife will be all right?

DOCTOR (*brusquely*): Please don't disturb me.

After a moment's silence, during which only the sound of instruments
can be heard, the doctor speaks again.

DOCTOR: Bring the lamp a little nearer.

Mikkel lowers the lamp. The doctor is evidently studying the position
of the child and making his decision. After a short interval, during
which only the clatter of instruments is heard, the doctor speaks again.

DOCTOR: You can put the lamp down.

Mikkel puts the lamp back where it was before.

DOCTOR: And get me a tub.

MIKKEL: How big? Like that? (*Indicating the size with his hands.*)

The doctor nods.

Mikkel leaves the sick-room.

44 THE LIVING-ROOM

Enter Mikkel and old Borgen simultaneously, from their respective
rooms. Before going over to his father, Mikkel turns to the maid,
Karen, who has been told to stay in the living-room in order to be at
hand. She has just lit a paraffin lamp. Mikkel calls to her.

BORGEN: Well, how's it going?

MIKKEL: Karen, go out and fetch the little tub – you know, the wooden tub my wife bought last week.

KAREN: Ay.

Karen, infected by Mikkel's nervous uneasiness, hurries out into the kitchen. Then Mikkel goes up to his father.

BORGEN: So the doctor's here, then – what about the midwife?

MIKKEL: They're both here.

BORGEN: Well, is there anything wrong with the child?

MIKKEL: It was lying in the wrong position.

BORGEN: And Inger?

MIKKEL: If *her* life is saved, we can be thankful.

Karen has returned with the tub.

KAREN: If you please, this is the one, isn't it?

MIKKEL: Yes, thank you.

Mikkel hurries into the sick-room. Karen goes out to the kitchen. Borgen takes a turn across the floor. Then Anders enters.

ANDERS: Is it serious, Father?

BORGEN: You and I, Anders – are going to have a busy night.

ANDERS: Are we?

BORGEN: Yes – praying.

ANDERS: Yes, Father, both for Anne and for Inger.

BORGEN: For Inger. Anne – that we can manage ourselves. Now go to your room and lie down and put your trust in God.

ANDERS: Shan't we pray together, Father?

BORGEN: My boy, when it's something really important I prefer to pray alone. Though of course it's always the Lord's will that is done.

Anders goes to his room. Borgen sinks into a chair. A moment later Johannes comes in quietly. He is carrying a thin reed in his hand. He approaches his father, who turns towards him.

JOHANNES: God be with you.

BORGEN: Yes, all right, Johannes.

JOHANNES: Then came the Lord himself – with His scythe and His hour-glass.

BORGEN: Hold your tongue, Johannes.

JOHANNES: Why art thou afraid, thou man of little faith? For I am not yet gone to my Father.

BORGEN: Go to your room, go to bed.

JOHANNES: But in His own country He did no mighty works because of their unbelief.

While saying this, Johannes has turned away from his father. He takes a few steps, after which he sits down on a chair and begins drawing invisible figures on the floor. During the following scene he is completely absorbed in this, and appears not to be listening to what is said by his father and Mikkel. Outside a storm is gathering. The wind can be heard more and more distinctly.

Mikkel has hurried in and is rummaging in the chest of drawers. Borgen goes up to him.

BORGEN: Well, Mikkel.

MIKKEL: Yes, the child has arrived now.

BORGEN: Well, and was it a boy, as Inger promised me?

MIKKEL (*in a hard, bitter voice*): Yes, it *was* a boy.

BORGEN: There you are, you see. The Lord is unfail . . .

MIKKEL: He's lying in there – in the tub – in four pieces.

Mikkel has found what he is looking for and has been sent to fetch, namely a pair of towels, which he finds in the chest of drawers. As he gets up, Borgen lays a hand on his shoulder.

BORGEN: Oh, Mikkel, if only you could pray to God.

MIKKEL (*with a hint of sarcasm*): *You* can do that, Father.

Mikkel goes into the sick-room.

Borgen sits down heavily in an easy chair. From outside a gust of wind is heard. Johannes has got up from his chair. He takes a couple of paces into the room and bows his knees, as if greeting a king from the East. Borgen suddenly becomes aware of his son's remarkable behaviour and asks:

BORGEN: What are you carrying on about now?

JOHANNES (*rising*): Did you not see Him?

BORGEN: Who?

JOHANNES: The Lord.

BORGEN: The Lord?

JOHANNES: The man with the hourglass and scythe. He went with the child. If you had believed in me, this would not have happened. Now I can do nothing.

Johannes has approached Borgen, but the latter turns away and supports his head in his hand as he groans:

BORGEN: Oh God, oh God, oh God . . .

JOHANNES (*bearing himself like a prophet*): How great must thy need be, before thou hearest me?

Borgen looks up at Johannes with an expression of entreaty, indeed of supplication.

BORGEN: Johannes dear, if you want to make your father happy, go to your room.

Without taking any notice of his father's suggestion, Johannes moves imperturbably away, but stops abruptly with an exclamation of surprise.

JOHANNES: Look, look . . .

BORGEN: What am I supposed to see?

JOHANNES: Can't you see him? There he is, look . . .

BORGEN: Who?

JOHANNES: The man with the scythe.

BORGEN: Oh no, oh no . . .

JOHANNES: He's come back . . .

BORGEN: Oh, oh . . .

JOHANNES: To fetch Inger.

BORGEN: Will you be quiet, man!

Johannes has again come up to his father.

JOHANNES: Do you still reject me?

BORGEN: Johannes, Johannes – no – this is madness! And yet: what is madness and what is sanity?

JOHANNES: Now you are drawing nigh to God.

BORGEN: No, no, go away!

JOHANNES (*cajoling*): One word only . . . it will cost you but one word.

Borgen, whose nerves are already stretched to breaking point, now gives unwilling vent to his suppressed rage and shouts:

BORGEN: No, no, no – go away – go to your room – you're driving me insane – me too!

Johannes shakes his head in compassion and gazes up at the ceiling.

JOHANNES: They seek to gather grapes of thorns. The vine they pass by.

Then, with sublime calm, he strides away and sits down on his chair.

Borgen glances at him, more in sorrow now than in anger. Johannes leans back against the wall and closes his eyes. As soon as he has become quiet, the door of Borgen's bedroom opens, and little Maren appears in her short nightdress. She looks from Johannes to Borgen and then trips across to her grandfather, who doesn't see her immediately.

MAREN: Grandfather.

BORGEN: Aren't you in bed, little Maren?

MAREN (*climbing up on his knee*): Yes, I am.

BORGEN: But . . .

MAREN: You were shouting so loud, Grandfather.

BORGEN: Ah, have I woken you?

MAREN: Yes, because we've been moved.

BORGEN: Have you been moved?

MAREN: Our bed's been put in your room. And do you know why?

BORGEN: No.

MAREN: Because we're going to have a little brother.

BORGEN: Who told you that?

MAREN: Mummy.

BORGEN: Well, and were you glad?

MAREN: Well, I wanted to have a little sister rather, but Mummy said she'd promised you a little brother.

BORGEN: Did she say that?

MAREN: Yes, and do you know what? Now she's ever so sick.

BORGEN: Yes, and that's why Our Lord has decided that the little boy isn't going to come this time.

MAREN: Has He?

BORGEN: Yes, and now you can go and ask Our Lord to make Mummy well again.

MAREN: Yes, but He's not going to.

BORGEN: Not going to?

MAREN (*in a whisper, as if revealing a great secret*): No, because she's going to die tonight.

BORGEN: What – she's going to do what?

MAREN (*nodding her head towards Johannes and still whispering*): That's what Uncle Johannes says, and then he's going to raise her from the dead. Like the man in the Bible, you know.

BORGEN: What's all this nonsense?

MAREN: That's what Uncle Johannes says.

BORGEN: Well – I see, I see. But now you must go and snuggle down nicely under the eiderdown, little Maren.

MAREN: Yes, Grandfather.

BORGEN: Good night, my precious ... (*kissing her*).

MAREN (*kissing him*): Good night, Grandfather.

Maren goes to the door of Borgen's bedroom. She doesn't go in, however, but remains standing in the half-open door, for just at that moment her father comes out of the sick-room. Old Borgen goes towards him. Mikkel is deeply shaken, and his behaviour towards his father is more imbued with natural filial feeling than before. Borgen puts his arm round him to comfort him.

BORGEN: How's it going?

MIKKEL: I can't bear it in there another moment.

BORGEN: Have courage, my boy.

MIKKEL: I see too clearly how it's going to end.

BORGEN: End?

MIKKEL: Father, I don't think I can bear to lose her.

BORGEN: You're not going to lose her, Mikkel, God will – it will –

MIKKEL (*pleading, without irony*): Father – if Inger dies ...

BORGEN: Mikkel ...

MIKKEL: Will you promise me that you will live to see Anders and Anne married, so that the children have a home ...

BORGEN: Almighty God: it mustn't happen, God, don't take Inger from us – let's go in to her, I'll come with you ...

MIKKEL: How strong you are, dear old Father.

BORGEN: Yes, but then I'm holding God by the hand, you see ... come. They go into the sick-room together.

5 During the preceding scenes Johannes has remained seated, leaning back with closed eyes. From time to time his lips move in a soundless muttering.

As soon as Borgen and Mikkel have left the room, Maren ventures in and trips on her little bare feet across to Johannes.

MAREN: Uncle Johannes ... Uncle Johannes, will Mummy die soon?

JOHANNES: Do you want her to, little girl?

MAREN: Yes, because then you're going to raise her from the dead, aren't you?

JOHANNES: I dare say it will come to nothing.

MAREN: Why?

JOHANNES: The others won't let me.

MAREN: Yes, but what about Mummy then?

JOHANNES: Then your Mummy will go to heaven.

MAREN (*shaking her head*): Yes, but I don't want that at all.

JOHANNES: Little girl, you don't know what it is to have a Mummy in heaven.

MAREN: Is it better than having her here on earth?

JOHANNES: You don't need me to tell you that.

MAREN (*nudging him*): What nonsense, Uncle Johannes! If we get hurt, then we'll have no Mummy to take care of us.

JOHANNES: Nobody can hurt the child whose mother is in heaven. When your mother is dead, then you have her with you always.

MAREN: But you have that when she's alive.

JOHANNES: Ah, but then she has so many other things to see to.

MAREN (*looking up*): Yes, that's right – she has to milk the cows and scrub the floors and do the washing up. Dead people miss all that.

JOHANNES: Of course, of course.

MAREN (*after thinking it over*): But I'd still rather you raised her from the dead, Uncle Johannes.

JOHANNES: Would you?

MAREN: Yes, because then we can keep her.

JOHANNES: Child of man, child of man.

MAREN (*ingratiatingly, stroking his cheek*): Won't you please raise her from the dead?

JOHANNES (*throwing out his arm*): I will if the others let me.

MAREN: Oh, but you don't need to worry about them. Oh, I *am* so looking forward to it.

JOHANNES: Are you?

MAREN: Will you come and tuck me up?

JOHANNES: Yes, and I will get one of my Father's angels to keep watch over you tonight.

MAREN: And will you bless us like you always do?

JOHANNES: Yes, I'll do that.

He has lifted Maren on his arm, and as he carries her out of the room he quotes.

JOHANNES: 'And he took them up in his arms, put his hands upon them, and blessed them.'

He carries Maren into Borgen's bedroom and shuts the door behind him.

At the same time the camera pans to the door of the sick-room. Borgen comes in quietly. It is evident that the sight of Inger has made a deep impression on him. He stands for a moment at a loss, looking round with a strangely vacant expression. Then he sinks into a chair and turns his eyes upwards. In a voice choked with tears he appeals to God.

BORGEN: God, do not send death to us.

He is cut short by the door of the sick-room being thrown open. The midwife appears with a kettle in her hand. She tears through the room like a whirlwind, and out into the kitchen.

A moment later the doctor appears in the door of the sick-room.

DOCTOR: Why the devil isn't she bringing the hot water?

The doctor runs to the kitchen door. At the same moment Mikkel opens the door of the sick-room and shouts in great anxiety:

MIKKEL: Hurry, doctor, hurry, can't you?

He leaves the door open, and disappears back into the sick-room. The next moment the doctor comes with the kettle of hot water, and finally the midwife. They hurry into the sick-room and the midwife closes the door behind her.

Borgen sits for a while lost in reflection. From time to time an incomprehensible muttering is heard from him. Then he raises his voice and says – taking the words from the sixth Psalm:

BORGEN: ... for the Lord hath heard the voice of my weeping. The Lord hath heard my supplication; the Lord will receive my prayer ...

He is again interrupted, this time by the doctor, who emerges from the sick-room, drying his hands on a towel. He goes up to Borgen.

DOCTOR: There now, Borgen ...

BORGEN: No, no – don't say it, doctor.

DOCTOR: It's over now. And she's sleeping soundly. Let's hope there are no complications.

BORGEN: Eternal praise and thanks.

DOCTOR: Yes, it was a hard job.

BORGEN: It certainly was, doctor. And thank you, thank you ... (*pressing his hand*). God bless you, God bless you.

DOCTOR: And now let's have some coffee.

BORGEN: Yes, of course – sit down, doctor.

The maid Karen has come into the room to hear the news.

BORGEN (*seeing her*): Karen, Karen, we're having – Inger's going to be all right, Karen, she's going to be all right – we're having coffee, with beans, you understand ... (*turning to the doctor*) Doctor, may I have a peep at her?

DOCTOR: Yes, but do be quiet ...

BORGEN: Yes.

DOCTOR: Quiet now!

Borgen is already on his way to the sick-room, when the priest enters.

PRIEST: Good evening.

BORGEN: Good evening – ah, pastor, welcome again.

PRIEST: Thank you, thank you.

BORGEN: You know ... (*nodding towards the doctor*).

PRIEST: Yes, I know the doctor – and his car. That was what made me look in – I wanted to know what was going on. Good evening, doctor.

DOCTOR: Evening, evening.

BORGEN: Ah, yes, that was kind of you. Well ... you see, my son's wife was ... you see, she had to ...

PRIEST: Yes, I think she was expecting ...

BORGEN: Yes ... (*pause*) ... The child died, but she's ... all right.

PRIEST: I see ...

BORGEN (*now in high spirits*): But off with your coat, pastor, and sit down. Coffee's coming any moment.

PRIEST: Thank you, but I really must get home.

BORGEN: But you can go in – you can go with the doctor.

DOCTOR: Yes, of course.

BORGEN (*to the priest*): There, you see. Do sit down ... I'm just having a peep in there ... (*pointing towards the sick-room*).

The priest sits down.

Karen comes in and lays the table, with coffee cups, cake dishes and plates.

46 THE SICK-ROOM

Enter old Borgen. He approaches the bed, looks at Inger, who is sleeping soundly – and he and Mikkel exchange glances, and smile and nod happily to each other. The events of the day seem to have brought father and son closer together.

47 THE LIVING-ROOM

Borgen returns.

BORGEN: She's sleeping like one of God's angels. (*Karen has poured the coffee, and Borgen offers his guests cake.*) Here you are, doctor. Help yourself. It's like a miracle.

DOCTOR: Yes, but forgive me, my dear Borgen, I don't want to hurt your religious feelings, only, now that it's all gone so well, I must be allowed to tease you a little. Which do *you* think has helped most this evening: *your* prayers or *my* treatment?

BORGEN: Our Lord's blessing, my dear doctor.

PRIEST: *Ora et labora* – as the old monks used to say.

DOCTOR: Perhaps you also believe in miracles, pastor?

PRIEST: Believe? Naturally miracles are possible, since God is the creator of all things and therefore the Lord of creation, but . . .

DOCTOR (*sarcastically*): But?

PRIEST: On the other hand, even if God *can* perform miracles. He doesn't in point of fact do so.

DOCTOR (*in the same tone of voice*): Well, and why not?

PRIEST: Because miracles would be a breach of the laws of nature, and obviously God doesn't break His own laws.

DOCTOR: But the miracles of Christ then?

PRIEST: Well yes, but that was under special circumstances . . .

DOCTOR (*in triumph*): Aha! You see: 'under special circumstances' . . . this normally reliable God of yours allows Himself to deviate a little from the straight and narrow. My dear pastor!

BORGEN: It's a funny thing about doctors, they always believe what's least worth believing.

From Borgen's bedroom comes the sound of Johannes's voice. The three men listen. Johannes is intoning the Aaronic blessing, as follows:

JOHANNES: The Lord make His face to shine upon thee, and be gracious unto thee. The Lord lift up His countenance upon thee, and give thee peace, both now and evermore. Amen.

The priest and the doctor look enquiringly at Borgen.

PRIEST: What was that?

BORGEN: That's Johannes . . . blessing the little children.

PRIEST: Indeed.

BORGEN (*turning to the priest*): You probably know, pastor . . . I believe you met him, in fact?

PRIEST: Excuse me, but don't you think – I mean, wouldn't it be better – for him in a home?

BORGEN: My boy is staying with me, as long as I'm at Borgensgård.

DOCTOR: Besides, Johannes is going to get better.

BORGEN: Do you think so?

DOCTOR: Just give him time, and one of these days he'll get a psychic shock that will turn the rubbish-bin known as his subconscious completely upside-down.

BORGEN: So you think he'll be his old self again?

DOCTOR: Exactly the same, within, let's say . . .

BORGEN: So you see, pastor, the doctor too believes in miracles.

DOCTOR: Yes, I believe in the miracles my science has taught me.

BORGEN: God grant that it may happen!

DOCTOR (*rising*): Well, Borgen. I'll just go in and have a look at the patient . . . (*turning to the priest*) and then we'll be off.

PRIEST: Right, I'm ready.

The doctor goes into the sick-room. The priest gets up and presses Borgen's hands.

PRIEST: My dear Borgen – my heartiest congratulations.

BORGEN: Many thanks, pastor.

PRIEST: I'm sure you must be rejoicing over what God has done for you here tonight.

BORGEN: Indeed I am, pastor, of that you can be sure.

PRIEST: It's been a hard time.

BORGEN: That it has – and yet I wouldn't willingly have missed it.

PRIEST: That too I can understand. Thank you for your hospitality.

The doctor comes in from the sick-room, carrying his doctor's bag. The priest and Borgen both look at him enquiringly.

BORGEN: Well, doctor?

DOCTOR: She's sleeping beautifully. And now you should go to bed. Good night.

Borgen helps the priest and the doctor on with their coats.

BORGEN (*to the doctor*): Good night, and on behalf of Borgensgård: thank you for tonight.

Karen comes in to clear the table. Borgen calls to her.

BORGEN: Here, Karen. Remember, Karen: two geese to go to the doctor at Christmas.

DOCTOR: I'm not a vet. They'll die under my treatment.

The doctor has already opened the door.

DOCTOR: Well, are you coming then?

PRIEST: Yes, all right – good night, Borgen.

They leave the room. Old Borgen goes to the window to see them drive off. Meanwhile Anders comes in. He goes up to his father.

ANDERS: How's it going with Inger?

BORGEN: It's going well, Anders – much better than we expected.

ANDERS: That's good.

While old Borgen and Anders are talking, Johannes comes in from Borgen's bedroom. He advances several paces into the room, then stands as if spellbound by one of his hallucinations.

JOHANNES: There he is again, the man with the hourglass. He's come back for Inger.

BORGEN: Johannes, go to bed.

Out in the yard the doctor has switched on the lights of his car. The beam of light shines in at one of the windows and falls on the wall containing the door into the sick-room.

JOHANNES: Look, now he's going through the wall.

ANDERS: It's only the doctor's headlights!

BORGEN (*in tones of gentle persuasion*): Johannes dear, Inger is asleep now, her life is not in danger any more.

From outside we hear the doctor starting his car.

JOHANNES (*again completely absorbed in his hallucination*): Listen – it's the scythe, he cut in error, cut the wrong swath.

ANDERS: It's the doctor, now he's backing out.

The blinding white light from the headlights sweeps from the wall round the room.

JOHANNES (*in a tone of command*): Stop, will you! Come back, do you hear! You *must*... He's not going to. Go then. In the hour of faith you will be forced to bring her back.

BORGEN: For goodness' sake, Johannes, let's call it a day.

The light on the wall and window has disappeared. Johannes has retired to another corner of the room.

Mikkel comes from the sick-room with a glazed expression on his face.

MIKKEL (*tonelessly*): So she's died after all.

BORGEN (*incredulously*): What?

MIKKEL: She went suddenly in her sleep.

BORGEN: Inger dead? You're lying – you must be lying.

ANDERS: It's your nerves...

BORGEN: I mean, the doctor – he was in there only a moment ago.

MIKKEL: All right, come and see for yourselves.

48 THE SICK-ROOM

Enter old Borgen, Mikkel and Anders. Old Borgen bends over Inger, studying her features and listening in vain for her breathing. With tear-stained eyes he looks up at Mikkel, who is standing beside the bed.

Mikkel steels his heart, struggling to avoid being overcome by his feelings. With dry eyes and a forced calm, which has the effect almost of callousness, and in the bitter, querulous tones of an injured party, he says:

MIKKEL: I felt her go stiff and cold in my arms, I saw her lips turn blue and her eyes become glassy...

BORGEN: The Lord gave, and the Lord hath taken away; blessed be the name of the Lord.

ANDERS: Shan't we ring for the doctor?

MIKKEL: If you think ringing for the doctor can bring back the dead, Anders, then ring.

Anders leaves the room.

49 THE LIVING-ROOM

Enter Mikkel and old Borgen one by one. Johannes is sitting in his usual place, drawing figures on the floor. Mikkel takes a step or two into the room and then stops. Behind him a Dutch wall-clock, with weights and a pendulum, is ticking away. Without pausing for reflection he stops the pendulum, and with it the clock. Borgen collapses into a chair.

BORGEN: The Lord gave, and the Lord hath taken away ...

Anders on the telephone.

ANDERS: ... No, he left here a few minutes ago ... yes. Will you tell him ... (*with tears in his voice*) will you tell him that she's just died, Inger ... (*sobbing*). Thank you. Goodbye. (*Puts the telephone down hurriedly and buries his face in his hands.*)

At the words 'she's just died' Johannes gets up.

JOHANNES: She is not dead, but sleepeth.

MIKKEL (*going up to his brother*): Do you think so, Johannes? (*with bitter irony*) Do you want to see her ... sleeping?

JOHANNES: Show me the place where you have laid her. If ye *believe*, ye shall see the glory of God.

Mikkel and Johannes go into the sick-room. Anders remains standing in the doorway.

BORGEN (*sitting in his chair*): The Lord gave, and the Lord hath taken away ...

50 THE SICK-ROOM

Enter Johannes and Mikkel. Since Johannes got up and said 'She is not dead, but sleepeth', a remarkable change has come over him. The tension in his sick, ecstatic mind has increased, and his self-confidence has mounted irresistibly to dizzying heights, until the tension is so great that something in his mind is bound to give.

As he comes to the foot of the bed in which Inger lies dead, his fanatic's eyes are blazing. His bearing is more self-assured, his voice more defiant than ever before. His words are borne aloft on the breath of an inner fire. Mikkel watches him in fear and wonder as, with his face raised to heaven, he says:

JOHANNES: From God am I, the Christ, come hither, and to God I shall return. In the clouds of heaven . . .

He advances a few steps – with the intention of telling Inger to arise – but suddenly stops, and stands with his eyes riveted on Inger's face. It seems as if his self-confidence and self-assurance are falling from him. Of the fanatic, the prophet, the ecstatic there is suddenly no trace. All that remains is a pathetic little human being.

He stands for a moment with his eyes closed, swaying to and fro. Then all his joints appear to become paralysed and to give way under the weight of his limbs. He has fallen into a swoon, and he collapses on the bed.

Mikkel calls to Anders, and between them they lift Johannes up.

51 THE LIVING-ROOM

Old Borgen is sitting in the same position as before, repeating monotonously:

BORGEN: The Lord gave, and the Lord hath taken away . . .

He has an air of apathy. The sight of Mikkel and Anders, however, carrying Johannes between them, brings him to life.

BORGEN: Oh, is he . . . is he dead?

MIKKEL: No, Father, he's not the dying type.

BORGEN: Even that mercy is denied us.

Mikkel and Anders have carried Johannes into the room where Johannes and Anders sleep. We do not actually follow them into the room, but through the open door we hear them laying Johannes on his bed. Then Mikkel appears in the door, which he shuts quietly behind him. He remains standing just this side of the door.

52 THE BEDROOM

Anders covers Johannes up well and then sits down in an armchair in order to keep watch. He has placed the chair in front of the door to prevent Johannes from slipping out, in case he himself should fall asleep in the chair. For the moment, however, he sits with his eyes fixed firmly on Johannes, who seems to be sleeping soundly.

53 THE LIVING-ROOM

Mikkel is standing on the same spot as before. His expression is one of indecision. Johannes's collapse has evidently made a strong impression on him. We hear Borgen's voice:

BORGEN: The Lord gave, and the Lord hath taken away . . .

Mikkel looks at his father. The hardness and bitterness are still present in his features. Now it really seems to dawn on him for the first time what a fearful loss he has suffered in Inger's death. Something like a shudder or a shivering fit passes over him. Then he goes across to his father. Old Borgen looks up. Mikkel gives way to his sorrow and bitterness, and breaks out in a lament which is felt almost as an accusation against his father.

MIKKEL: Why should she die – why should we be torn apart, it's all so meaningless . . . meaningless.

Old Borgen tries to console his son.

BORGEN: Mikkel, you know . . .

MIKKEL (*turning hard again, since he expects his father to come out with a quotation from the Bible*): What do I know? I know that everything I've loved and worshipped is about to be clamped down in the earth – to rot, to *rot* . . . yes, *rot* . . .

Gradually Mikkel's lamentation dies away. He goes into the bedroom where Inger lies dead.

54 Slow dissolve to a close-up of a lamp-lit death certificate. Dissolve to the following shot.

55 THE BEDROOM

Moonlit night. Johannes has been put to bed after his fainting fit. The shot shows first the armchair, in which Anders has fallen asleep, overcome by fatigue and grief. Then the camera pans to the other end of the room. Here Johannes stands, in the process of getting dressed. He is in the act of putting on a thick woollen sweater, as a change from the loose-hanging prophet's mantle in which we have hitherto seen him,

He is in his stockinged feet – thick, home-knitted socks. A stout pair of high boots is standing on the window-sill. The prophet's mantle is lying over a chair.

Very carefully he proceeds to open the window. Without a sound he puts the boots outside. His driving-cape follows. Then he gets up on the chair, thence onto the window-sill, and so gently out and down.

When he is on firm ground, his eye falls on a piece or pad of paper and a pencil, lying on the window-sill. Following a sudden impulse, and using large capital letters, he writes a sentence or two on the paper. Then he steals away with the driving-cape over his arm and the boots in his hand. He disappears off screen, whereupon dissolve to the next shot.

56   Close-up of the pencil and piece of paper on the window-sill. We read what Johannes has written:

> Ye shall seek me, and shall not find me:
> and where I am, thither ye cannot come.

57   This is the first in a series of shots, dissolving into each other and all showing the search for the missing Johannes. Old Borgen, Anders and one or two farm hands are taking part in the search. Their shouts echo among the dunes and the trees in the adjacent plantation.

Slow dissolve to the next shot.

58   Two death-announcements are shown, printed in the same local newspaper, one above the other. They are seen in big, vertically-panning close-up, and read as follows:

> My faithful wife and our dear mother
> INGER BORGEN
> née Kjaer
> has departed from us.
> MIKKEL BORGEN
> Maren   Inger

Our dearly loved daughter-in-law and sister-in-law
INGER BORGEN
has with faith in her divine Saviour
JESUS CHRIST gone to her eternal rest,
deeply missed by all at Borgensgård.
Morten Borgen
Anders Borgen

The shot of the newspaper dissolves slowly into the next shot.

59   Big close-up of the top third (or less) of a printed page of the New
Testament. Right at the top can be read, in bold type: 'ST.
MATTHEW 5.'

The extract shown on the screen includes verses 37–42. In the margin
a finger can be seen following the text, while a voice is heard reading
aloud. Both the finger and the voice belong to Peter the tailor.

Verse 39 reads: 'But I say unto you, That ye resist not evil: but who-
soever shall smite thee on thy right cheek, turn to him the other also.'

When the voice has reached the end of this verse, the reading aloud
ends abruptly, and we switch to a long shot of Peter the tailor, dressed
in his Sunday best, sitting in his living-room with the New Testament
in front of him. He sits looking straight ahead with a thoughtful expression, as if the verse he has just read has given him something to
think about – as indeed it has. As he ponders deeply over it, he taps the
table-top with his nail.

After he has been sitting like this for a few moments, Kirstine comes
in from the kitchen. She too is dressed in black and has a hat in her
hand, and over her arm a black outdoor coat, which she puts on as she
talks to her husband.

KIRSTINE: It's high time we were off, if we're to get seats in the church.
PETER (*absent-mindedly*): Yes, Kirstine.

But Peter remains seated, absorbed in his own thoughts. Then he turns
to his wife.

PETER: Do you remember when Morten Borgen was here?
KIRSTINE: Yes – what about it?
PETER: I offended against the Lord.
KIRSTINE: I should rather say it was Morten who offended.

PETER: Well, that may be, but my offence was greater. Kirstine – I ought to have turned the other cheek.

KIRSTINE: Aren't you being a little hard on yourself now?

PETER: No, remember what Christ said: 'What are you going to church for?' He said. 'First be reconciled to thy brother.' And now let's be off. We're going up to Borgensgård.

KIRSTINE: Aren't we going to the church?

PETER: No, we're going to Borgensgård.

Peter goes to the kitchen door, opens it and calls to his daughter.

PETER: Are you ready, Anne?

ANNE: Yes, Father.

Enter Anne, carrying a wreath. She too is in black. She looks with a smile of surprise at her father's mild, conciliatory expression.

Meanwhile Peter, helped by his wife, has put on his overcoat, and now gets ready to leave the house with his wife and daughter.

Slow dissolve to the next shot.

60 THE DUNE LANDSCAPE

A funeral hearse, drawn by two caparisoned horses, on its way to Borgensgård. Slow dissolve to the next shot.

61 THE LIVING-ROOM AT BORGENSGÅRD

The relatives and closest friends are waiting to follow Inger to the church and the churchyard. They are all in mourning and talk in solemn voices. Some are carrying wreaths. The maid Karen goes round with red-rimmed eyes, offering coffee to the funeral guests.

They thumb through their hymn books. Mikkel goes into the front parlour, which adjoins the living-room. The guests sing.

ALL: How joyful, how joyful,
                            The soul that's at rest,
                    Though no man knows the day till
                            The sun's in the West.

                    Good morning, good morning,
                            Sang birds on the spray,
                    Which oft beheld from cages
                            The sunset that day.

Oft danced and gave perfume
  Small flowers at dawn,
Which shortly 'neath a hailstorm
  Lay crushed and forlorn.

Oft sported an infant
  In gay morning light,
Which lay all still and lifeless
  That very same night.

62 THE FRONT PARLOUR

Here Inger's coffin stands. The lid has not yet been placed over her.
The coffin is standing on a kind of catafalque, which is covered with a
black, silver-edged cloth. At the head of the coffin a candle has been lit.
Following the custom of the region sheets have been hung in front of
the windows. The lid of the coffin is standing against the wall.

Old Borgen sits as motionless as a pillar, gazing into Inger's face.
Some movements of the jaw are the only sign of life that he gives. It is
as if the thought processes in his normally active mind have come to a
halt.

Anders is sitting slumped on a chair.

Mikkel enters from the living-room and goes up to his father.

MIKKEL: It's going to be a large gathering, Father.

BORGEN (*silent and sorrowful*): Hm.

The subdued hymn-singing is heard from the living-room.

MIKKEL: The priest must be due any moment.

BORGEN: Yes.

MIKKEL: I suppose we'd better let them finish their coffee in there
first.

BORGEN (*with a vacant expression, nodding*): Yes.

Mikkel and Anders are listening for sounds out in the courtyard.

63 THE ENTRANCE TO BORGENSGÅRD

The hearse, which we saw earlier out on the dunes, drives into the
courtyard. The hymn is heard from the living-room.

64 THE FRONT PARLOUR

The hymn can still be heard. Mikkel reacts to the sound of the hearse's wheels on the uneven cobblestones by turning towards the coffin.

MIKKEL: Well, Inger, I suppose we'd better be fastening the lid on you. Mikkel has taken a few steps towards the coffin. Anders looks up, unhappy about the expression on his brother's face and his cold tone of voice.

ANDERS: Oh Father, Father . . .

BORGEN: Mikkel, let the pastor – say a prayer first.

Mikkel, who feels his raw nerves stretched to breaking point, only wants to get the whole thing over – for his own and Inger's sake, so that he can get some peace.

MIKKEL (*in a voice full of tears as well as derision*): Oh, yes, of course – she's got to be sent off with bands playing.

The sound of a car is heard, driving into the courtyard and stopping. A door slams.

MIKKEL: Ah, that must be the priest arriving . . . (*going to the living-room door*) Shall I let the public in?

BORGEN: Mikkel, you're breaking my heart.

MIKKEL: All right – then we'll wait.

Enter the priest and the doctor. The doctor puts down his hat and coat. The priest, who is wearing all his vestments, advances to greet old Borgen.

PRIEST: Good morning, Borgen . . . ah, there she is.

BORGEN: There must surely be some purpose in it. Otherwise it would never have happened.

PRIEST: Spoken like a true believer.

Meanwhile the doctor has been silently greeting old Borgen and Anders, and now presses Mikkel's hands.

DOCTOR: Remember, Mikkel Borgen, even pain can be beautiful.

MIKKEL: Yes, doctor. And all that business about beauty is very important, of course.

DOCTOR (*turning to Anders*): There's no news of Johannes, I suppose?

ANDERS: No, we've searched everywhere for him, but nobody's seen or heard any sign of him.

DOCTOR (*turning to Borgen*): It looks as if you'd better be prepared for the worst.

BORGEN: Pray God he's been granted his release.

The doctor shrugs his shoulders, as if to say: 'Well, I suppose that's one way of looking at it.'

The hymn-singing in the living-room has ended, and the priest goes up to the coffin and stands looking at the dead woman. Mikkel goes up to him.

MIKKEL: Shall I let them in?

PRIEST: Ah, let me just first . . .

He goes to the head of the coffin, and clears his throat before speaking.

PRIEST: Death is the gateway to eternity, and through that gate the young woman who lies here has gone ahead of her dear ones. If *we* now sorrow, it is only because we are thinking of ourselves and our loss, since for her we have no reason to sorrow. And so you must be thankful for the memories, the bright and wonderful memories, you have of her, in the life that has ended, and for the bright and wonderful hope you have for her, in the life that is to come. And to you, Mikkel Borgen, to you I would like to say this: that if you can live your life in the memories you have of her, and if you can bring up your children in a way that would make her glad if she saw it, then the two of you, who loved each other, will meet again and be united, never to part . . . Shall we say the Lord's Prayer in silence?

The priest bows his head and folds his hands. The others do likewise. Without speaking, without even moving their lips, they say the Lord's Prayer. The room is absolutely quiet.

65 THE ENTRANCE TO BORGENSGÅRD

Peter the tailor, Kirstine and Anne arrive. Kirstine takes the wreath from Anne. Peter separates from Kirstine and Anne.

66 THE FRONT PARLOUR

The priest and the others are still in the middle of the Lord's Prayer. When the priest has finished the prayer, he says amen, in which the others follow him.

Now Mikkel goes up to the priest and takes his hand with deep feeling.

MIKKEL: Thank you, pastor, for those heartfelt words.

PRIEST: There is nothing to thank me for.

The priest pats Mikkel's hand sympathetically. At this moment Peter the tailor enters from the hall.

ANDERS: Father, look . . .

BORGEN: Peter, is it you coming here?

PETER: Forgive me for intruding, Morten Borgen, but will you take my hand?

BORGEN: It was I who struck you.

PETER: Yes, but it was I who forgot my Saviour's words. Now I have asked Him to forgive me. And you must do the same, Morten.

BORGEN: It's all a thing of the past now.

PETER: No, it is not, because I have something to say to you in front of this coffin, something you must all know up here, before Inger is carried out.

MIKKEL: I know you mean it well, Peter, but enough has been said here already.

PETER: I'm just coming to what I wanted to say, which is that Inger's place shall not stand empty.

Peter goes to the door into the parlour, opens it and calls:

PETER: Anne, come here a moment.

ANDERS: Have you brought Anne, Peter?

Anne appears in the door. Her father takes her by the hand and leads her over to Anders.

PETER: Yes, here she is.

ANDERS: Only Our Lord can repay you for that.

PETER: Now she is yours.

ANDERS: Anne . . .

PETER: Now I have only my Saviour. From Him I shall never be parted.

Borgen goes up to Peter and shakes his hand.

BORGEN: Oh Peter, this does the heart good.

PETER: Be gentle with her up here.

ANDERS (to Anne): Now, Anne, you must be the sun that sheds light on us all.

ANNE: Thank you, Anders.

Mikkel sinks to the floor beside the coffin. After many days spent in hardening his heart, painfully gritting his teeth in his pride, he has now given up resisting and abandoned himself to violent grief. He collapses, sobbing in despair at the thought of his imminent separation from the one he loved so deeply.

MIKKEL: Oh, oh, oh . . . Inger.

BORGEN: Ah, thank God, tears at last.

Borgen goes to the door leading out to the kitchen, opens it and calls:

BORGEN: Karen, come now!

We hear Karen's answering call. Then Borgen turns towards the room and continues.

BORGEN: Because now it's all over.

He goes to the coffin and bends over Inger.

BORGEN: Goodbye, Inger. Thank you for everything, because it was all good. We shall meet again soon.

Mikkel raises his head and looks imploringly up at his father.

BORGEN: Yes, Mikkel, we do meet again. Goodbye for the present, Inger . . . (*stretching out his hand as if to caress her*) God gladden your soul.

Karen has entered with Maren.

BORGEN: Maren, come and say goodbye to Mummy.

MAREN: Goodbye, Mummy.

Borgen leads Maren back to Karen.

BORGEN: She doesn't understand a thing, she's too small.

Borgen turns to the priest.

BORGEN: And the rest of us, pastor – we don't understand a thing either.

PRIEST: That is true, Borgen.

ANDERS: Goodbye, Inger – and thank you.

BORGEN: Anders . . . the lid.

ANDERS: Yes, Father.

MIKKEL: No, you mustn't take her from me, you mustn't separate us – oh, oh, oh, no, no . . .

57 THE ENTRANCE TO BORGENSGÅRD

Johannes comes in from outside, strong and confident, with firm, resolute strides.

68 THE FRONT PARLOUR

Mikkel seems calmer. Borgen approaches him.

BORGEN: Come, Mikkel, her soul is with God. It isn't here, surely you can see that.

MIKKEL (*again convulsed with tears*): But her body – I loved her body too.

BORGEN: Be a man and say your farewells. Remember you are a son of Borgensgård.

MIKKEL: Goodbye, little darling, goodbye, little darling, goodbye, Inger girl.

Johannes has entered unobserved and is now standing in the middle of the room.

BORGEN: Johannes!

JOHANNES: Yes, Father.

BORGEN: Father? Did you say Father? Are your eyes healed, Johannes, have you got your reason back?

JOHANNES: Yes, I've got my 'reason' back.

During this exchange Borgen and Johannes have approached the coffin. Johannes looks at the dead Inger – and then at the surrounding relatives.

JOHANNES (*reproachfully*): Not one of you has thought of asking God to restore Inger to you.

BORGEN: Johannes, now you are mocking God.

JOHANNES: No, it is you who are mocking God with your half-heartedness. If you had prayed to God, He would have heard your prayers.

Through all this Mikkel has remained seated, completely uninterested in what is going on around him. At Johannes's last outburst, however, he seems to come to life. He rises in anger.

MIKKEL: What's the idea of this – standing here and shouting over my wife's dead body?

Johannes goes up to him.

JOHANNES: Mikkel, my brother – why, among all the believers, is there not one who believes?

Johannes turns to the coffin.

JOHANNES (*addressing Inger*): Inger, you must rot, because the times are rotten. (*He looks sadly round.*) Put the lid on, then.

69   Maren has followed anxiously the scene by the coffin. Now she makes
      a rapid decision, escapes from Karen's hand, runs across to Johannes
      and tugs at his sleeve.

MAREN: Do hurry up now, Uncle Johannes.

Johannes looks down at Maren, and his face breaks into a smile of confidence.

JOHANNES: The child – the child – the greatest in the Kingdom of
Heaven.

MAREN: Do hurry up a little.

JOHANNES: Do you believe I can do it?

MAREN: Yes, Uncle Johannes.

JOHANNES: Thy faith is great, it shall be done according to thy will . . .

Johannes feels his strength returning. He bends down and talks to the
child.

JOHANNES: Look at your mother, then – when I speak the name of
Jesus, she will rise.

The child fastens her eyes on her mother's face. Johannes has straigh-
tened up and now speaks to Inger.

JOHANNES: Hear me, thou dead one.

The priest tries to go to Johannes, but is restrained by the doctor, who
is sitting next to him.

Johannes breaks off and turns towards the priest.

PRIEST: But he's insane.

JOHANNES: Is it insane to want to save lives?

MIKKEL: Johannes . . .

JOHANNES: Trust in God!

Mikkel is perplexed what to think or do, but, since he clings to the
slenderest thread of hope, he decides to remain passive.

Johannes turns his gaze upwards.

JOHANNES: Jesus Christ, if it is possible, let her come back to life . . .

After a very short silence he continues:

JOHANNES: . . . give me the Word – the Word that can bring the dead
alive.

And now he addresses himself directly to Inger.

JOHANNES: Inger, in the name of Jesus Christ I say unto thee: arise.

A moment passes, then she begins to stir. Without waking up, she unclasps her folded hands as if in her sleep, and lies for a while with outstretched arms.

Little Maren, who is holding tight onto Johannes's hand, looks up at him, and he nods down at her, as if to say: keep your faith up.

Inger lies for a long time as if lifeless. We cannot even hear her breathing.

A breathless silence reigns in the room. Then a spasm passes rapidly over Inger's face.

After some time she opens her eyes, gives a deep sigh. She is now breathing deeply and naturally.

Little Maren smiles up at Johannes, who nods down at her.

Mikkel bends over Inger and calls out.

MIKKEL: Inger, Inger . . . Inger girl.

Inger's eyes meet Mikkel's – she sees only Mikkel's eyes and Mikkel's face. He draws her up to him, and she throws her arms round his neck.

Inger raises her face. Her eyes are still blurred and far away.

The camera picks out Peter the tailor and old Borgen.

PETER: Morten – He is still the God of old – the God Elijah – eternal and the same.

BORGEN: Yes – eternal and the same . . .

Mikkel and Inger have not altered their positions, but there seems to be more life now in Inger's eyes. Her consciousness is slowly returning. She turns to Mikkel and asks:

INGER: The child? Where is it? (*when Mikkel doesn't answer immediately*) Is it alive?

MIKKEL (*searching for the words, which for him are new and unfamiliar*): Yes, Inger – it is alive – it lives with God.

It takes a little time before Inger grasps the meaning of the words. She asks in surprise:

INGER: With God?

MIKKEL: Yes, I have found your faith.

Inger almost caresses him with her eyes. Then she again presses her face against his cheek.

MIKKEL: Now life is beginning for us.

INGER: Yes, life – life, life.

Slow fade out.

BIOGRAPHICAL NOTE
AND
FILMOGRAPHY

BIOGRAPHICAL NOTE

Carl Theodor Dreyer was born in Copenhagen on 3 February 1889. His mother, who was Swedish, died as he was born; he was brought up by adopted parents and given a strict puritan education. He studied the piano and left home after taking a job in a café as a musician. At seventeen, while working for a telegraph company, he began to frequent radical circles. About 1909 he started to write theatre reviews and articles on sport, first for various provincial papers, subsequently for Copenhagen's largest daily, the *Berlingske Tidende*, and from 1912 to 1915 for the afternoon paper *Ekstrabladet*, to which he contributed a series of satirical profiles of personalities of the day.

In 1912 he began to work for the Nordisk Films Kompagni as a writer of titles and scenarios. As more and more of his time became devoted to this activity he ceased his journalistic work, and by 1918 he had completed a considerable number of scripts and adaptations from novels. In 1919 he made his first film as director, *Præsidenten*, following it with *Blade af Satans Bog*, inspired by Griffith's *Intolerance*. He then went on to direct a succession of films, some in Denmark, some in Germany. After the success in 1925 of *Du Skal Ære Din Hustru* (*Master of the House*), his seventh film, he was invited to France, where in 1928 he made *La Passion de Jeanne d'Arc*.

Vampyr, his first sound film, followed in 1932; after which he came to England. He worked for a time with John Grierson, Basil Wright and other directors of the British documentary movement, but no film resulted; and in 1935, after an equally unproductive visit to Africa, he returned to Copenhagen and to journalism. He abandoned the cinema for seven years, and then, after finishing a twelve-minute documentary, in 1943 he made *Vredens Dag*. In 1946 he attempted to found a nationally-supported documentary school, and in 1948 began preparatory work for a film, never to be made, on the life of Christ. In 1952 he became proprietor of a cinema in Copenhagen. *Ordet* appeared in 1955, and nine years later still his last completed film, *Gertrud*. At the time of his death, on 20 March 1968, he was once more engaged in planning his film about Christ.

FILMOGRAPHY

In preparing the filmography which follows the Publishers gratefully acknowledge the invaluable help given them by Ib Monty of the Danish Film Museum. The following abbreviations have been used: *Dir*, director; *Scr*, author of the screenplay; *Ad*, artistic designer; *Cost*, costume designer; *Ed*, editor; *Ph*, cameraman; *Mus*, musical composer; *Sd*, sound; *Narr*, narrator. Running times are sometimes given in minutes (mins.) and sometimes in metres (m.).

FILMS AS SCENARIST

1912
Bryggerens Datter
   (dir. Rasmus Ottesen)

1913
Balloneksplosionen (dir. unknown)
Krigskorrespondenten (dir. unknown)
Hans og Grethe (dir. Wolder)
Chatollets Hemmelighed
   (dir. Hjalmar Davidsen)

1914
Ned med Vaabnene
   (dir. Holger-Madsen)
Penge (dir. Karl Mantzius)
Pavillonens Hemmelighed
   (dir. Karl Mantzius)

1915
Juvelerernes Skraek
   (dir. A. Christian)
Den Hvide Djævel
   (dir. Holger-Madsen)
Den Skønne Evelyn
   (dir. A. W. Sandburg)
Rovedderkoppen (dir. August Blom)
En Forbryders Liv og Levned
   (dir. A. Christian)
Guldets Gift (dir. Holger-Madsen)

1916
Den Mystiske Selskabsdame
   (dir. August Blom)
Hans Rigtige Kone
   (dir. Holger-Madsen)
Fange No. 113 (dir. Holger-Madsen)
Lydia (dir. Holger-Madsen)

Glædens Dag (dir. A. Christian)
Gillekop (dir. August Blom)

1917
Hotel Paradis (dir. Robert Dinesen)

1918
Grevindens Ære (dir. August Blom)

1947
De Gamle
   (dir. Torben Anton Svendsen)

1950
Shakespeare og Kronborg
   (dir. Jørgen Roos, Erling
   Schroeder)

1954
Rønnes og Nexøs Genopbyning
   (dir. Poul Bang)

1956
Noget om Norden
   (dir. Bent Barfod)

SHORT FILMS

Mødrehjælpen (*Maternity Aid*)
Nordisk Films Kompagni Mogens
Skot-Hansen, 1942
Dir: Carl Theodor Dreyer
Scr: Carl Theodor Dreyer
Ph: Verner Jensen, Poul Gram
Mus: Poul Schierbeck
Narr: Ebbe Neergaard

(Documentary on health care for
married and unmarried mothers.
12 mins.)

Vandet På Landet
   (*Water in the Country*)
Dansk Kultur Film – Preben Frank
Film, 1946
Dir: Carl Theodor Dreyer
Scr: Carl Theodor Dreyer
Ph: Preben Frank
Mus: Poul Schierbeck
Narr: Henrik Malberg, Asbjørn
   Andersen

(Documentary on the problems of
irrigation in the Danish country-
side. It was never released because
the farmers' organizations disliked
its picture of farm hygiene.)

Kampen mod Kræften
   (*The Fight against Cancer*)
Dansk Kultur Film, 1947
Dir: Carl Theodor Dreyer
Scr: Carl Theodor Dreyer, Carl
   Krebs
Ph: Preben Frank
Mus: Peter Deutsch
Narr: Albert Luther

(A propaganda film on cancer.
315 m.)

Landsbykirken
   (*The Country Church*)
Dansk Kultur Film – Preben Frank
Film, 1947

Dir: Carl Theodor Dreyer
Scr: Carl Theodor Dreyer, Bernhard Jensen, Victor Hermansen
Ad: Carlo Jacobsen
Ph: Preben Frank
Mus: Svend Erik Tarp
Narr: Ib Koch-Olsen

(Documentary on Danish village churches. 14 mins.)

De Nåede Færgen

(*They Came to the Ferry*)
Dansk Kultur Film – Ministetines Filmudvalg, 1948
Dir: Carl Theodor Dreyer
Scr: Carl Theodor Dreyer, from a story by Johannes V. Jensen
Ed: Jørgen Roos
Ph: Jørgen Roos

(Documentary on traffic problems based on a story by the Danish poet Johannes V. Jensen. 12 mins.)

Thorvaldsen

Dansk Kultur Film – Preben Frank Film, 1949
Dir: Carl Theodor Dreyer
Scr: Carl Theodor Dreyer
Ph: Preben Frank
Mus: Svend Erik Tarp
Narr: Ib Koch-Olsen

(Documentary on the Danish sculptor Bertel Thorvaldsen, 1768–1844. 10 mins.)

Storstrømsbroen

(*The Storstrøm Bridge*)
Dansk Kultur Film – Preben Frank Film, 1949
Dir: Carl Theodor Dreyer
Scr: Carl Theodor Dreyer
Ph: Preben Frank
Mus: Svend S. Schultz

(Documentary on the longest bridge in Europe linking the Danish islands of Seeland and Falster. 10 mins., 196 m.)

Et Slot i et Slot

(*A Castle within a Castle*)
Dansk Kultur Film – Teknisk Film, 1954
Dir: Carl Theodor Dreyer (completed by Jørgen Roos)
Scr: Carl Theodor Dreyer
Ph: Jørgen Roos, Paul Solbjerghoej
Narr: Sven Ludvigsen

(Documentary on the remains of the old castle of Krogen which lie within the present castle of Elsinore. 98 m.)

FEATURE FILMS

Præsidenten (*The President*)
Nordisk Films Kompagni, 1919
Dir: Carl Theodor Dreyer
Scr: Carl Theodor Dreyer, from a novel by Karl Emil Franzos
Ad: Carl Theodor Dreyer
Ph: Hans Vaagø
Cast: Halvard Hoff (*the magistrate*), Elith Pio (*his father*), Carl Meyer (*his grandfather*), Hallander Hellemann (*his servant*), Fanny Petersen (*Birgitta, his maid*), Olga Raphael Linden (*Victorine, his daughter*) Betty Kirkeby (*his mother*), Richard Christensen (*the lawyer*), Peter Nielsen (*the attorney-general*), Jon Iversen (*the fiancé*), Jacoba Jessen (*Maïka*).

(A magistrate has to try a young woman accused of murdering her child. He recognizes her as his own daughter, the child of a woman whom he had once abandoned. After wrestling with the impulse to preserve his respectability he takes flight with his daughter, with whom he eventually dies. 1,700 m.)

Blade af Satans Bog
  (*Leaves from Satan's Book*)
Nordisk Films Kompagni, 1919
Dir: Carl Theodor Dreyer
Scr: Edgar Høyer, after a novel by Marie Corelli, rewritten by Carl Theodor Dreyer
Ad: Carl Theodor Dreyer, Alex Bruun, Jens G. Lind
Ph: George Schnéevoigt
Cast: (1) 'In Palestine.' Halvard Hoff (*Jesus*), Jacob Texiere (*Judas*), Erling Hansson(*John*), Helge Nissen (*The Pharisee, or Satan*).

(2) 'The Inquisition.' Hallander Hellemann (*Don Gomez*), Ebon Strandin (*Isabelle*), Johannes Meyer (*Don Fernandez*), Nalle Haldén (*major-domo*), Helge Nissen (*the Grand Inquisitor, or Satan*).

(3) 'The French Revolution.' Tenna Kraft (*Marie Antoinette*), Emma Wiehe (*the Countess of Chambord*), Elith Pio (*Joseph*), Helge Nissen (*Ernest Durand, or Satan*).

(4) 'The Red Rose of Soumis.' Carlo Wieth (*Paavo Rahja*), Clara Pontoppidan (*Siri*), Carl Hillebrandt (*Tautaniemi*), Karina Bell (*Naima*), Helge Nissen (*Ivan, or Satan*). Also Hanne Tramcourt, Viggo Wiehe, Emil Helsengreen, Vilhelm Scholander, Landskabsmaler Hermansen, Tomrer Weigel, Bogbinder Gylche, Wilhelm Jensen.

(Inspired by *Intolerance*, Dreyer's second film consists of four episodes showing the workings of evil in history. 'In Palestine' is also called 'The Passion of Jesus Christ'. 'The Inquisition' anticipates *La Passion de Jeanne d'Arc*. 'The French Revolution' relates most closely among Dreyer's subsequent films to *Vampyr*. 'The Red Rose of Soumis' is set against a background of Finland in 1918; in its use of close-ups of Siri's suicide it anticipates *Jeanne d'Arc*. 110 mins., 3,254 m.)

Præsteenken

(*The Parson's Widow*)
Svensk Filmindustri Stockholm, 1920
Dir: Carl Theodor Dreyer
Scr: Carl Theodor Dreyer, from a story by Kristofer Janson
Ph: George Schnéevoigt
Cast: Hildur Carlberg (*Margarete Pedersdotter, the parson's widow*), Einar Rød (*Søfren*), Greta Almroth (*his fiancée Kari*), Olav Aukrust and Kurt Welin (*seminarians*), Emil Helsengreen and Mathilde Mielsen (*servants*), Lorentz Thyholt (*bell-ringer*).

(A young curate preaches a rousing sermon, routing his rivals to win his first living, only to discover that he must marry the previous incumbent's widow, an old lady who has already buried three husbands. Reluctantly he agrees, but consoles himself by persuading the old lady to hire his girl-friend as a maid. The frustrated young lovers plan to do away with the old lady, only to realize with bitter regret that they have misjudged her. Shot entirely on location and inspired by Sjöström and Stiller, the film combines a rough humour with realistic treatment. 1,500 m.)

Elsker Hverandre

(*Love One Another*)
Original German title:
Die Gezeichneten
Primus Film Berlin, 1921
Dir: Carl Theodor Dreyer
Scr: Carl Theodor Dreyer, from a novel by Aage Madelung, *Elsker Hverandre*
Ad: Jens G. Lind
Ph: Friedrich Weinmann
Cast: Polina Piekowska (*Hanne-Liebe*), Wladimir Gajdarow (*Jakow Segal*), Torleif Reiss (*Sascha Krasnow*), Richard Boleslavsky (*Fedja*), Duwan (*Suchowersky*), Johannes Meyer (*Rowitsch*), Adele Reuter-Eichberg (*Mme Segal*), Emmy Wyda, Friedrich Kühne, Hugo Döblin.

(A complicated story about a Jewish girl, Hanna, during a Russian pogrom coinciding with the 1905 revolution. Griffith is again a strong influence. Copies of this film were lost for many years, but one turned up in the Russian archive in 1961. 105 mins.)

Der Var Engang
(*Once Upon a Time*)

Sophus Madsen Film Copenhagen, 1922

Dir: Carl Theodor Dreyer
Scr: Carl Theodor Dreyer, Palle Rosenkrantz from a play by Holger Drachmann
Ed: Carl Theodor Dreyer, Edla Hansen
Ph: George Schnéevoigt
Ad: Jens G. Lind
Cast: Clara Pontopiddan (*the princess*), Svend Methling (*the prince*), Peter Jerndorff (*the king*), Hakon Ahnfeldt-Rønne (*Kaspar Røghat*), Karen Poulsen, Gerda Madsen, Valdemar Schiøler-Linck, Torben Meyer, Musse Scheel, Viggo Wiehe, Mohamed Archer, Henry Larsen, Lili Kristiansson, Zun Zimmermann, Bodil Fater, Karen Thalbitzer, Emilie Walblom, Lars Madsen, Wilhelmine Henriksen, Frederik Leth

(A romantic fairy-tale about a bored princess and a handsome stranger of which only two-thirds have survived. It was made in one month with the company of the Theatre Royal, Copenhagen, to no one's satisfaction. Length of surviving portion of only known print, at Danish Filmmuseum, 1,080 m.)

Mikaël (*Michael*)

Original German title: *Michael*
Decla Bioscop Universum Film Aktien Gesellschaft Pommer Production, 1924

Dir: Carl Theodor Dreyer
Scr: Carl Theodor Dreyer, from a novel by Herman Bang
Ad: Hugo Häring
Ph: Karl Freund, Rudolph Mate
Mus: Hans Joseph Vieth
Cast· Benjamin Christensen (*Claude Zoret*), Walter Slezak (*Eugene Mikaël*), Nora Gregor (*Princess Lucia Zamikoff*), Grete Mosheim (*Adils Kjold*), Robert Garrison (*Swift*), Alexander Murski, Didier Aslan, Karl Freund, Mady Christians.

(The film is based on a 'decadent' *fin-de-siècle* novel about an elderly sculptor who adores his protégé and former model, Mikaël. The young man drifts into an affair with the worldly Princess Zamikoff, and the sculptor, driven to despair by his desertion, shuts himself away as a hermit and dies, leaving everything to Mikaël. The film director Benjamin Christensen, who plays the sculptor, had completed *Witchcraft through the Ages* two years earlier. In attempting the manner of the German *Kammerspiele*, or intimate theatre, Dreyer was anticipating his own *Gertrud* by forty years. 75 mins.)

Du Skal Ære Din Hustru
(*Master of the House*)
Palladium Film Copenhagen, 1925
Dir: Carl Theodor Dreyer
Scr: Carl Theodor Dreyer, Svend Rindom, from Svend Rindom's play *Tyrannens Fald*
Ad: Carl Theodor Dreyer
Ph: George Schnéevoigt
Cast: Johannes Meyer (*Viktor Frandsen*), Astrid Holm (*his wife Ida*), Karin Nellemose (*their daughter Karen*), Mathilde Nielsen (*Mads*), Vilhelm Petersen, Clara Schonfeld, Johannes Nielsen, Petrine Sonne, Aage Hoffmann.

(The title of the play which is the film's source means 'The Tyrant's Fall'. The film is a study of a selfish and narrow bourgeois and the suffering he causes his household. Alternative English title: *Thou Shalt Honour Thy Wife*. 2,356 m.)

Glomdalsbruden
(*The Bride of Glomdal*)
Victoria Film Oslo, 1925
Dir: Carl Theodor Dreyer
Scr: Carl Theodor Dreyer, Jacob Breda Bull, from two novels by Jacob Breda Bull
Ad: Carl Theodor Dreyer
Ph: Einar Olsen

Cast: Stub Wiberg (*Ola*), Tove Tellback (*Berit*), Harald Stormoen (*Jacob*), Einar Sissener (*Tore*), Einar Tveito (*Gjermund*), Rasmus Rasmussen (*the pastor*), Sofie Reimers (*the pastor's wife*).

(A lyrical film about the son of a poor farmer who falls in love with the daughter of a rich farmer, who is betrothed to another man. Cast out by her family, she is looked after by the young man's parents until a reconciliation is effected and the two are married. Dreyer himself described it as 'a little folk-tale'. 1,237 m.)

La Passion de Jeanne d'Arc
(*The Passion of Joan of Arc*)
Société Générale de Films Paris, 1927
Dir: Carl Theodor Dreyer
Asst dir:
        Paul la Cour, Ralf Holm
Scr: Carl Theodor Dreyer, distantly after a book by Joseph Delteil
Ad: Hermann Warm, Jean Hugo
Ph: Rudolph Maté, assisted by Barth Kottula
Cast: Maria Falconetti (*Joan*), Eugène Silvain (*Pierre Cauchon*), André Berley (*Jean d'Estivet*), Maurice Schutz (*Nicolas Loiseleur*), Antonin Art ud (*Jean Massieu*), Michel Simon (*Jean Lemaître*),

Jean d'Yd (*Guillaume Erard*), Ravet (*Jean Beaupère*), André Lurville, Jacques Arna, Alexandre Mihalesco, R. Narlay, Henri Maillard, Leo Larive, Henry Gaultier, Paul Jorge.

(110 mins., 2,036 m.)

Vampyr (*Vampire*)
Carl Theodor Dreyer Filmproduktion Paris-Berlin, 1932
Dir: Carl Theodor Dreyer
Scr: Carl Theodor Dreyer, in collaboration with Christen Jul, from the story 'Carmilla' by Sheridan le Fanu
Ad: Hermann Warm, Hans Bittmann, Cesare Silvani
Ph: Rudolph Maté, Louis Née
Mus: Wolfgang Zeller
Director of Dialogue:
Paul Falkenberg
Cast: Julian West, alias Baron Nicolas de Gunzburg (*David Gray*), Henriette Gérard (*Marguerite Chopin*), Jan Hieronimko (*the doctor*), Maurice Schutz (*lord of the manor*), Rena Mandel (*his daughter Gisèle*), Sibylle Schmitz (*his daughter Léone*), Albert Bras (*servant*), N. Babanini, Jane Mora.

(*Vampyr* was made in three versions: French, German and English. 70 mins., 2,732 m.)

Vredens Dag (*Day of Wrath*)
Palladium Copenhagen-Tage Nielsen, 1943
Dir: Carl Theodor Dreyer
Scr: Carl Theodor Dreyer, Mogens Skot-Hansen, Poul Knudsen from the play *Anne Pedersdotter* by Hans Wiers-Jenssen
Ad: Erik Aaes, Lis Fribert
Cost: K. Sandt Jensen, Olga Thomsen
Ph: Karl Andersson
Mus: Poul Schierbeck
Ed: Edith Schlüssel, Anne Marie Petersen
Cast: Thorkild Roose (*Absalon*), Lisbeth Movin (*his wife Anne*), Sigrid Neiiendam (*his mother Merete*), Preben Lerdorff Rye (*his son Martin*), Anne Svierkier (*Herlof's Marte*), Albert Høeberg (*the bishop*), Olaf Ussing (*Laurentius*), Dagmar Wildenbrüch, Emilie Nielsen, Kirsten Andreasen, Sophie Knudsen, Harald Holst, Preben Neergaard, Emanuel Jørgensen, Hans Christian Sørensen.

(2,790 m.)

Två Människor (*Two People*)
Hugo Bolander Pr. Svensk Filmindustri Stockholm, 1945
Dir: Carl Theodor Dreyer
Scr: Carl Theodor Dreyer,

Martin Glanner after a play *Attentat* by W. O. Somin
Ed: Carl Theodor Dreyer, Edvin Hammarberg
Ad: Nils Svenwall
Ph: Gunnar Fischer
Mus: Lars-Erik Larsson
Cast: Georg Rydeberg (*Arne Lundell*), Wanda Rothgardt (*his wife Marianne*).

(An experimental film, with only two characters. Arne, an assistant physician at a mental hospital, is accused of having stolen his thesis from his superior. Arne, however, discovers that his wife Marianne was the doctor's mistress, that she had been forced to show Arne's work to her lover, and that finally she had killed him, disguising the murder as suicide. Arne and Marianne kill themselves. Because of its lack of commercial success the film was never shown outside Sweden, not even in Denmark. Dreyer himself disowned the film, chiefly because he was unable to have the actors he wanted. 2,125 m.)

Ordet (*The Word*)
Palladium, Copenhagen, 1954–5
Dir: Carl Theodor Dreyer
Scr: Carl Theodor Dreyer from the play by Kaj Munk
Ad: Erik Aaes, N. Sandt Jensen
Ph: Henning Bendtsen
Dialect expert:
 Svend Poulsen

Mus: Poul Schierbeck
Cast: Henrik Malberg (*Morten Borgen*), Emil Hass Christensen (*his son Mikkel*), Preben Lerdorff Rye (*his son Johannes*), Cay Kristiansen (*his son Anders*), Birgitte Federspiel (*Inger, Mikkel's wife*), Ann Elisabeth (*Maren*), Susanne (*little Inger*), Ove Rud (*the priest*), Ejnar Federspiel (*Peter the tailor*), Sylvia Eckhausen (*his wife Kirstine*), Gerda Nielsen (*Anne, their daughter*), Henry Skjaer (*the doctor*), Hanne Agesen (*Karen*), Edith Thrane (*Mette Maren*), Kirsten Andreasen and the peasants and fishermen of the district of Vedersø.

(An earlier film version of Munk's play was made in 1943, directed by Gustaf Molander. 124 mins., 3,440 m.)

Gertrud
Palladium, Copenhagen, 1964
Dir: Carl Theodor Dreyer
Asst dir:
 Solveig Ersgaard, Jens Ravn
Scr: Carl Theodor Dreyer from the play by Hjalmar Söderberg
Ed: Edith Schüssel
Ad: Kai Rasch
Ph: Henning Bendtsen, assisted by Arne Abrahamsen

Mus: Jørgen Jersild; lyrics: Grethe Risbjerg Thomsen

Sd. Knud Kristensen

Cast: Nina Pens Rode (*Gertrud*), Bendt Rothe (*Kanning*), Ebbe Rode (*Lidman*), Baard Owe (*Janssen*), Anna Malberg (*Kanning's mother*), Axel Strøbye (*Nygren*), Karl Gustav Ahlefeldt, Edouard Mielche, Valsø Holm, Vera Gebuhr, William Knoblauch, Lars Knutzon, Ole Sarvig.

(Gustav Kanning, a successful lawyer, is invited to become a government minister; he hopes that this news will revive the affection that his wife Gertrud used to feel for him. But she tells him that she loves someone else, and goes to her suitor, the young composer Erland Janssen. The next day she learns that Janssen has been boasting of his new conquest, and their affair ends. Rejecting another offer from an old friend she leaves for Paris, where years later she tells yet another faithful friend that her epitaph shall be 'Love is Everything'. 115 mins., 3,440 m.)